Red Odyssey

JEFF GOULDING

Red Odyssey

Liverpool FC
1892–2017

First published by Pitch Publishing, 2018

Pitch Publishing
A2 Yeoman Gate
Yeoman Way
Worthing
Sussex
BN13 3QZ

www.pitchpublishing.co.uk
info@pitchpublishing.co.uk

A CIP catalogue record is available for this book
from the British Library.

ISBN 978-1-78531-387-5

Typesetting and origination by Pitch Publishing

Printed in India by Replika Press

Contents

I dedicate this book to my wife Angela, and my children; Joe, Mollie, Lucy and Sophie. Thanks for inspiring me and tolerating me in equal measure.

This is also for the 96 and all those who continue to live with the legacy of 15 April 1989.

You will never walk alone.

Foreword

LIVERPOOL Football Club means so much, to so many people across the globe. Each supporter will have their own unique connection to the club. For most of us, our emotions fluctuate between love, adulation and euphoria, anger and frustration; such is the life of a football supporter. Some worship, or despise, individual players, while others focus on the tactics of the coach and team selection. Then there are those, like me, who have simply come to love the history, ethos and spirit of the club.

There are many ways to approach the task of writing a celebration of this milestone in the club's history; 125 years of football played at Anfield. In doing so, I have decided to explore my own connection to Liverpool FC. This book will be unashamedly subjective.

As a child, growing up in Liverpool in the 1970s and '80s, the club meant everything to me. The players and the manager could do no wrong. But, beyond that, the club felt special and unique. We weren't like other teams or their supporters, and it wasn't just about the trophies.

Our songs were different, and our banners were witty and often irreverent. The Kop was a joyous and anarchic place, but its humour was as fair as it was cutting.

Of course, with the passing of time and the globalisation of the game, football is a very different beast today than it was back then. I confess to being far more cynical than I was as a child and an adolescent. However, I have never lost that sense of being part of something bigger than me every time I set foot inside Anfield. Maybe that's how every football fan feels when watching their team, I don't know, but it is how *I* feel.

So this book will not be a recitation of facts and figures, although there are many in there. It will describe the club's journey in the only way I know how, and with what I believe is the fuel that drives our love for it; the stories that made Liverpool FC what it is today.

I have come to realise that this is what Liverpool Football Club is; a collection of experiences and stories, passed down from one generation to the other. Of course, they get blurred along the way, but that too is part of the magic.

So I have collected 125 of them to coincide with the club's anniversary. Wherever possible, I have included the voice of the supporter and many of these tales contain first-person perspective on some of the greatest moments in the club's history.

I offer them as my contribution to this illustrious journey, our Red Odyssey. Enjoy!

Introduction

IN June 2017, Liverpool FC turned 125 years old. This is a remarkable achievement for any enterprise, let alone a sporting institution. The club has survived relegations, scandals, two world wars and great tragedies. In all that time, it has become one of the most successful football clubs in history.

Having been born in 1967, my earliest memories of supporting Liverpool FC stem from the 1970s and I remember my early Anfield experiences vividly. While the games themselves are not so clear to me, the feelings, the sounds, smells and noise are deeply imprinted.

If I close my eyes for a moment I'm transported back to a pub near the ground, with my dad and uncle. The game is an hour or so away. I'm drinking Coke and a packet of crisps lies untouched on the table. I'm far too excited to touch them. All I want is for kick-off to arrive, so that I can make my pilgrimage up Walton Breck Road and climb the steps on to the Kop.

The bar is filling up and more of my dad's mates have joined us. The noise escalates, and I can just make out fragments of conversation over the clink of glasses and the mutterings of Kopites crammed into the pub. There's laughter, swearing and apologies. Someone winks at me and says, 'No good saying sorry to him now, he'll hear much worse in the ground.'

More laughter and someone tousles my hair. My heart is bursting. There's a picture of the team on the wall with cups at their feet. It's Liverpool and soon I'll see them up close.

This was a rite of passage and I was part of a community, much bigger than anything I'd encountered before, and the sense of togetherness had to be experienced to be fully understood. I was following in my dad's footsteps and those who had gone before him. I felt ten feet tall.

Now I'm being handed a succession of drinks. Soon I've got a collection of unfinished lemonades and juices on the table. My uncle tells me, 'Go easy lad or you'll be peeing in your shoes with all that in your belly.' I would later see the wisdom in his words.

We were in the Kop for this game and packed in tight. The air is full of sweat, cigarette smoke and the smell of stale ale. It's a heady brew. We find ourselves somewhere near the middle of the terrace, between the two great pillars supporting the roof, and the toilets are a distant dream. It doesn't matter though, because kick-off is approaching.

The crowd is swaying back and forth and side to side. I'm only small and can't see much. Then a man I'd never met lifts me up and sits me on a crash barrier. I think nothing of it. It seems the most natural thing in the world. Suddenly the whole stadium lies before me. I see the pitch and my heart soars.

I have seen Anfield on *Match of the Day* many times but this is something else. The grass is so green. Sounds stupid I know, but this is the first thing that strikes me. The crowd are so loud, and the noise seems to be coming from everywhere.

Emotions swell up inside and I'm getting a lump in my throat. I think I'm going to cry, but that's unthinkable. I swallow hard and join in with the singing. My voice is small and lost in the cacophony. I don't care, I'm doing my bit. I'm part of it all.

Even now, in the big games, when the stakes are high enough and the Kop rolls back the years, the ghosts of those first Anfield experiences return and I get that same lump in the throat and tear in my eye.

This is the Liverpool I fell in love with as a kid. It's been a love affair that has burned for more than 40 years. I've been lucky enough to see this team win everything. As I've aged and had kids of my own, naturally I have done all I can to immerse them in that great community and let them witness that green grass up close, as have countless Kopites down the years.

However, as the football I knew and loved gave way to the mega-rich, corporate entity it is today, I found myself falling out of love with the club and the game. I still went, handed over my money, but each step along Walton Breck Road began to feel like an act of duty, rather than the joyful pilgrimage it once was.

It became increasingly difficult to get a handle on what Liverpool FC was anymore. Was it the shirt that cost an arm and a leg? The badge previous owners sought to patent? Or was it the players or the managers who swapped teams during tough times? Even Anfield, once a cauldron of energy, wit and passion, had fallen into a brooding and sometimes eerily silent affair.

However, in writing *Red Odyssey*, I have reconnected with that old world once again. I've been reminded of the richness of our history. I've discovered long forgotten moments, like when Reds supporters stood at Lime Street station in 1914, eager to taste their first FA Cup Final. Their songs and raucous behaviour reminded me that today's Kopites stand on the shoulders of giants.

Completing the book has transported me across the ages. I've joined heroes and villains, unearthed forgotten victories and terrible defeats, relived great tragedies and moments of redemption and vindication.

Through all of that I have realised that the club I loved was never lost. It has been there all along, hiding in the archives and in the stories of the people who built it and nurtured it through more than a century of sporting endeavour.

So, I humbly present to you 125 tales that capture the richness of the people who are the cornerstone of this great club. Writing them has been my odyssey, a journey from the scepticism of middle age to the forgotten treasure of my youth, and the lives of our ancestors. Along the way I found a renewed sense of love for our club.

May reading it bring you as much joy as writing these tales has brought to me.

The Call to Adventure

Liverpool Football Club 1892–1939

From the flames of conflict: the birth of Liverpool Football Club

Citizens of Liverpool, in 1892, divided their loyalties between two football teams, Everton FC and Bootle FC. Their supporters enjoyed a spirited but ultimately friendly rivalry. They would cheer on their heroes during home games at Anfield and Hawthorne Road. Then, when their team played away, they often switched their support to the other.

However, things were about to get much more complicated with the emergence of a new upstart that would challenge their dominance of Merseyside football. With talk of boycotting the new team's games, those supporters would watch in envy as this 'new kid on the block' grew to eclipse them both.

The story is chronicled in an innocuous column, situated in the top left-hand corner of the now defunct *Liverpool Mercury*, dated 16 March 1892. A remarkable tale is told under the headline:

THE FUTURE OF EVERTON FOOTBALL CLUB

LIVELY MEETING

MR HOULDING REMOVED FROM THE PRESIDENCY

The article tells of the birth of a sporting dynasty in stunning detail. It spells out how, in a packed committee room, in the Presbyterian School on Royal Street, Everton Valley, an extraordinary battle was being waged. It would ultimately lead to the city of Liverpool's only top-flight team tearing itself apart and the establishment of a rivalry that would turn the city into the most successful footballing town in England.

Everton had won the title in 1891 but had failed to defend it. Some directors had blamed the team's poor showing on the fact that they got changed into their kits at the Sandon pub, which was situated just across the road from the Anfield pitch.

The implication was they were sampling the local hospitality, instead of preparing themselves for games.

But that was the least of the club's problems. Before the assembled businessmen at the meeting was a motion to remove the president, John Houlding, a brewer and politician, from the board. Plans were also afoot to relocate the club altogether.

Houlding had set up a new company, the Everton Football and Athletic Grounds Company Limited. However, he couldn't get it registered as two companies with such similar-sounding names couldn't exist. The board discovered this and, suspicious of his motives, they were outraged.

Rival factions within the club's hierarchy had been at war for months. The row stemmed from the fact that Houlding, who owned the ground at Anfield, wanted to raise the rent.

His opponents on the board believed he was trying to steal the club away from them, along with its fixtures and fittings, while making a tidy profit at their expense. As well as steadfastly refusing to pay up, they also wanted him out. If he lost the vote on the night it would leave him with a ground, but no team.

In truth he knew what was coming and had already worked out his 'Plan B'. Anyone reading the proceedings of these meetings would be left with the impression that Houlding was enjoying himself.

The board had called an Extraordinary General Meeting, ostensibly to carry out a coup by removing their president in the full glare of the local press. In the chair for the night was one of Houlding's rivals and a future leader of Everton, George Mahon.

Tensions reached fever pitch when Houlding entered the room. Mahon stood and asked if, as club president, he would like to take the chair. There were cries of 'Hear, hear' and 'No, no.'

Sensing the drama of the occasion, Houlding rose to the challenge. 'I am here to reply,' he said, then with a twinkle in his eye, he added, 'And a criminal never takes the chair, he steps into the dock.' It brought half the house down at least. Laughter and applause mixed with cries of 'Shame!' rang out.

A furious debate raged with claim and counterclaim flying in all directions. The committee accused their president of 'underhanded deeds'. He had, they said, sought to set up his own company and register it with the Football Association. He steadfastly denied any wrongdoing, but it was clear that a historic split was on the cards.

In the end the motion to split was carried easily and just three days later, on 15 March 1892, Liverpool Football Club and Athletic Grounds Limited was formed. The Football Association granted it official recognition three months later, on 3 June.

A great sporting institution came into existence on that day. A rivalry that began in the boardroom would go on to divide families throughout the city for more than a century.

Houlding quickly assembled a squad, made up of largely Scottish players, dubbed the 'team of Macs'. He appointed William Edward Barclay as the manager and immediately applied to join the Football League. His application was rejected and Liverpool instead entered the Lancashire League.

For a time they would play 'third fiddle' to Everton, who were in the First Division, and Bootle FC, who had just entered the newly formed Second Division. But the new upstarts would eventually eclipse their rivals.

Barclay's men and the club's officials also met and got changed in the Sandon pub, where they donned the blue and white kits, left behind by their rivals before crossing the street to Anfield. They would wear those colours until 1896.

Liverpool's first competitive game came on 3 September 1892 at home to Higher Walton, in front of a crowd numbering the low hundreds. It finished 8-0 to the Anfield men.

Houlding and the club's new supporters would wait just seven months to face his bitter rivals from across Stanley Park, in the Liverpool Senior Cup Final at Hawthorne Road, Bootle. It proved to be an encounter as fiery as the boardroom split that had created the two teams, but more about that later.

Two games and 15 goals in three days: Liverpool's barnstorming debut in English football

Liverpool FC came into existence in March 1892, but they would have to wait six months to play their first official game. That came at Anfield where they faced a team called Higher Walton in the Lancashire League, in front of a crowd of just 300, thrashing them 8-0 on Saturday, 3 September 1892.

However, on the Thursday before, John Houlding's new creation would warm up with a friendly game against Rotherham Town. The game may have been lost in the mists of time, but for a report filed in the *Liverpool Mercury*.

The official attendance is unknown; however, there are suggestions that as many as 200 may have turned up. Entrance was probably free but supporters would have to pay one penny for the official matchday programme.

Liverpool, playing in blue and white, won the toss and were straight at the visitors from the first whistle. Within minutes they were a goal up through John Miller; then Andrew Kelvin hit a brace, with his second and Liverpool's third coming from a free kick.

Rotherham had been blitzed early on and it seemed to spark them into life. They mounted a series of attacks on Liverpool's goal, with at least two efforts going very close, but the defence was equal to it and the visitors soon ran out of steam.

Then the 'Anfielders' rushed into a five-goal lead with two goals from Tom Wyllie. Half-time couldn't come quick enough for the away side and they'd have been desperate for the break.

After the restart Rotherham had the wind at their backs and attempted to restore some pride.

This is how the *Mercury* described their attempted fightback, 'Langdon missed an easy chance a moment later, and for the next few minutes the home defenders had a very anxious time. Leather and Pickering in turn sent in capital shots, and the Liverpudlians were somewhat lucky in keeping their position intact.'

Liverpool woke up, though, and Kelvin missed a sitter as they threatened to run riot. The visitors' penalty area was under siege and eventually it caved in, with Miller adding his second and Wyllie his third. Liverpool then hit the crossbar, before Rotherham snatched a late consolation. The final score was 7-1 and Liverpool's footballing story had truly begun.

The local paper gave Merseyside's newcomers a report card that said 'good, with room for improvement', continuing, 'As a team the 11 played well together, and are sure to improve with more practice. Ross, in goal, had little to do, but in the few cases in which he had to handle, he showed great coolness and courage. The backs played well together, thoroughly understanding each other, and showing great resource when pressed.

'The trio of halves could hardly be improved on, McBride in particular playing a brilliant game. Forward the combination is sure to improve in time, but Smith showed a slight tendency to keep the ball too long, much to the detriment of his comrades.'

Improve they did. Liverpool won the Lancashire League in their first season and captured the Liverpool Senior Cup at the expense of their neighbours Everton, beginning a journey that would take the club to the pinnacle of European and world football.

Liverpool triumph but the spoils of victory are stolen as first Merseyside derby ends in protest

Everton and Liverpool's official first encounter came in 1894, in the First Division of the Football League. Liverpool went down to a 3-0 defeat at Goodison Park. However, this wasn't the first time the two rivals had ever met.

During Liverpool's inaugural 1892/93 season in the Lancashire League, they also contested the Liverpool Senior Cup. After disposing of both Chester and Bootle, they set up a mouth-watering final against their Goodison neighbours on 22 April 1893.

Technically this was a friendly match, so it is not recorded in official derby records by either club. However, reports show it was hotly contested and anything but a friendly encounter.

The game was hosted at Bootle FC's ground in Hawthorne Road, a site also used for cricket. The city was abuzz at the prospect of such an important game taking place between Everton and Liverpool so soon after their acrimonious split in 1892.

Liverpool's home attendances had grown from a few hundred to nearly 2,500. However, the Blues were still by far the bigger club, averaging attendances of almost 13,000.

Liverpool were clearly seen as unpopular upstarts by their rivals, as evidenced by talk of boycotts of Anfield by Evertonians and Bootleites, as they were known. It was common back then for local supporters to transfer allegiance to their neighbours when their side was away from home. However, rumours were rife of a pact between Everton and Bootle supporters not to visit Anfield.

The *Liverpool Echo* review, written on the eve of battle, captures the mood surrounding the fixture:

'On account of the rivalry existing between the contestants – Everton and Liverpool – the game has created a vast amount of interest, and arrangements have been made for a large attendance.

'The game is sure to be one of the keenest and most exciting descriptions, as Liverpool are determined to try their best to dispossess Everton of the handsome trophy.'

The psychological battle was in full swing in the run-up to the match. Everton had threatened to field a 'combination team' as they didn't see it as an important fixture. Liverpool threatened to retaliate, by fielding a reserve side. In the end, both sent out a strong XI.

On the day, over 10,000 supporters turned up. Conditions outside the ground were described by the *Lancashire Post* as appalling, with fans finding it difficult to get into the ground.

Everton came out first, followed by Liverpool. Teams would emerge separately and run past a box placed on the pitch to allow a photographer to line up his shot. Reports suggest both teams were given a sporting welcome.

Then battle commenced, and it was Liverpool, perhaps wanting it more, who went on the early offensive. The *Liverpool Mercury* gives an almost minute-by-minute account of the action, beginning, 'Liverpool had the best of the play so far, being quicker and better combined than their opponents.'

The Everton goal was under siege, with their keeper pulling off a succession of saves to deny the men from Anfield. However, they couldn't withstand the barrage for long and in the 35th minute Liverpool took the lead. Here's how the *Mercury*'s scribe saw the goal, 'McCartney was penalised for holding, but the free kick was adroitly turned to Liverpool's advantage, as on Miller passing to Wyllie, the latter scored a goal with a low shot.'

The underdogs were 1-0 up and it stayed like that until half-time. The press couldn't make out whether they were the better team, or if Everton hadn't taken the game seriously enough. It didn't matter as far as Liverpool's new following were concerned.

The second half was different and, perhaps after a dressing-room telling-off, Everton emerged with more impetus. Still they couldn't break Liverpool down and, as the game wore on, they became increasingly frustrated at Liverpool's tactics.

The Anfield outfit had resorted to some agricultural defending by the end of the game. Meanwhile, Everton were pushing hard, desperately trying to avoid defeat.

In the dying moments they won a corner and from the resulting scramble, Everton alleged a handball by one of Liverpool's defenders and demanded a penalty. The referee, after consulting his linesman, waved away their appeals.

It was the last action of the match. As the final whistle sounded, there was uproar.

In what many felt was a cynical ploy to prevent Liverpool receiving the trophy on the pitch, Everton lodged a formal protest. The victors would have to wait to receive their spoils.

Writing in *Cricket and Field Review*, on 29 April 1893, one journalist recorded his disappointment at the behaviour of Everton officials at the end of the game, 'I would much rather have seen the full strength of Everton on the field, and so would lots of their supporters, but the executive I suppose considered the team quite good enough to again win the cup, but when they failed it is bad form then to step in with a protest, and this on the most flimsy ground.'

Everton complained that the referee was incompetent. However, Liverpool Football Association rejected this at a hearing, held at the Neptune Hotel, on the Monday after the game.

Andrew Hannah, club captain, received the trophy, described as 'a splendid specimen of the silversmith's art', at a home game against Preston on Tuesday. He had also lifted the Lancashire League Cup, completing a historic double in Liverpool's first season.

However, the drama was far from over. On 1 September 1893, on the eve of Liverpool's debut season in the Second Division, both trophies were stolen from a pawnshop in the Paddington area of the city.

They had been on display there, allowing supporters to view them in the shop window. The *Daily News* on 4 September 1893 reported, 'The burglars forced open the door of the shop with a jemmy, and took away the prizes, which are of considerable value. So far the police have failed to obtain a clue to the missing cups.'

Sadly, the trophies were never found. Liverpool would be forced to pay the princely sum of £130 to replace them. Who could have carried out such an act?

Changing colours: Liverpool become 'the Reds' in 1896

Imagine a world where Everton played in red and Liverpool entered the field of play wearing blue and white. Hard to picture that ever happening, isn't it? It's unthinkable actually. Well it did and here's why.

In 1892, Everton had walked out of Anfield and decided to set up a new club at Goodison Park. Liverpool's new owner, John Houlding, quickly set about building a new team. He recruited most of his players from Scotland, leading to the creation of a so-called 'team of Macs'. There was just one problem; there was no money left over to buy a kit.

Everton's new board had decided to change their shirt to 'ruby red', so Houlding decided to go rummaging in the

Anfield store room and found Everton's old blue and white shirts and that became the new team's official kit. So, for four full seasons, until 1896, Everton played in red and Liverpool in blue.

Liverpool were referred to during this period as 'the Anfielders'. However, at the end of the 1895/96 season Liverpool manager John McKenna moved upstairs to the boardroom. Liverpool swiftly appointed Tom Watson as their new boss.

The last game under McKenna, against West Bromwich Albion at Stoney Park, would turn out to be the last time Liverpool played in blue. They lost 2-0.

Watson ushered in an exciting new era at Anfield and a new kit. Everton had decided to ditch the red shirts and opted for royal blue. Houlding quickly saw his opportunity and immediately purchased 20 red shirts from Jack Sugg's clothing store in the city centre.

It turned out to be a masterstroke because red and white were the municipal colours of the city. This meant his club now bore both the city's name and its colours.

There is some confusion over the colour of the shorts, or knickers as they were called at the time, as they were initially intended to be black. However, as the team kicked off the new season away to 'The Wednesday' on 1 September 1896, the *Liverpool Daily Post* reported that they were wearing red shirts and white shorts for the first time.

Liverpool FC were now officially the Reds. They would win their first game wearing the new shirt 2-1 and the first player to score for the club in the red top, white shorts and red socks was George Allen, who netted twice.

Sadly the first game in red at Anfield was a 2-0 reverse against Bolton Wanderers. The Reds faced similar disappointment at Goodison when they faced the Blues for the first time in their new kits. The game ended 2-1 to Everton, with Jimmy Ross scoring for Liverpool.

Liverpool's first victory over Everton after changing to red came on 25 September 1897. They won 3-1 in front of a crowd of 30,000.

The shirt was a simple one, with a 'dark red or black stand collar and buttons down the front'. There was no badge though. Liverpool players did not wear a Liver bird upon their chest until the 1950 FA Cup Final against Arsenal.

It would disappear after that game, which the Reds lost 2-0, and wouldn't be seen again until 1955. Eventually Bill Shankly would oversee the change to the all-red kit in a European Cup game against Anderlecht during the 1964/65 season.

Shanks initially only wanted red shirt and red shorts, because he thought it would make the team look more powerful. However, according to Ian St John's autobiography, 'the Saint' suggested they 'go the whole hog' and change the socks to red too. The evolution of Liverpool's kit is indeed intricately woven into the fabric of the club's history. It has been shaped by the many stories and great men who built the institution we love today.

Heartbreak as defeat snatched from the jaws of victory in 1899

By 1899 Liverpool Football Club was seven years old. They had won the Lancashire League in their debut season and were crowned Second Division champions in 1894 and 1896. However, they had never mounted a serious assault on the First Division title.

That changed in the 1898/99 season under manager Tom Watson when they would go agonisingly close to the biggest prize of all.

Going into the season there was great optimism among Liverpool supporters, as reflected in a season preview in the *Lancashire Evening Post*, published on 27 August 1898:

'Liverpudlians are awaiting the forthcoming season with eagerness and confidence, and unless Tom Watson is a false prophet Liverpool will achieve fame and honour before many moons have passed. No expense, no effort, has been spared in the attempt to get a first-class team together; and Mr Watson has every reason to feel proud of his handiwork.'

The paper cited the capture of Alex Raisbeck and the retention of several star players as reasons for Scousers to be cheerful. The club had also poached trainer James Chapman from Heart of Midlothian and apparently, he 'already had the men well in hand'.

The Reds performed well and raced to the summit. With one game left they had won 19 of their 33 matches.

Going into their last fixture of the season, away to Aston Villa, Liverpool sat at the top of the table. They were two points clear of second-placed Villa, but the side from the Midlands had a far superior goal difference. This set up a mouth-watering clash with the winner taking the title.

The omens were not good though, as Liverpool had lost the home fixture 3-0 earlier in the season. Nonetheless, the *Liverpool Mercury* reported that many supporters made the journey from the city to Birmingham and the attendance at Villa Park was a bumper 41,357.

There was clearly a huge sense of occasion with the encounter taking on the air of a cup final, rather than a league match. Both teams entered the field to tumultuous applause with Villa coming out first. Imagine those hopeful Scousers taking up their places in the ground, hopelessly outnumbered, bellies full of ale and trying their damnedest to shout the lads to glory over the Villa din.

However, they would have their hopes cruelly dashed. Maybe Liverpool were simply outplayed, or perhaps the occasion got to them. Whatever the reason, they were out of the game by half-time. The local press was damning, stating that 'the Anfielders lost heart and were outplayed'.

Two goals from Jack Davey in the first 20 minutes set Villa on their way. Then Billy Garraty and Jimmy Crabtree grabbed a goal apiece in the space of a minute and Fred Wheldon sealed the five-goal rout in the 44th minute.

Liverpool mounted a fightback in the second half but it was a case of too little too late. Those Liverpudlian supporters on their 19th-century away-day would make their way home to Merseyside, heartbroken.

They would return to damning headlines in the *Liverpool Echo*, words that would perfectly sum up the scale of their disappointment:

FIGHT FOR THE LEAGUE CHAMPIONSHIP

AGONY FOR LIVERPOOL

ASTON VILLA MAKE NO MISTAKE

ROUT OF THE LIVERPOOL MEN

Fortunately for those poor 'Anfielders' they wouldn't have to wait too long for the club's first top-flight championship. Tom Watson would lead them to the title in 1901. That team would receive an astonishing welcome on their return to the city, but that's another story.

A hero's tale; Raisbeck leads Reds to their first league title, in 1901

On Monday, 29 April 1901, Liverpool went into their last game of the season, away to West Brom. They sat in second in the First Division.

They were level on points with Sunderland but their rivals' season was already over. If they avoided defeat the championship would be theirs for the first time.

Liverpool's manager was the great Tom Watson. He joined the Reds in 1896 from Sunderland. There he had won three First Division titles and led the men from the north-east to a world championship in 1895.

Unsurprisingly, Tom commanded the respect of everyone in the game. Few players could turn him down, allowing him to build a formidable team. Writing in the *Liverpool Echo* in 1924, Victor Hall had this to say, 'One of the secrets of his success in discovering new players was his own personal popularity. Everyone he met liked him and was always ready to do him a service.'

Like the great Bill Shankly, Tom was also something of a pioneer. He believed strongly that diet and exercise held the key to success.

However, his prescription of chops and eggs on toast for breakfast and wine for lunch would probably raise a few eyebrows today. In his defence, he did tell his men to use tobacco sparingly.

As club secretary, he would use his powers of persuasion to sign Liverpool's first superstar player, Alex Raisbeck, in 1898. The Scot was a regular for Hibernian and was coveted by Stoke, who had taken him on a four-game trial.

Watson was a guest of the Hibs chairman in May 1898 and was impressed with Raisbeck. However, Stoke's secretary was expected to arrive and sign the player on the same day.

Fortunately for Liverpool, he failed to turn up and Raisbeck was ours.

There is no doubt that this was something of a coup. Raisbeck was regarded as one of the finest players in Scotland. He was also something of a pin-up boy, if this review in the *Liverpool Echo* was anything to go by, 'A man of Raisbeck's proportions, style and carriage would rivet attention anywhere. He was a picture at 5' 9" and fully 12½ stone; a fine and beautifully balanced figure.'

Hall, writing for the *Echo* in 1924, would say Raisbeck elevated Liverpool above their station, adding, 'Raisbeck was wholeheartedly a destroyer of attacks when it came from the opposing wing … There may be and may have been others so gifted. We have not seen them'.

He would play 312 times for Liverpool, scoring 19 goals and captaining the side from 1900 to 1909. Raisbeck also won two league titles during his time at Anfield. He would have been idolised in much the same way Steven Gerrard or Kenny Dalglish are today.

The last game of the 1900/01 title-winning season was anything but easy. Perhaps nerves got to the players but they would labour to victory. This is how Raisbeck described the goal that won the league, 'The ball was lying on the goal-line. Johnny Walker and the "Throstles'" goalkeeper had got mixed up some way and were lying near the back of the net, and there was no friendly foot to put the ball through.

'I know I stopped dead. I was fascinated, I suppose, by the sight of both goalkeeper and Walker starting to wrestle towards the ball at the same instant. Which would reach it first? There was such a deathly stillness.

'I fancied I heard the tick of the referee's watch, although he was twenty yards from me, and it seemed as though half an hour had passed. But it must have lasted only a second or two.

'The goalie was on his hands and knees crawling towards the ball, when Walker, with a cat-like movement, wriggled his body along the ground and just tipped the ball over the line and the goal and championship were ours.'

With no telephones or televisions, supporters back home would rely on the recently invented radio to find out that their team were champions. Nevertheless, somehow word reached home, and people turned out in their thousands to welcome their idols home.

This is how Liverpool's heroic captain described the scenes that greeted the team at the city's Central station, 'What a night after the match! We were unprepared for what was awaiting us at Liverpool. I should imagine there was a crowd of between 50–60,000 packed in front of the Central station, and right along nearly as far as Lime Street. The street was literally black with people.'

The players were then carried through the streets and eventually ended up in the Sandon Hotel, where the victory party took place. Oh to have been a fly on the wall that night.

The birth of the Kop in 1906

In 1900, on a far-flung battlefield in South Africa, the Boer War was raging. The British army was attempting to capture a strategic hilltop called Spion Kop and 300 men died trying. Many were from Liverpool.

Meanwhile, back home, Liverpool Football Club were on their way to winning their very first league title. The club were also busy constructing a new stand alongside Kemlyn Road.

Then in 1906, after Liverpool's second league title was secured, they turned their attention to the heap of rubble on Walton Breck Road. Little did they know, but they were about to give birth to something quite magical.

As a reward for the loyalty of supporters, who had stood at that end of the ground since 1892, the owners decided to erect a new stand made of cinder and brick.

The sports editor of the *Liverpool Daily Post and Echo*, Ernest Edwards, gazed upon the magnificent pile and immediately christened it the Spion Kop, after the famous hill where so many Scousers had perished years before.

In that moment a legend was born. Sure, other football grounds have stands they call a Kop end, but Anfield's is the original and by far the best. It is also easily the most famous terrace in all of football.

The first game to take place in front of the mighty stand was a league opener against Stoke City. According to the local press, the city of Liverpool was sweltering under record temperatures. Shock was expressed at the fact the game wasn't postponed, but the heat didn't deter the first Kopites from turning out in their droves.

With no roof above their heads, they'd have been exposed to the burning sun and packed together they'd have struggled with the unbearable heat. The *Liverpool Echo* gives a sense of the conditions, with a headline that declared:

LIVERPOOL V STOKE

———

LEAGUE DIVISION 1

———

TROPICAL HEAT

———

HEWITT SCORES FIRST GOAL
FOR LIVERPOOL

———

CROWD ESTIMATED AT 30,000

Liverpool won 1-0 thanks to a 20th-minute goal by Joe Hewitt, the first player to score in the shadow of the Kop. The match report states that 25,000 supporters were packed into the ground at kick-off. However, they continued to pour in during the game and by half-time there were 30,000 in attendance. This was 10,000 more than the previous season and many of those supporters were crammed into the new stand. It must have been a fearsome sight.

The numbers climbing on to the Kop ebbed and receded as the season unfolded, but on 29 September 1906, 40,000 crammed into the stadium to see Liverpool take on Everton. Sadly, despite the home side going a goal up in the first half through Jack Parkinson, Everton's Sandy Young hit two in the second half to take the spoils.

The ground remained unchanged until 1928 when the Kop got a makeover. It became a terrifying sight for any opposition and the largest single bank of terrace anywhere in football. It was capable of holding 30,000 people all standing, more than some grounds could hold in their entirety. The club also erected a roof over it, providing protection from the elements. To those used to the old stand, this must have seemed like luxury. The noise, amplified under that tin roof, must have been incredible.

In the 1960s and '70s the Kop would reach new heights, in terms of its majesty and power, when it would terrify opponents and inspire new generations of Liverpool players to glory.

In all the years since that famous old terrace has inspired awe and wonderment. It has been celebrated for its colour and song, for its wit and invention and for its fierce loyalty.

For many of us, blessed to be able to call it home on a matchday, it is, without doubt, the greatest place in football. And long may it reign.

Liverpool 6-5 Newcastle United: Anfield breathless as Reds refuse to be beaten in 1909

When we think of great games against Newcastle United, it doesn't take long for thoughts to drift back to the 1990s. In those days it was Roy Evans and Kevin Keegan going toe-to-toe and producing some of the most breathtaking football Anfield has ever witnessed.

Perhaps some of us look back fondly on the 1974 FA Cup demolition of the Geordies at Wembley. However, none of those great games can hold a candle to an epic encounter that took place at Anfield on 4 December 1909.

Liverpool are now famed for their ability to mount a heroic fightback, but few of us realise just how ingrained in the club's DNA this is. So let's spend a short while revelling in another glorious moment in the Reds' 125-year history and a comeback that will take some beating.

This was Liverpool's 18th season in the Football League. Their manager was the great Tom Watson, who had delivered the club's first league title. They would ultimately finish runners-up to Aston Villa in 1909 but they boasted a great side, captained by Arthur Goddard, and they had the prolific Jack Parkinson up front.

In goal was Sam Hardy – who Charlie Buchan, a founder member of the Football Writers' Association, described as the finest goalkeeper he had ever seen.

He served Liverpool for seven years, notching up 240 appearances, but none will have been more difficult than this one. His team were a goal down in the first minute.

Anfield was a shadow of the ground it is today and that season the average attendance was 25,000. Supporter Frank Ryan, who was just 11 years old, was at the game. He wrote to Liverpool in 1972 to tell them of his experiences supporting the club and his story is lovingly set out in a club programme.

In it, he tells of scrambling beneath the Kemlyn Road stand looking for cigarette packets that might contain a clean football card. Occasionally he would find a shiny silver coin that had fallen through the cracks.

However, his fondest memory is sitting on his dad's shoulders as Goddard scored the winner against Newcastle in that historic encounter, completing a monumental comeback.

Another fan, Charles Wannop of Childwall, describes how he was in a sweepstake and had Liverpool to win. At half-time the Reds were 5-2 down and he thought he'd seen the last of his bet; instead, he would leave Anfield clutching his two shillings with pride.

Just picture the scene inside the ground as Liverpool surged forward. Imagine the roar that would have greeted each goal.

The *Liverpool Echo* spoke of the Reds' 'pluck' and their 'wonderful rally in the second half'. It was, the newspaper reported, an 'amazing game'.

Imagine no more. Here, in the words of a local journalist, is exactly how victory was wrestled from the jaws of defeat, 'The seemingly impossible happened when McDonald, Parkinson and Orr, with almost superhuman energy, swept all before them, Orr equalising under very great difficulty. The excitement of the crowd was intense and the noise almost deafening at times. Would you believe it. Robinson's forward pass, crossed to Goddard, and lo and behold, the Reds were ahead.'

It sounds like a truly amazing game.

Liverpool's first taste of FA Cup fever, but Clarets down Reds at Crystal Palace

This moment in Liverpool history takes us from the humblest of beginnings in the Lancashire League, playing in front of tiny crowds at Anfield in 1892, to the splendour of an FA Cup Final in front of 72,000 people at Crystal Palace in 1914.

In just 22 years the Reds had been catapulted to the very top of English football.

This would also be the first time a reigning monarch would watch the final, with King George V taking his seat in the Royal Box. Burnley were the Reds' opponents and they would break Liverpudlian hearts that day.

Liverpool had competed in the FA Cup four times previously and had always fallen short. However, after a 2-0 victory over Aston Villa at White Hart Lane in the semi-final, they faced a second trip to the capital but this time with the biggest prize in football on offer.

In charge was Tom Watson, a manager who had masterminded two First Division titles for the Reds.

However, Liverpool would be without star defender and club captain Harry Lowe. He pulled out of the game at the 11th hour and it must have been heartbreaking for the player and the supporters, who wouldn't have known until the teams emerged onto the field.

The thought of a first cup final in the capital had supporters' hearts racing.

The *Liverpool Echo* gives an insight into the cup fever gripping the 'Anfielders'. Under the headline 'A ROYAL DAY: MERRY SCENES AT THE STATION' the paper reports that more than 20,000 Liverpudlians made the trip to Crystal Palace by train and coach.

So large were the crowds that 'one of the biggest trains on record' was pressed into service, carrying 1,200 fans. This may have been the first train referred to as a 'football special'.

In addition, 18 and a half coaches transported 'the population of a village from Liverpool to London in one swoop'. It seems those travelling by coach got the better deal, with the *Echo* stating that, on the train, passengers were 'crammed like cigars in a box'.

Many had just finished night shifts and, rather than go home to bed, they piled on to the train. Imagine the anticipation, the eager chatter and their hopes and dreams of silverware.

The local paper paints a glorious image of the journey. Drink it in, 'It was a train of streamers. Every carriage was a blaze of red and white ribbons and rosettes.

'Portraits of the Liverpool team were stuck on the windows and *Echo* badges bearing football battle cries were worn on nearly every hat and button hole.'

Fans hung out of the window and serenaded the railway porters with the music of the day.

Inside the carriages they mocked their opponents, with one of the earliest recorded Liverpool songs. It went like this:

> *'The Burnley men came like wolves on the fold*
> *And their faces gleamed like the Klondyke gold*
> *To the football field they all wended their way*
> *To see their old foes at football to play*
> *But nins and slack, when they got on the fluid*
> *And saw their opponents, they knew they's to yield*
> *For they rushed them and pushed them until all were sore*
> *And beat them all hollow, as they'd oft done before.'*

Many of those travelling were factory workers and had fashioned tiny replicas of the cup out of metal, pinning them as badges to their coats. Their pockets bulged with sandwiches and others were carrying 'a little extra', according to observers. It wasn't an all-male excursion either, with reports of many 'lady supporters of the club, who took a leading part in the display of enthusiasm'.

It was said that Burnley's supporters outnumbered Liverpool's, but they couldn't match the red men and women for their spirit. These scenes may have occurred more than a century ago, but they are instantly recognisable to any Red travelling to cup finals today.

How heart-warming to know that, when we travel all over the world to follow our team, we are walking in the footsteps of such passionate people. Sadly though, on this occasion Liverpool would return empty-handed and their loyal following would be bitterly disappointed.

Burnley netted following a throw-in and, to rub salt in to the wound, it was an ex-Everton player, Bertie Freeman, who scored it with his head. Reds would have to wait more than half a century to see their team win the cup, tasting more pain along the way.

Many of those merry men and women at Lime Street on 25 April 1914, won't have lived to see Shankly's boys eventually win the FA Cup, but today's Kopites stand proudly on their shoulders.

Thanks to their legacy, we are still recognised as some of the most passionate supporters in the game. So, next time you step on to a coach, train or plane, remember you are following in the footsteps of these great fans.

Match-fixing scandal rocks Liverpool and Manchester United, in 1915

Fixtures between Liverpool and Manchester United have often been mired in controversy. However, few will outdo a game in 1915 which will forever live in infamy.

With war raging in Europe, many felt it was only a matter of time before the Football League would be suspended. Many players had left to fight and those left behind may have thought their careers would end once the season was over.

Liverpool and United were struggling in the table and with games running out, United looked in trouble. They had drawn 1-1 at Anfield earlier in the season and neither side had any chance of honours as they faced off on Good Friday in 1915.

The bookies had laid odds of 7/1 on United winning 2-0 and there were stories emerging, even before kick-off, that players from both teams had been seen drinking together ahead of the fixture.

Rumours were rife that they had been discussing plans to fix the game in United's favour. An Old Trafford crowd of 18,000 watched in amazement as both sides seemed to go through the motions, with United emerging 2-0 winners.

However, the players' odd behaviour had not escaped the attention of match officials and journalists covering the game.

In the first half United were 1-0 up through George Anderson when they were gifted the chance to extend their lead from the spot after Bob Purcell had deliberately handled in the penalty area.

Patrick O'Connell, United's captain and centre-half, stepped up to take the penalty. He smashed the ball well wide, almost hitting the corner flag. However, it was his reaction as he walked towards the centre circle that caused outrage.

He was seen to be laughing and many thought he didn't care because United could get another at any time in the game. Liverpool had appeared lifeless and offered little resistance.

Not all players were in on the fix though and there were reports of angry exchanges in the dressing rooms at half-time.

In the second half United extended their lead thanks again to Anderson, who was not said to be in on the scandal.

With the score at 2-0 it looked like several players would be laughing all the way to the bank. However, one of them hadn't read the script.

Reds striker Fred Pagnam, who knew of the plot and was determined to wreck it, almost scored. He was also concerned that Liverpool were struggling in mid-table. It wasn't beyond the realms of possibility that they could be dragged into a relegation fight. So, late on in the game he rattled the crossbar with a fierce shot, much to the conspirators' anger.

His own team-mates were seen angrily remonstrating with him, clearly worried that he could have cost them dearly. The game finished 2-0 as planned and evidence soon emerged that large bets had been placed on that scoreline.

An FA investigation found that seven players from both teams were involved. United's Sandy Turnbull, Enoch West and Arthur Whalley were found guilty. For Liverpool, Jackie Sheldon, Thomas Fairfoul, Bob Purcell and Miller were also found to have been involved.

All received lifetime bans. The clubs escaped punishment as the FA accepted it had been the players alone who had transgressed.

The story ends in tragedy though. The Football League was soon suspended due to the war and a number of the players went off to fight on the western front.

In 1919 all but West had their bans lifted in recognition of their military service. Turnbull was posthumously reinstated as he had been killed in battle. West was aged 59 when the FA lifted his ban in 1945.

The scandal would allow United to escape the drop at Chelsea's expense. However, the league was expanded for the 1919/20 season to allow them to re-join.

Elisha Scott and the 'Untouchables' win back-to-back titles, in the 1920s

When we think of the emergence of Liverpool Football Club as a major force in the history of English football, we tend to think of the 1960s and the charismatic Bill Shankly.

It's true that the man from Glenbuck delivered the long-awaited FA Cup and established the Reds as a force in Europe, but the honour of putting Liverpool firmly on the footballing map goes to David Ashworth, the all-conquering manager of the 1920s.

This was a team so awesome that they earned themselves the title 'Untouchables'. Ashworth's Reds were groundbreaking with players interchanging positions and outwitting opponents during games. They could mix it up too, with John Williams, author of *Red Men*, singling out their 'toughness and sheer will to win' as the cornerstone of their success.

In goal was the great Elisha Scott, the first player to earn a chant from the Kop, such was their love of the man.

Scott would travel to games from his New Brighton home on the Wirral, taking the Mersey ferry to the Pier Head before hopping on the tram to Anfield. On the way he would mix freely with the supporters and chat to them. During games they would roar "Lisha, 'Lisha'.

It was said that during matches he would wander over to the supporters and ask what they thought of the game, prompting many to consider him a friend.

Regarded by many as the greatest goalkeeper in British football, he served Liverpool for 22 years. In his final game, he was afforded the rare opportunity to address the crowd via a loudspeaker. He gave a speech in which he talked of his 'great friends on the Kop' and how he 'simply could not thank them enough for their support'. It is said that grown men wept as they listened.

Ashworth was clearly a believer in the importance of physical fitness and he employed a man called W. Connell to whip the lads into shape. The *Liverpool Courier* praised the trainer for his efficiency, stating, 'The Reds invariably outstay and outpace the opposition in the second half.'

With Dick Forshaw and Harry Chambers scoring for fun and a tough no-nonsense captain in Donald Mackinlay, the Reds were practically invincible. They won the league in 1922, finishing six points clear of their nearest rivals, Tottenham, winning 22 out of 42 games and scoring 63 times.

They were presented with the league title at Old Trafford of all places, after a Charity Shield game against Huddersfield Town. As both teams were from the north, for the first time the FA moved the game out of London. The Yorkshiremen won the shield but Liverpool didn't care; they were English champions.

The local press reported that on their arrival back at Lime Street, the squad were mobbed and captain Mackinlay was 'picked up and carried in triumph out of the station'.

There was more to come though, and the Reds would go again in the 1922/23 season. This time they swept all before them, again finishing six points clear at the top of the table, with Sunderland trailing in their wake.

They had won 26 games out of 42, scoring 70 times and losing on just eight occasions. Elisha Scott had conceded just 31 goals, keeping 21 clean sheets.

However, in February 1923, their all-conquering manager sensationally departed and returned to his former club, Oldham Athletic, who were battling relegation. He would be unable to prevent them going down and his replacement Matt McQueen managed only one win in the last seven games for Liverpool. Fortunately, the Reds were so far ahead they won the league anyway.

In the final match of the season, against Stoke City, Liverpool's heroic goalkeeper injured his thigh and was carried off the pitch on the back of a ground assistant. Bill Lacey, an outfield player, went in goal as there were no substitutes allowed.

Lacey was known to be a hard man, as illustrated by this snippet from an article in 1923, 'As for kicking Lacey as a hobby, I can assure you it's a waste of time, the boy is made from solid rock. Dynamite could not shift him off the ball.'

He lived up to his reputation and managed to keep a clean sheet in Scott's absence.

After the game, Liverpool were presented with their second title in as many years in front of a jubilant Anfield crowd of 30,000.

Ashworth would never recapture the success he had with Liverpool and McQueen would stay in the hot seat for a further five years.

Besides the 1923 championship, McQueen's greatest contribution to Liverpool was signing Gordon Hodgson, one of the club's greatest strikers, who scored nearly 250 goals in almost 400 appearances – more about him next.

Gordon Hodgson: Liverpool's 1930s goal machine

When supporters think of Liverpool's greatest goalscorers, thoughts will turn to Roger Hunt, Kenny Dalglish, Ian Rush or perhaps Robbie Fowler. However, long before all of those players were even born, Liverpool possessed a player so prolific he was a legitimate rival for Everton's Dixie Dean.

That man was Gordon Hodgson, who signed for Liverpool in 1925 and played 377 games for the Reds, scoring 241 goals. The likes of Hunt and Rush have since surpassed Hodgson's goal tally, but neither player has a better goals-per-game ratio than the South African's 0.64.

The player would finish the Reds' top scorer in seven of his nine seasons at Anfield. He notched a total of 233 goals in the First Division, including 19 hat-tricks.

In the 1920s and early 1930s, Merseyside boasted two of the greatest goalscorers in the country. At Anfield, Hodgson was utterly prolific and across Stanley Park, Everton boasted the great Dean.

So popular were these men that a local entrepreneur would sell biscuits for the price of five for a penny at Anfield one week, calling them Hodgson's choice. Then the following week he would be at Goodison, calling them Dixie's choice.

Everton supporters are justifiably proud of Dean, a legend and hero. In 1927/28 the striker would score 60 league goals in one season, a record that stands to this day. However, during the same period, Liverpool's Hodgson was also banging them in for fun.

The two men would face each other in the First Division a number of times, with the highlight for the Liverpool man coming in his final season.

Hodgson only managed nine games in 1935/36 but one of them was the Merseyside derby at Anfield. In front of 46,000 supporters, Liverpool's defence would shut out Dean and the Reds scored six without reply. Hodgson got two of them. In all, he scored six goals against the Blues.

It's worth remembering that these players plied their trade on pitches that the modern player would baulk at, wore shirts and boots that were heavy and often uncomfortable and headed balls that were more like concrete than leather. When considered alongside these factors, their achievements are all the more remarkable.

Gordon's greatest season came in 1930/31. Everton were fighting for the Second Division championship and the Reds were in the top flight. Liverpool would finish a disappointing ninth in the table, but their striker would yield a bumper crop.

In a 42-game season, Hodgson played 40 times and scored 36 goals, including four hat-tricks. It was his most prolific campaign at the club.

There were many highlights for Hodgson but one of the best must have been a game against Bolton Wanderers, at Anfield, in September 1930.

Liverpool won 7-2 and Gordon netted two of the Reds' goals. However, it wasn't his goalscoring exploits that caught the eye of the local media. Instead, it was an incident between Hodgson, a burly Bolton centre-half and a Kopite.

The two players had apparently become embroiled in an incident with the Kop taking exception to the visiting player's treatment of their heroic striker. Suddenly one of them climbed out of the Kop and appeared on the pitch.

Determined to defend Hodgson's honour, this furious fan started aiming punches at the Bolton defender. Naturally the police appeared, and this loyal Red decided to take a swing at them too.

He was eventually carted away, with one account suggesting he did six months in jail for his exuberance.

Such an incident gives an indication of how revered Hodgson was by the Liverpool faithful. Either that or it is a testament to the strength of the beer on sale around the ground in the 1930s.

In another game against Sheffield Wednesday, with his team 2-1 down at half-time, Hodgson inspired a second-half fightback. The Reds won 5-3 and Gordon scored four of the goals.

It's a great shame that Hodgson never won a trophy with Liverpool. His efforts in front of goal should have been rewarded with medals.

Hodgson was in the running to become Liverpool manager in the 1940s but Don Welsh was eventually appointed, and the prolific striker would instead go on to manage Port Vale.

After football he became a successful county cricketer for Lancashire but, sadly, he died at the tragically young age of 47 in 1951. Liverpool's chairman at the time, George Richards, said this of the former Anfield great, 'We remember with great pride the great service Gordon Hodgson gave Liverpool. He was a grand sportsman, always a genuine trier. And he never gave us a moment's anxiety.'

The battle of Bold Street: A story of Merseyside rivalry

One of the greatest rivalries in Merseyside football history was the one between Liverpool goalkeeper Elisha Scott and Everton striker Dixie Dean. Both players were footballing superstars and idolised by their respective team's supporters.

Imagine Ronaldo and Messi both living and playing on the banks of the Mersey and you get a sense of what this must have felt like for Reds and Blues. The difference was that, while these two were fierce enemies on the pitch, they were best of friends off it.

Stories about their rivalry and banter have now passed into legend. Inevitably some are exaggerated and have been distorted over time. Others have been documented for posterity, like their pre-derby ritual, for example.

LFCTV documentary *Elisha* tells how both men would meet in a city-centre bar after most games to discuss the results. Dixie would drink bitter and for Elisha it was Guinness. However, on the eve of derby day, Scott received an envelope from Dean, containing aspirin.

There was a note attached saying, 'You better get these down you. You'll need a good night's sleep, because I'll be scoring against you tomorrow.'

There are many more stories of their rivalry on the pitch, but by far the greatest story of the two men happened off it. This one concerned an encounter between the two on Liverpool's Bold Street.

Of course, it may well be a tall tale, but it is still recounted on Merseyside today. Its origins are unknown but apparently Dixie Dean once recounted it, giving the anecdote some credence. It goes like this:

The Everton striker is walking down the street. He hears someone shout his name, turns to see who it is and realises it is Elisha Scott.

Now, depending on who you listen to, he either tips his hat to the Liverpool goalkeeper or he pretends to head an invisible ball at him.

Whichever it was, Scott dived full length on the stone street to save this imaginary header.

Another story, recounted by Frank Keating in the *Guardian*, says Elisha dived through a plate-glass shopfront to save the phantom ball. Imagine the scenes as passers-by witnessed these two sporting legends acting out a footballing duel on the city's streets.

It almost doesn't matter if it's true or not. It should be.

Such stories serve to tell us how significant and important these two men were in the history of the game. They were worshipped as gods, but they were men of the people and belong to a forgotten but glorious period in the history of the Merseyside derby.

They also symbolise the closeness between two clubs, who could be mortal enemies for 90 minutes and best friends the rest of the week. Dean and Scott continued their friendship long after their playing careers ended and often drank together in Dixie's pub in Chester.

John Keith, Liverpool journalist and historian, said this of the two, 'I've spoken to Dixie Dean about Elisha Scott and they had this fantastic rivalry in the 1920s. Dixie Dean said he was the best goalkeeper he had ever seen and played against.'

We may never witness such a rivalry in Liverpool again. More's the pity.

The Age of Kings
Liddell, Paisley, Shankly and his Boys

Liverpool Football Club
1946–1974

Bob Paisley and Billy Liddell kick-start their Liverpool careers in 11-goal thriller, in 1946

Although the Football League had been suspended during World War II, unofficial games still went ahead. Liverpool featured in many of them. They often gave run-outs to two men who would go on to define the club: Bob Paisley and Billy Liddell.

Both had played countless games in the famous red shirt between 1939 and 1945. Liddell managed 152 and scored 82 goals. Paisley had already made 58 appearances and scored 12 times. However, none of these were official.

So, paradoxically, they would have to wait until 1946 and the resumption of the Football League to make their

Liverpool debuts. For both men this would come in the second home game of the 1946/47 season, against Chelsea. And what a game that was.

Almost 50,000 supporters packed in to Anfield to watch the game would have had no idea that they were witnessing the emergence of two living legends. Paisley and Liddell are now rightly woven into the fabric of the history of the club. They are threads of gold.

Liddell would go on to be idolised by the Kop, making 492 official appearances and scoring 215 goals. Billy was so popular that fans referred to the club as 'Liddellpool'. He would become a league champion in his first season and an FA Cup runner-up in 1950.

Paisley also received a 1946/47 league championship medal and went on to make 252 appearances.

However, his greatest contribution would be in management. Succeeding the great Bill Shankly, Paisley amassed 13 major honours in just nine years, including an unprecedented three European Cups. His feats would make him the most successful manager in Liverpool's history.

But, as the saying goes, every truly great journey must begin with a single step and theirs would turn out to be momentous. Liverpool tore into Chelsea from the off and Liddell opened the scoring in just two minutes. The Scot had now officially scored on his debut and the Reds sensed blood.

By half-time it was 4-0 to Liverpool, including a brace for another lad making his bow, Bill Jones. The Londoners looked out on their feet.

As the second half got under way they were soon in danger of being out for the count. The brilliant Jack Balmer grabbed the fifth just two minutes after the restart. Balmer had also been a regular during wartime, scoring an astonishing 64 goals in 101 games.

Just three minutes later, Liddell added his second and the Reds' sixth. Game over, or so the Liverpool supporters thought.

What happened next was simply astonishing and would have had the Kop in a state of panic. In the space of just 17 minutes the home defence fell apart and Chelsea scored four goals.

Liverpool goalkeeper Charlie Ashcroft picked the fourth out of the net in the 72nd minute and there must have been an inquest among the back four, because they somehow pulled themselves together and Chelsea ran out of steam.

With just three minutes left on the clock, Liverpool finally put the game to bed. Willie Fagan scored his second of the match and the supporters breathed a sigh of relief.

It finished 7-4; what an incredible game! But for those Kopites there would be even more glory to come in May.

Albert Stubbins defies gravity to send Reds into FA Cup semi-final in 1947

It's March 1947, the dark cold days of war are over, but Liverpool remains a city in the icy grip of winter. The Reds are sitting in fourth place, but they're on their way to becoming league champions for the fifth time in their history.

A series of four straight wins is the perfect antidote for Reds fans still smarting from a 1-0 reverse at Goodison Park in January. Liverpool are still in the FA Cup and have reached the quarter-finals. Only a home game against Birmingham City stands in the way of a place in the last four.

Officials estimated that more than 55,000 Reds huddled together for warmth as the game got under way on a frozen, snow-covered pitch, swelling the coffers to the tune of £5,500.

Liverpool were a team packed with legends and included two future managers, Phil Taylor and Bob Paisley.

Taylor would go on to spend three years at the helm, before making way for Bill Shankly. Bob, of course, went on to become the most successful Reds manager of all time.

Joining these two on the pitch were Billy Liddell, one of the club's greatest ever players, and Albert Stubbins, a goal machine who would later appear on a Beatles album cover.

Both would play a key role in one of the most magical moments in Liverpool's history, in what was a fierce encounter. According to the *Birmingham Daily Mail*, 'Feeling had crept into the game and the football was robust.'

Liverpool led at half-time through Stubbins but the away side levelled on 56 minutes. The Reds were having none of it though and would take just one minute to go back in front thanks to one of the most spectacular goals ever scored at Anfield.

After conceding, they immediately won a free kick in a dangerous position. Standing over the ball was the immortal Liddell. Lurking in the box was Stubbins.

I'll leave it to King Billy to tell you what happened, 'When I put the ball over it was going a bit off course, but Stubbins literally threw himself through the air to meet it with his head when parallel with the ground, about two feet off the turf.

'It went in like a rocket, giving Gil Merrick absolutely no chance, and Albert slid on his stomach for several yards on the frozen pitch, before coming to a stop.'

The crowd went wild. All game they had bemoaned the fact the players were bypassing captain and playmaker, Willie Fagan. Little did they know this was a deliberate tactic. The Reds knew Birmingham would mark him out of the action.

Fortunately they had a secret weapon in Stubbins and the Midlanders had no answer to him as Albert netted his third and Liverpool's fourth in a hugely satisfying afternoon. He went on to collect 24 goals that season.

Sadly, the Reds went out in the semi-final to Burnley, but Stubbins's heroics would help them to secure a memorable league title.

Beating the Blues and two trophies in one day – Liverpool's epic 1946/47 season

Imagine beating Everton in a cup final and winning the First Division title on the same day. Sounds like the stuff of Kopite fantasy, doesn't it? Believe it or not, this happened in 1947 and 40,000 Scousers were there to see it.

The Football League had only just resumed following the end of the war in 1945. Liverpool's league season was over. They had beaten Wolverhampton Wanderers 2-1 at Molineux on 31 May to go top of the table.

However, they would have to wait a fortnight to see if they were champions. Due to a prolonged winter the season would roll into June for some teams and the Reds' rivals for the league still had a game to play.

That team was Stoke City: they could still win the title on goal difference, if they beat Sheffield United on 14 June.

A headline in a Dundee local paper, 'Liverpool Must Wait', tells you what a story this was. It also says so much about how the whole nation was gripped by the return of football after the horrors of war.

Coincidentally the Reds had reached the final of the Liverpool Senior Cup on the same day as the title decider in Sheffield, which would kick off 15 minutes earlier.

They had already secured the Lancashire Senior Cup with a 2-1 victory over Bury a week earlier. Standing in the way of a local double was Everton.

A game against Everton is usually a must-win, but Reds legend Billy Liddell recalled how the players could barely concentrate. 'Our minds were more on what was taking place at Bramall Lane than at Anfield,' he said.

This was Billy's debut season. He had joined Liverpool's youth team in 1938, but the war interrupted his career. He broke into the first team in an FA Cup third-round tie away to Walsall, managing to score in a 5-2 win.

Somehow, despite their lack of focus, the Reds found themselves 2-1 up against Everton. Then, with 15 minutes left on the clock, an announcement over the loudspeaker declared that Sheffield United had defeated Stoke. Liverpool were champions of England.

They could still be champions of Merseyside yet, but no one in the stands seemed to care. Reports suggest there were scenes of wild celebration all around Anfield. Even the players on the pitch could feel it.

This is what Liddell himself made of it, 'The last ten minutes were a mere formality, for the news had been given over the loudspeakers that Stoke had been defeated and the title was ours. The crowd didn't care two straws what happened after that.

'All they wanted was the final whistle, so they could come swarming over the ground from the Kop and Kemlyn Road and carry us off the field. It was a scene of amazing enthusiasm.'

Somehow the Reds hung on to clinch an incredible treble, and bag two trophies in one day. Liddell had won the league in his first season with the Reds.

What an incredible end to a campaign that also saw Liverpool reach the semi-finals of the FA Cup. Surely the pubs in Liverpool would have been drunk dry on Saturday, 14 June 1947.

Who would have been a Bluenose going into work on the Monday after that game?

Worcester City too hot for Reds in 1959 FA Cup shocker

One of the oldest clichés in football talks of the 'magic of the cup'. It is usually applied to an act of so-called 'giant killing', which describes a smaller, less successful team, overcoming the odds to dump a bigger side out of the FA Cup.

In truth you only think it's 'magic' when it happens to someone else.

Liverpool, a club regarded as giants of the game, have found themselves on the wrong side of a few of these 'David and Goliath' encounters, but few have been more bruising than the reverse they suffered to non-league Worcester City in 1959.

Despite their Second Division status, this was an FA Cup third round tie Liverpool should have negotiated comfortably.

They were going well in the league and pushing for promotion, and few could have seen the draw against Worcester as anything to worry about.

The game was scheduled for Saturday, 10 January but was postponed due to freezing conditions and rescheduled for a Thursday afternoon.

It was attended by a Worcester record of 15,000 supporters, although it was later eclipsed by City's fourth-round defeat at the hands of Sheffield United, a game watched by over 17,000 fans.

Reds manager Phil Taylor clearly wasn't too concerned about his side's chances because he dropped club legend Billy Liddell.

This gave the minnows a boost and they raised their game considerably. Perhaps a combination of this and a degree of complacency on the part of the Reds proved to be our undoing.

Ten minutes into the game, City were in front. A bad back-pass by Reds defender John Molyneux left goalkeeper Tommy Younger high and dry; 18-year-old striker Tommy Skuse seized his chance and prodded the ball into an empty net at the Canal End.

Worcester could hardly believe their luck and Liverpool were rattled into a response. The Reds bombarded City for the next 20 minutes, but the home side stood firm and Taylor's men eventually ran out of ideas. At half-time, Liverpool had much work to do.

It proved to be an afternoon of frustration, however, with the weather deteriorating significantly in the second half.

With just ten minutes to go, Dick White's attempted clearance in the six-yard box looped over his own goalkeeper's head and into the net. Liverpool were heading out of the cup at the first attempt.

There was still time, though, for the Reds to pull one back and make the last six minutes of the game the longest of any City supporter's life.

Liverpool's moment came in the 84th minute when defender Les Melville bundled over Freddie Morris in the box and up stepped Geoff Twentyman to smash the ball home from the penalty spot.

It would prove to be just a consolation though.

The final whistle sparked a pitch invasion by the home crowd and saw the officials leave the field, flanked by police officers.

Phil Taylor had praise for brave Worcester but he wasn't happy with the pitch or his own players. He said, 'Worcester deserved to win. They outfought us on a pitch that may have reduced the odds against them, but was still as good a playing

THE AGE OF KINGS

surface as you can get in England right now. We lost because our forwards refused to fight.'

The last word goes to Fleet Street though.

With Worcester famous for a spicy condiment, the headline writers came up with 'What Sauce!' and 'Worcester Too Hot For Liverpool'.

It's not funny, unless you're a City fan.

How Ronnie Moran's first taste of the Merseyside derby was oh so sweet

It's back to the mid-1950s we go for this magical moment and to what would have been a rare treat for the red half of Merseyside.

It was also a first derby-day outing for a 20-year-old Ronnie Moran. 'Bugsy', a young left-back, had signed as a professional for Liverpool in 1952. He had to wait three years to line up against our neighbours and surely, even in his wildest dreams, he couldn't have envisaged a more memorable baptism.

With the scars of war written in the rubble and craters all over the city and etched into the psyche of its citizens, both Liverpool's teams found themselves in miserable form. The Reds had ended the 1954 season bottom of the First Division and were deservedly relegated. Everton, having spent three years in the second tier, had managed to clamber out after finishing runners-up to Leicester City on goal difference.

In doing so they gleefully reclaimed the much-cherished bragging rights from their red rivals. Their bravado would prove short-lived, though, and when the two sides were drawn together in the FA Cup fourth round the stage was set for Kopites to wreak their revenge.

Ronnie gave an interview to a newspaper in 1967 in which he vividly described the atmosphere surrounding the match.

By then the Kop was renowned for its humour and song but, he recalls, back in '55 things were very different. Neither side was doing well and though the crowds on Merseyside could be loud, there was little to differentiate them from other grounds around the country.

Ronnie comments that the fierce rivalry had dimmed in the 1950s, but surely in the cup it must have been different. Everton had already won the famous trophy twice, in 1905/06 and 1932/33. Liverpool had never won it; a fact their rivals never tired of pointing out.

Certainly the absence of a derby game for three seasons must have cranked up the rivalry a few notches. Schools, factories and pubs around the city must have been alive with banter in the days leading up to the fixture, and so it was that on 29 January 1955, 73,000 Scousers crammed into the old ground on the wrong side of Stanley Park to witness their heroes do battle.

Pathe News footage reveals the total absence of segregation and a crowd bereft of flags and banners. The stands around the pitch are rammed to bursting point and Reds and Blues are stood shoulder to shoulder.

As the goals go in it seems that all sides of the ground are applauding.

The players were certainly up for this one. Billy Liddell, who scored the first after 18 minutes, recalls how he and his team-mates were almost sick and tired of the relentless preparations. Manager Don Welsh had made them work tirelessly on free kicks as he knew Everton's tactic was to catch teams offside from set pieces. Their training-ground efforts would pay off big-time.

As the half-hour mark approached, the Reds were a goal to the good and won a free kick in Everton's half. Liddell picks up the story.

'Alan A'Court, Jack Smith and myself lined up with the Everton defence on the penalty area, while John Evans stood in line with the player who took the free kick,' he recounted.

'The referee blew his whistle and the ball was kicked and all the Everton players rushed out to play us offside, but we ran with them as Johnny Evans raced forward to meet the ball.'

The Blues' defence were stunned as Evans, comfortably onside, squared it to A'Court to slot in the second. If you watch the footage, you will hear the plum accent of the commentator and see the crowds surge all around the ground. This was a game played in the spirit of friendly rivalry and sportsmanship off the pitch and, as Liddell himself recalls, on it too.

Liverpool didn't have it all their own way though, and Everton twice had the ball in the net only to see their goals ruled out. Still, the *Liverpool Echo* recorded that the Reds left the pitch at the interval deservedly in front and 'to a storm of cheers from all parts of the ground'.

In the second half Johnny Evans took over and added a third on 57 minutes and the fourth on 75. Evans served the Reds for four years from 1953–57 and was a goal machine. Signed for the princely sum of £12,500 from Charlton Athletic, he managed a goals-to-games ratio of almost one in two by scoring 53 times in 107 appearances.

Everton huffed and puffed but there was no way back and the sound of Reds supporters chanting 'we want five' would have been a rare moment of Schadenfreude for Kopites in 1955. The game would end with excited journalists claiming Liverpool could go all the way to the final.

Sadly they would crash out at Anfield to Huddersfield Town in the fifth round, losing 2-0. They endured another miserable season in the second tier by finishing 11th and Don Welsh later became the first Liverpool manager to be sacked, in 1956, after finishing third and missing out on promotion.

He was succeeded by Phil Taylor, the man who recruited Reuben Bennett, Joe Fagan and Bob Paisley to the world-famous boot room. Not a bad legacy. All three would be retained by Bill Shankly after he took over from Taylor in 1959.

The great Scot would quickly identify Liverpool's inferiority complex when it came to their nearest rivals and set about taking it apart, piece by piece. The Blues have lived in our shadow ever since and a young 20-year-old left-back, who played in this classic encounter, would play a huge part in that.

Rest in peace Ronnie, YNWA.

Bill Shankly arrives in 1959, armed with a vision and an unshakeable belief in the power of the collective

The club had tried to bring Shankly in earlier, but their refusal to allow him to pick the team meant he would walk away. However, in the dying days of the 1950s, with the team going nowhere, they came calling once more and this time agreed to give him the control he needed.

Shanks was a man of humble beginnings, a fierce intellect and sharp wit. Born in the small mining town of Glenbuck, in Scotland, Shankly's roots forged his philosophy on life and his outlook on football.

Shankly had four brothers and five sisters. He was the youngest of the boys. His upbringing had taught him the power of collective effort and he had a deep understanding of the nobility of labour.

One of his many great quotes came when he was asked whether he felt under pressure before a cup final.

His reply was to lecture the journalist on what real pressure was, 'Pressure is working down the pit. Pressure is having no work at all. Pressure is trying to escape relegation on 50 shillings a week. Pressure is not the European Cup or the championship or the cup final. That's the reward.'

The club he took over in 1959 had just been eliminated from the FA Cup by Worcester City. They had been languishing in the Second Division for five years and he would describe Anfield as the biggest toilet in Liverpool.

However, he immediately saw a community that was as fiercely loyal, passionate and witty as he was. In the Kop he saw a group of supporters who knew what it was to work, fight and play hard and with whom he could forge a timeless bond, 'Liverpool have a crowd of followers which rank with the greatest in the game. They deserve success and I hope, in my own small way, I am able to do something to help them achieve it. I make no promises except that from the moment I take over I shall put everything into the job I so willingly undertake.'

He understood the uniqueness of Liverpool supporters and their spirit of collectivism and community appealed to him deeply.

Take this quote for example, 'The word "fantastic" has been used many times, so I would have to invent another word to fully describe the Anfield spectators. It is more than fanaticism, it's a religion.

'To the many thousands who come here to worship, Anfield isn't a football ground, it's a sort of shrine. These people are not simply fans, they're more like members of one extended family.'

Bill's belief in loyalty and fairness saw him keep faith in Bob Paisley, Joe Fagan and Reuben Bennett, who had all been part of the old set-up. They would become the cornerstone of the famous boot room cabal that would successfully plot the conquest of Europe.

The story of Shankly would fill many volumes as well as hours of film footage. His talent for spotting a player, his charismatic style and his ability to articulate deeply complex thoughts and ideas in the language of the people are all factors that mark him out as a unique and special leader.

His quotes are legion and each one was designed to serve a purpose. His barbs about Everton, for example, had nothing to do with a lack of respect for Liverpool's neighbours.

Instead they were intended to puncture what he believed was an inferiority complex his players had when it came to their rivals. Others, such as the famous 'life and death' quote, and the one about his socialism, have all passed into folklore. I love them all.

However, there is a less famous lecture given by the great man that, for me, says everything about his vision and attitude to life, people and purpose.

It's this, 'If I became a bin man tomorrow, I'd be the greatest bin man who ever lived. I'd have everyone working with me, succeeding and sharing out the success.

'I'd make sure they were paid a decent wage with the best bonuses and that we all worked hard to achieve our goals.

'Some might say, "Ah but they're only bin men, why do we need to reward them so well for a job anyone can do?" But I'd ask them why they believe they are more important than a bin man.

'I'd ask them how proud they'd feel if their dirty city became the cleanest in the world. Then ask who made them proud? The bin men.'

This was about a commitment to service, a desire to be the best no matter what your job is and a belief that everybody has value and deserves to be rewarded for their efforts.

I believe this is the vision that pulled Liverpool Football Club, its players and supporters together and drove them to greatness. This was Shankly's vision.

The arrival of Shankly's colossus

Bill Shankly, the club's legendary manager and widely regarded as the father of modern Liverpool, was a master of psychology. His quotes have filled volumes and ex-players, lucky enough to have worked with him first-hand, still get misty-eyed recounting stories of his brilliance.

Among his many talents was his ability to get inside the heads of players and opponents alike. He knew the power of belief, 'If you believe, you can conquer the bloody world.'

When addressing what he perceived as Liverpool's inferiority complex with their neighbours across the park, Everton, he raged, 'I never understood it. You have to tell yourself every day that you're the best, until you believe it. Then you have to go out and prove it.'

He would famously greet opposing players as they arrived at the away team dressing room. He would grip their hands tightly and, if they were a player he was worried about, he'd ask if they were feeling okay, because they looked a bit pale to him.

His handling of the media was no different and when he signed a new centre-half, Ron Yeats from Dundee United for £22,000 in 1961, the great Scot was at it again. Shanks was having none of the usual stale press call. Instead he instructed Yeats to change into full all-red kit and invited the press on to the Anfield turf to photograph him.

Yeats recalled the boss's reaction when he first saw the defender in his kit, 'Jesus son! You look ten feet tall.' The shy youngster had made a big step moving away from home and was nervous about settling in a new town.

Was he good enough to make the transition and play for Shankly's Reds?

Those words lifted him and, he remembers to this day, that it was exactly how he felt every time he pulled on the shirt: ten feet tall. Liverpool supporters still refer to Yeats as big Ron or Colossus to this day. Maybe, just maybe that image of the man from Dundee, as a giant, created doubt in the minds of opposition strikers.

Yeats played 454 games for Liverpool and scored 16 goals in a career that spanned a decade. He won one Second Division title, two First Division championships and lifted the club's first FA Cup, secured by defeating Leeds United in 1965. After Liverpool, Yeats went on to play for Tranmere for three seasons and spent time playing for the Los Angeles Sky Hawks in the United States.

However, he received his footballing education at Anfield and still regards his time with Shankly's Reds as the greatest days of his life.

Ian St John grabs a debut hat-trick in the Liverpool Senior Cup Final at Goodison Park

The partnership between Ian St John and Roger Hunt is the stuff of legend. Both players were integral to Liverpool's rise from the second tier of English football under Bill Shankly to glory in the FA Cup. It also inspired one of the great footy jokes of all time, but you might have to be a Scouser to appreciate it. It goes like this:

> *Q. What's the longest goal ever scored?*
> *A. When St John scored from Hunts Cross*

Hunts Cross is a district in the city of Liverpool and it lies about eight miles from Anfield. Get it? No? Oh well, Kopites in the 1960s thought it was funny.

They also fell in love with 'the Saint', a player who once talked about how he would die for the supporters and said he believed they would die for him.

Shankly bought St John from Motherwell in 1961, for the record sum of £37,500. The manager had witnessed the young lad score a hat-trick in 150 seconds against Hibernian two years earlier and had never forgotten it. He knew St John could provide the ammunition that would fire the Reds into the First Division.

In persuading the board to part with their cash, Shanks would say St John was 'not just a good centre-forward, he's the only centre-forward in the game'. They replied, saying the club couldn't afford that much money, to which the Scot replied, 'We can't afford not to buy him.'

He was, of course, right. The player would go on to be idolised by the Kop, playing 425 games for the Reds and scoring 118 goals in all competitions. His signing helped Liverpool win the Second Division and achieve promotion in 1962.

He missed just two games that season and scored 18 times. He would go on to win two First Division titles and was a member of the 1965 FA Cup-winning team, scoring the clinching goal at Wembley.

His first outing for Liverpool came against Everton, on 9 May 1961, at Goodison Park in the Liverpool Senior Cup Final. Almost 52,000 supporters packed into the ground to witness a seven-goal thriller. There could be no greater opportunity for a young striker to endear himself to the Liverpool supporters and St John would take full advantage of it.

The pressure must have been immense, but the young Scot had nerves of steel. He was a scrapper and despite his height he wasn't afraid to get physical on the pitch if necessary.

Rather than be intimidated by the derby atmosphere, the Saint rose to it.

Unfortunately Liverpool lost 4-3 but their supporters had been captivated by their new record signing. St John had scored all three of the Reds' goals in the second half of the game.

Word spread quickly that Liverpool had bought a goal machine and a perfect partner for Hunt. This was the birth of Shankly's Reds, a team that would earn the admiration and respect of the footballing world and restored pride to the red half of the city and St John was a vital part of that story.

Liverpool emerge from eight years of mediocrity to join the elite of English football

In 1962, Liverpool finally returned to the big time after winning the Second Division title. They had languished in England's second tier for eight years. The board had turned to Bill Shankly in December 1959 and he immediately set about transforming the club, from top to bottom.

The Reds had finished third in his first two seasons in charge, but in 1961/62 everything just clicked. Shanks rescued Gerry Byrne from the transfer list, saw huge potential in Roger Hunt and Ian Callaghan, and brought in Ian St John and Ron Yeats.

However, it would be a forgotten hero, Kevin Lewis, who would fire the goals that secured the title and promotion against Southampton on 21 April 1962.

St John was serving a suspension and the boss brought in the former Sheffield United man as replacement striker. He had signed the lad for £13,000 in June 1960.

Lewis was born on Merseyside, in Ellesmere Port, and was one of Bill's earliest captures. He had a short but effective career for the Reds, scoring 44 goals in 82 appearances.

He would move on in 1963 due to the emergence of Ian Callaghan on the right wing.

Another player who played a huge role that season was club legend Ronnie Moran. He recalled Lewis's contribution and his own later, 'Kevin was only playing because Ian St John wasn't available, but he scored the goals that took us up. I was particularly proud because I'd played a lot of games for the club in Division Two and we'd tried so hard for so long to get into the top league.'

Lewis was just 22 and had big shoes to fill. There were still six games to go but the Reds only needed a point for promotion and a win would give them the championship. However, Liverpool had lost their last four games against the Saints, so confidence wouldn't have been high.

Liverpool Echo journalist Michael Charters bemoaned the absence of St John, but made this prophetic statement on the eve of the game, 'His [St John's] deputy is Kevin Lewis, who has mainly been at outside right for his first team appearances, but manager Bill Shankly preferred the experience of this Ellesmere Port lad for such a vital game.

'Young centre forward Alf Arrowsmith is off form at present, and the crisp shooting of Lewis should mean St John's absence will not have too marked an effect on the forward line. This could be a famous day at Anfield – the day they have all been waiting for.' His words proved to be uncannily accurate, with Lewis scoring two goals in ten minutes to put Liverpool in the driving seat. His first was a bit of a scramble but the second was a classic poacher's goal. Callaghan had crossed to Hunt, whose shot was saved, but Lewis was there to head in the rebound.

The Reds held on to their lead and secured the championship and promotion with five games to spare. It truly was the beginning of a new era.

Charters summed up the atmosphere in his post-match analysis, 'The skies wept, the atmosphere was grey and dismal, but it was still a glorious unforgettable day at Anfield on Saturday.'

The press reported scenes of celebration on the pitch and in the stands. Shankly was in bullish mood and declared that the title had been decided at the start of the season. He told the local paper, 'We won the championship in the first month when we were fitter competitively than our rivals. We beat Sunderland and Newcastle twice in that spell and we never looked back.'

Looking forward, there would be unimaginable glory. However, for Kopites at the end of the 1961/62 season, it was the prospect of renewing acquaintances with their rivals across the park that excited most.

It had been seven years since they last met Everton. That had been in the fourth round of the FA Cup. The Reds owed the Blues one too, as that game had ended 4-0 to the Toffees. However, in the years that followed that glorious promotion, Shankly would ensure there would be no inferiority complex in the red half of Merseyside.

Kopites build snowmen on the Anfield pitch as war rages in the corridors of Anfield

It's 1965 and Bill Shankly is conducting his team's advance across Europe. He's building a bastion of invincibility that would one day 'conquer the bloody world'.

Liverpool have reached the quarter-final stages of the European Cup and have been drawn against FC Cologne. The first leg, on 3 March, in Germany had ended goalless. The return game was scheduled for a week leater.

The only problem was that Anfield resembled something of a winter wonderland. The pitch was covered in a thick blanket of snow and had been all day. However, no one had considered calling the game off.

As kick-off approached the turnstiles opened and 50,000 supporters filed into the ground. For more than 40 minutes they stood freezing, as the away side warmed up on the pitch. At 7.40pm the Danish referee came out to inspect conditions and to nobody's surprise, except the Germans', the game was called off.

Newspaper reports spoke of how the Liverpool fans accepted the news with good grace. In truth, they were probably more concerned with collecting the all-important voucher for the rescheduled match on their way out past the turnstiles.

Sadly Anfield's turnstiles only spun one way and supporters were reduced to climbing over them to get out, clutching their vouchers as they left. This slowed things down considerably and huge queues developed.

Some fans accepted their lot and climbed on to the pitch. A ball appeared and a huge kick-about got under way. Then a snowball fight broke out and some supporters built snowmen on the frozen turf. None of them were aware of a growing drama, unfolding in Anfield's inner sanctum.

Cologne's players and officials were furious. They were convinced that Shankly didn't want to play the game and had influenced the referee to call it off. It was clearly ridiculous, but tempers had got out of hand.

One reporter describes how Shankly himself was conducting a furious argument with FC Cologne's treasurer, a Mr H. Pelzer. Bill didn't speak a word of German and his adversary no English so they had enlisted legendary German goalkeeper Bert Trautmann to interpret.

Journalist Horace Yates wrote that Shanks 'bristled and hit back pugnaciously'. I can only imagine the scene, as the legendary Scot asked a German goalkeeper to translate words that, according to Yates, 'would have been better left unsaid'.

Somehow things were eventually calmed down and the game went ahead a week later. Shankly described it as the most one-sided game he had ever witnessed, with the Reds bombarding the visitors' goal. It would end goalless with Cologne's number one, Toni Schumacher, having the night of his life.

Liverpool eventually went through to the semis thanks to – incredibly – a toss of a two-coloured disc (the away goals rule did not exist then). It set up a classic and hugely controversial tie with Inter Milan, but that's another story.

EE-AYE-ADDIO! The Reds win their first FA Cup, in 1965

In the 1960s the city of Liverpool was at the epicentre of a musical earthquake that swept the world. Four young lads, called John, Paul, George and Ringo, were being mobbed by crowds of screaming fans everywhere they went. The feeling that something magical was happening on the banks of the Mersey was overwhelming.

On 2 May 1965 more than a quarter of a million supporters brought the city centre to a standstill as hordes of adoring supporters gathered to pay homage to their heroes. This time though they had come to see Shankly's Reds and the FA Cup.

For those who have grown up in the Premier League era, it may be hard to imagine just how significant the '65 FA Cup triumph was. However, for Liverpool supporters who lived through that period, this achievement outshone all that had gone before.

Liverpool had not yet won the cup despite over 70 years of trying. To make matters worse, Everton had won it twice.

Whenever a Reds supporter attempted to give a Blue some stick, the reply would always be, 'Come back when you've won the FA Cup.'

It was a painful running score, made worse by two near misses in 1914 and 1950. It seemed the cup was becoming an impossible dream.

Shankly described the lack of success in the competition and the fans enduring the taunts of their neighbours as a 'disgrace'. He set about building a team that would bring the famous old trophy home. These men would become immortal, their names still echoing through the ages. They were:

Tommy Lawrence, Chris Lawler, Gerry Byrne, Geoff Strong, Ron Yeats, Willie Stevenson, Ian Callaghan, Roger Hunt, Ian St John, Tommy Smith and Peter Thompson.

On 1 May 1965 they met Don Revie's Leeds United at Wembley. The Reds had endured a difficult league season, finishing seventh. Revie's side had narrowly missed out on the title having been pipped by Manchester United on goal difference. Though Shanks would have heard none of it, Liverpool were underdogs.

Some 100,000 people turned out at the national stadium to see the occasion, only for Leeds's tactics to almost kill the game. This was a point rammed home by *Daily Mirror* journalist Frank McGhee. Under the headline 'Final that almost died of tactics', he heaped praise on Liverpool's brilliant individuals, Stevenson, Byrne, Hunt and Smith, who were the shining lights of a dull game.

Yeats sarcastically summed up Leeds's lack of adventure, saying, 'You won't create many scoring chances from your own 18-yard line.' However, amidst the suffocating tension of normal time, Reds fans would suffer in the stands as the game went into extra time.

Then it exploded into life as in the 93rd minute Hunt put Liverpool into the lead. There was delirium among the supporters. Victory was so close they could almost taste it. Back home whole families, some crowded around black and white television sets, would have erupted in scenes of joy and euphoria.

Sadly though, they would be made to suffer for one of the greatest victories in the club's history. Just nine minutes later, Billy Bremner equalised. For the Liverpool players it was a body blow. They had toiled so hard and one of them, Gerry Byrne, was playing with a broken collarbone (more about that soon).

In the crowd the sense of peril must have been acute. Were their hopes and dreams about to be dashed once more? Would they have to endure the taunts of Everton fans, again? It must have felt intolerable.

Somehow though, the combined will of fans and players lifted the team for one more assault on the Yorkshiremen's goal. And it would be a combination of Scottish and Scouse flair that would deliver the killer blow.

In the 111th minute of an emotion-sapping, energy-consuming encounter, Ian Callaghan broke free of his marker Willie Bell and received a pass from Tommy Smith. He made it to the byline and whipped in a cross that was met by the head of Ian St John. The ball looped into the net and Liverpool were back in front.

Leeds had no answer. They were out for the count and at full time the cup was Liverpool's for the first time. Reds celebrated in the stands, singing 'EE-AYE-ADDIO we won the Cup!'

Shankly described it as the club's proudest moment. However, nothing could have prepared him for the reception they received back in Liverpool.

The team travelled home by train and it became evident as early as Crewe that the team were in for quite a spectacle. Crowds gathered on the platforms and flags hung out of windows as they sailed past.

At the city's Town Hall, a civic reception awaited the players. In Dale Street and Castle Street below, an incredible army of supporters had gathered as far as the eye could see. Nothing like this had ever been seen before and it left Beatlemania in the shade.

The Ambulance Service had drafted in support from all across the Mersey and 350 police officers stood guard. Joyous and delirious supporters climbed on to every vantage point to see their heroes, including lampposts and ambulance roofs.

The atmosphere was peaceful and carnival-like, although there were apparently rowdy scenes at the Pier Head bus terminus, as supporters struggled to get a ride home at the end of the day.

At the height of the celebrations, the crowds were so big an inevitable crush took place and it is estimated that 650 people were injured, including people who suffered fractures. Nothing could dampen the enthusiasm though.

Imagine that roar, filling the air and rolling out across the river, as the Reds emerged on the balcony of the Town Hall, holding aloft the FA Cup for the first time. For supporters lucky enough to be there, this was the greatest moment of their lives.

Many would say they could die happily in that moment, safe in the knowledge that the Reds had won the cup at last.

To them this was the league title and the European Cup rolled into one.

The Gerry Byrne story: Liverpool's bravest player finishes the FA Cup Final with a broken collarbone

Few players in Liverpool's history have epitomised bravery more than left-back Gerry Byrne, whose determination helped win the FA Cup in 1965.

We live in the era of sports science, where a player's every move is monitored, along with their heart rate and other vital statistics. Footballers are managed through games and regularly rested throughout the season, in order to maintain peak fitness. It wasn't always this way though.

In the days when teams weren't allowed substitutes and a side like Liverpool could go through an entire league season using the same 11 players, injury could spell a prolonged period out of the side; maybe even prompt a move away. To be in the first team often meant playing through the pain barrier and overcoming physical injury.

Gerry was one such player, although in the 1965 FA Cup Final he took his dedication to the cause further than anyone else. Gerry, a local lad, began his senior playing career in 1957 and managed a total of 333 appearances for the club, before hanging up his boots in 1969.

When Bill Shankly arrived in 1959, he immediately recognised Byrne's gritty qualities and quickly made him an ever-present. Byrne would win two First Division championships and one Second Division but the pinnacle of his Liverpool career was winning the 1965 FA Cup.

Liverpool had never won the cup, a fact of which Evertonians loved to remind the red half of the city. Supporters who followed the team back then will tell you that the FA Cup was the most coveted trophy in the English game. For a player, a chance to compete in such a game was not to be missed. Gerry would get his chance when the Reds lined up against Leeds United in May 1965. Of course,

Liverpool went on to win the game, but in terms of this moment in Liverpool's history that's not important. Instead what happened to Byrne in that match takes centre stage.

The heroism of Byrne that day will be spoken of for as long as the club exists, because it epitomises the strength and determination required to play for Shankly's Liverpool. Early in the game he was injured in a crunching tackle.

Bob Paisley, the Reds' physio at the time, explained what happened, 'Gerry had clattered into the chunky Bobby Collins. As soon as I reached him I knew that my initial touchline diagnosis had been painfully accurate. He had broken his collarbone.'

Even in the old videos of the game his pain is clear. Paisley ran to his player and delivered the heartbreaking news.

'Gerry it's broke,' he said. Byrne just got up and replied, 'I'll get by, Bob.' He begged Paisley not to tell anyone, so desperate was he to finish the game.

And finish the game he did, even managing to play a part in Roger Hunt's extra-time goal. Shankly didn't find out until after the cup and medals had been presented. He couldn't believe the lad had played most of the game in agony. 'It was a performance of raw courage from the boy,' he would say.

Gerry later paraded the cup around Anfield with one arm in a sling and the other clutching the famous trophy.

Milan 1965: Tommy Smith spoiling for a fight as Reds are 'robbed' of their first European Cup Final

On 12 May 1965 Bill Shankly stood on the brink of his greatest achievement as Liverpool manager with the Reds heading for triumph in Europe. Just six years earlier he had taken over a club struggling in the Second Division and now he was leading the Reds out at the San Siro in the semi-final of the European Cup.

His men had vanquished the Italian giants in the first leg at Anfield, beating them 3-1 amidst a cauldron of noise and emotion. Liverpool were just 90 minutes from their first European Cup Final.

However, the game would be forever mired in controversy as the Reds lost 3-0 and were eliminated from the competition. It was, though, the manner of the defeat that angered Shankly, who wasn't the only one to suspect foul play.

He reflected on the game later in his autobiography, 'There was no joy at the match in Milan's San Siro stadium. The Milan supporters had been told the fans at Anfield had been like animals because of the noise they had made when Milan had been sent out first and we then brought out the FA Cup.

'But what did they expect? We had got the cup for the first time and it was the greatest night of their lives.'

The great man felt that the Italian fans had been whipped up into a frenzy and was outraged at their behaviour. The atmosphere inside the ground certainly sounded intimidating. He went on, 'The crowd in the San Siro was really hostile. They even had smoke bombs, purple things in jars that went up in smoke when they burst. One of these landed on the steps and Bob Paisley's clothes were covered in the stuff.'

However, it was the performance of the referee, Jose Maria Ortiz de Mendibil of Spain, that drew his ire. To say some of the decisions were dubious is an understatement. Here's the boss's take on it, 'Inter beat us 3-0 but not even their players enjoyed the game, and we didn't think two of the goals were legal. They put an indirect free kick straight into the net for the first, and the ball was kicked out of Tommy Lawrence's hand for the second.'

Tommy Smith was so furious that he would attack the referee both verbally and physically on the pitch that night. Ian Herbert, writing in *The Independent*, quotes Smith as saying, 'I hoofed him in the left ankle, but he just kept on walking, just as he did when I was screaming "el bastido" at him. I also dragged him around [to face me] after the second goal but he just fluttered away.'

The 'Anfield Iron' had contemplated knocking the referee out, thinking it would force an inquiry into the game and the official's conduct. He wouldn't go that far, which is probably for the best as a lengthy ban would have undoubtedly followed.

To lose in these circumstances must have been infuriating. However, Shankly could always find a way to turn a defeat into a victory. This is what he said to the boys on their way home, 'Afterwards, the people were sweeping the streets with enormous flags and I said to our players, "All right, we've lost, but see what you have done. Inter Milan are the unofficial champions of the world and all these people are going mad because they are so pleased that they have beaten Liverpool. That's the standard you have raised yourselves up to."'

Still it would clearly gnaw away at the boss and the players for years. The jury is still out on whether the referee threw that game.

However, allegations of bribery have persisted ever since, with some pointing to the fact that Mendibil didn't send off Smith for his obvious red-card offences as highly suspicious.

In addition, in the late 1960s, Dezso Solti, a known Hungarian 'fixer', was later accused by key officials of persuading referees to fix matches in Inter's favour. He was also known to have worked with Inter's secretary, Angelo Moratti.

The Italians would go on to win the European Cup that year and the Reds would have to wait 12 years for their first taste of glory. There were of course no guarantees that, had they progressed, Liverpool would have won the final in '65. However, who would have bet against Shankly's boys doing it, all things being equal?

Reds overcome Celtic in a hail of fury to reach their first European final; 1966

In 1965, Bill Shankly went agonisingly close to achieving his dreams of European domination only for the Reds to crash out of the semi-final of the European Cup, with Inter progressing in controversial circumstances.

The boss was furious, his anger made worse by suspicions of match fixing. Fuelled by rage and with a point to prove he would lead Liverpool all the way to the final of the European Cup Winners' Cup the following season, in 1966.

On their way they faced Jock Stein's Celtic in the semi-final. The Bhoys had an added incentive as the final would be contested at Hampden Park, Glasgow.

Liverpool had lost the first leg 1-0 at Celtic Park in front of a crowd of 76,446. The thought of going out in yet another semi-final will have haunted Shanks's dreams.

So, as more than 54,000 people gathered on the terraces of Anfield on 19 April 1966, Shanks made sure the players knew exactly what was at stake. In truth there was a lot riding on this game for both teams and their supporters, with everyone desperate for European glory.

The atmosphere was nothing short of combustible, with fireworks sporadically exploding in the away end. The Kop roared back, urging their players to 'attack, attack!' Despite the pitch looking like a swamp, the Reds responded, running themselves into the ground.

It was a performance of steel and determination. One journalist wrote, 'Nobody is likely to forget this tussle, for the match, in mud-sapping conditions, was staged with all the calculation and much of the ferocity of a military campaign. The pace was blisteringly hot, too hot for any human to sustain, but nobody could have surpassed Liverpool's tremendous effort.'

The first half ended goalless. Tackles had been hard, and no prisoners were taken, but nothing could compare with the fury of the second half. Liverpool raced into a two-goal lead, thanks to strikes from Tommy Smith and Geoff Strong, in a six-minute spell that had the Kop in raptures.

The fact that Strong was even on the pitch at all was a miracle. He had gone down hard in the 35th minute, suffering a heavy blow to the knee. However, with no substitutes allowed and so much at stake, he played on.

The first goal was a 25-yard free kick in the 61st minute, dispatched by Smith through the Celtic wall. The second, in the 66th minute, saw Strong defy injury to leap high above the Hoops' defence to head the ball home. The player said, 'I somehow managed to jump on one leg to head my goal. I will never score another I could value more. The doctor says I have "nipped" my cartilage. I hope it doesn't have to come out.'

As the ball hit the net, the Kop went wild. Read this description in the *Express*, by Desmond Hackett, then close your eyes and picture the scene, drink it in and revel in it, 'The famed and feared Anfield Kop erupted. It broke up like a giant jigsaw swept away by a petulant child.

'It was a broken pattern, an inferno of joy-crazed humanity – dancing, leaping and roaring, a mad jungle noise of sound.'

John Simpson, an ex-dock worker from Liverpool 8, remembers the night vividly. He recalls, 'I started the game on one side of the Kop but ended up moving towards the goal. I actually found myself in line with where Geoff Strong scored his goal.

'You couldn't buy an atmosphere like that, unbelievable! There is a famous saying, "wooden ships and iron men", and that night there were 22 men of that kind on that pitch.

'Shanks was funny afterwards. I can remember reading about or hearing him offer to return the empty bottles to the Celtic supporters, if they needed them back.'

However, despite the blistering pace of Liverpool's attack, there was still more than half an hour to go. All Celtic needed was a single goal to take them through. They got their chance in the last moment of the game.

With less than a minute left, Celtic broke down the right towards the Anfield Road end. Their supporters surged forward as the ball flew into the box. Striker Bobby Lennox tapped it into the net and the away end erupted in a sea of green and white.

But to their rage, the linesman's flag was up for offside and the goal was ruled out. Celtic's players protested furiously, and pandemonium broke out among the visiting supporters. Soon a hail of bottles and beer cans would rain down on the pitch.

Liverpool fans chanted 'hooligans, hooligans' and Reds goalkeeper Tommy Lawrence grabbed the ball and clutched it to his chest, as he ran to the edge of his area to avoid the barrage. The game was temporarily halted as police and St John's Ambulance tried to restore order.

According to the *Evening Times*, it took Celtic trainer Neilly Mochan and physio Bob Rooney to run towards the Glasgow contingent, waving their arms in the air to calm the crowd. Unfortunately Rooney took a bottle to the head, but he was undaunted.

Sadly, further skirmishes broke out in the streets around Anfield after the game and windows were broken. Order was eventually restored and at midnight up to 1,000 Celtic fans left Exchange Station, bloodied and bruised.

Norman Dickson, writing in the *Liverpool Echo*, quoted a British Rail official as saying, 'They seem to have had all the fight taken out of them. They seem in a very docile mood now.'

Perhaps the realisation that their European dream was over had begun to set in, or maybe it was their hangovers kicking in. Whatever it was, the fact remained, Liverpool were through to their first European final.

A proud Bill Shankly said, 'We were determined to show Celtic we meant business … I think we made our point tonight.'

The Kop's majesty drives Liverpool to their seventh league title

Imagine the scene; the streets around Anfield are packed. There's a full half-hour to go before kick-off and the gates are locked. Inside the ground the place is rammed, with almost 54,000 supporters jammed into every available space.

There is an air of raucous anticipation. Liverpool have had a relentless season and the supporters are hungry for more silver. The previous season had brought an FA Cup and a European Cup semi-final.

On the horizon, just days away, is a European Cup Winners' Cup Final against Borussia Dortmund. However, all anyone can think of is the league title. It's so close that Kopites can taste it.

This is of course Saturday, 30 April 1966 and Liverpool need only two points against Chelsea to clinch the championship. The Kop is swaying, a mass of people crammed together and moving synchronously and singing in harmony.

Songs from the hit parade, punctuated by chants of 'Shankly, Shankly!' fill the air, along with individual tributes to each player in the team.

Suddenly, there's a commotion down at the front, a Kopite breaks free of the throng and runs on to the pitch. He's carrying a homemade replica of the league trophy. He charges for the centre circle, nobody chases after him and he gleefully plants it in the middle of the pitch.

There's a deafening roar of approval and he runs back into the massed ranks of supporters, his fist clenched in the air. Then the players emerge to thunderous cheers.

This is how the *Liverpool Echo* recorded the moment, 'There was no doubt who Chelsea thought were going to be champions because they came out first and lined up in two rows and applauded the Liverpool players as they ran between them on to the pitch.'

How could Liverpool lose with support like this? How could any opponent think clearly, let alone play football against such an awe-inspiring backdrop? This was Anfield at its finest, these were Liverpool supporters just loving football and life and believing they can achieve anything.

Somehow Chelsea stayed in the game until half-time, but the second half would explode into life. Three minutes after the restart a goalmouth scramble saw the ball in the net. Some thought it was an own goal, but the Liverpool players ran to Roger Hunt and he claimed it.

The Kop were in raptures, but 14 minutes later Chelsea stunned the hosts with an equaliser through Bobby Tambling. The visitors had a couple of chances to go ahead, but the Reds pulled themselves together and were back in front on 69 minutes.

Hunt gave the Chelsea defence a torrid time, weaving one way and then another, before unleashing a fierce left-footed drive that the goalkeeper got his hand to, but was powerless to keep out.

According to the gentlemen of the press, the Kop's response was to go through 'their entire repertoire' of songs. After that, Liverpool coasted. With a European final at Hampden Park to come on the Wednesday, there was no sense in burning themselves out.

Chelsea couldn't get near the Reds and with minutes to go, the supporters began chanting 'EE-AYE-ADDIO we've won the league!'

The local and national press could only eulogise about the Reds' fantastic support. The *Echo* gushed, 'When the final whistle went, several Liverpool supporters raced on to the pitch, and as Yeats was congratulated by the Chelsea players one boy gave him a replica of the trophy. Manager Bill Shankly came on to the pitch to join his players and he congratulated each one of them in turn.

'Then the players went on a lap of honour and the sight as they reached the Kop was a tremendous kaleidoscope of red and white colours.

'I doubt if anywhere else in the world could a football ground produce scenes like these. After running round the ground, the players lined up in the middle of the field and when the crowd chanted "Geoff Strong, Geoff Strong", he came out from the tunnel limping and joined them. His reception, too, was terrific.'

Strong had played through the pain barrier to score the winning goal against Celtic and take the Reds to the European Cup Winners' Cup Final. He couldn't play because of his injury, but the supporters wouldn't leave him out.

Jack Rowe of the *Express* was so moved he wrote an entire piece about how the Kop were the greatest supporters in the world, under the headline 'Kop's Finest Moment Had a

Sentimental Touch'. He opined, 'If the Kop boys get more credit and more notice it is because they are more vociferous and more uninhibited [than any other supporters].

'For several seasons now the boys on the Kop have been the talk and the envy of the clubs who come to visit Anfield. They have had some great moments, but for me this was their finest.'

Defeated manager Tommy Docherty could only say, 'Liverpool are a great side. Their record over the last four years speaks for itself and their support is the best in the world.'

Liverpool had won their seventh league title, drawing level with Arsenal. However, they were just getting started. The managers and players who graced Anfield in the coming decades would achieve great distinction and win many honours.

League title, FA Cup and World Cup paraded as Reds clinch 1966 Charity Shield at Goodison Park

In 1966 the city of Liverpool must have felt like the centre of the universe with Bill Shankly's Reds at the heart of this Merseyside triumph.

Four young Scousers, the Beatles, had taken the music scene by storm, conquering Europe and America, while in football the Blues had won the FA Cup and the Reds won the league.

In addition, Liverpool and Everton had five players in England's 1966 World Cup squad. Ray Wilson and Alan Ball, who had joined the Toffees on the back of his international performances, represented the Blues and Roger Hunt, Ian Callaghan and Gerry Byrne carried the flag for the Reds.

In the dugout for the Charity Shield clash that year were two of Merseyside's great managers; Bill Shankly for

Liverpool and Harry Catterick for Everton. This was a meeting of English football giants.

Liverpudlians of both persuasions would have been strutting around the country, chests puffed out and acting like they owned the place. They did. And, as the 1966/67 season was launched, a most extraordinary curtain-raiser took place at Goodison Park.

The 1966 Charity Shield was to be an all-Merseyside affair and the people would be unable to think of anything else. Imagine the banter in schools, workplaces and pubs. The opportunity to be crowned the pride of Merseyside in a one-off contest was tantalisingly close.

However, a special surprise also awaited those lucky enough to witness the encounter first-hand. The 63,638 supporters packed into Goodison would see the greatest parade of football silverware the city had ever seen.

In a move that received no pre-match publicity, the clubs had arranged for Hunt, Ball and Wilson to carry the World Cup, FA Cup and First Division trophy around the pitch before the game. This was unprecedented and no other set of supporters on earth could claim to have witnessed such a spectacle, which is unlikely to ever happen again.

Everton supporter Harry Colquhoun, who had also been at the 1966 World Cup Final and the FA Cup Final, was there. He recalls the complete sense of wonder and surprise as the three trophies were paraded around the pitch, 'Nobody knew it was going to happen and a huge roar went up. My heart swelled with pride. I knew then that I was in the presence of something really special, something I would remember for the rest of my life and it was happening in my city, to our two teams. Unbelievable.'

Jack Rowe, writing in the *Liverpool Daily Post*, captured the moment superbly, 'The followers of Everton and Liverpool will have something to talk about the rest of their lives ... and in time to come I will be able to say with those 63,000 – I was there.'

Liverpool dominated the game with 22 shots on goal and 13 of them on target. Everton's small forward line struggled against Liverpool's towering back four, which included 'Colossus' Ron Yeats.

The breakthrough for the Reds came in the ninth minute through ace marksman Hunt, of course. The *Post* described the goal, 'Liverpool's goal in nine minutes was a corker. The ball went from Hunt to Callaghan, Callaghan to Thompson, Thompson to Hunt who took it up about 20 yards left. He brought it to his left foot and poor West had no chance with a shot that whizzed into the top corner of the net.'

Liverpool remained dominant for the rest of the game. They could and probably should have won far more comfortably but a single goal would ultimately settle the occasion.

The Times's match report summed up the Reds' dominance, 'Such was Liverpool's command of affairs that even before the first half had spent itself they were slackening their tempo, tailoring their efforts to a pattern just sufficient to deal with the moderate challenge Everton offered.'

In truth though, this was one occasion when the game was a mere sideshow to the pre-match spectacle. That was probably scant comfort to the blue half of Merseyside, though. What a time to be a Red or a Blue for that matter.

Houllier watches from the Kop as Reds demolish Dundalk

There's nothing like a European night under the Anfield floodlights, so the saying goes. It may be a cliché, but on 16 September 1969 Kopites were treated to a night they would never forget. In the crowd that night was a young schoolteacher from France. His name was Gerard Houllier. Gerard would of course go on to lead Liverpool out in European competition, but he would never enjoy a scoreline as emphatic as this. The Reds clearly left their mark on the man.

He recalls how he was shocked at how Shankly's men continued to pound the opposition even though they were 5-0 up at the interval, 'In France, if you are 5-0 up at half-time the game is over in the sense that you don't bother trying to increase your score. It's not like that in England.'

The crowd also made an impact on the man who would go on to win a record five trophies in a single calendar year for the Reds, 'What impressed me first of all was the atmosphere inside the stadium. We were on the Kop, and it was fantastic to see the unconditional support of the fans.'

It's fair to say this wasn't elite European competition. It was the Fairs Cup, a forerunner of the UEFA Cup. Nor were the opposition considered the cream of Europe; Dundalk were a side from the Irish League. However, you can only beat what's in front of you and Liverpool did that in style.

Perhaps sensing an easy ride, Shankly caused a bit of a stir by dropping Roger Hunt and Ian St John to the bench. There was also a rare start for a young Ray Clemence, with regular stopper Tommy Lawrence ill with gastroenteritis. One journalist would describe Clem as 'an unnecessary luxury'.

The Irishmen had come to 'park the bus', as we say today. Their aim was to keep the score 'respectable for the second leg'. They say no plan survives contact with the enemy and Dundalk's took one hell of a beating.

Horace Yates, writing in the *Daily Post*, described how the game was so easy that the Kop got bored and started taking the mickey out of their own players, 'With nothing to arrest the goal avalanche the Kop turned on their favourites with playful bantering at every opportunity. They added a typical touch of comedy when Liverpool were leading 2-0 and strolling through by chanting "attack, attack", the battle cry they normally reserve for occasions when Liverpool are in trouble.'

This was exhibition stuff and goals rained down on Dundalk in both halves. By the 70th minute the Reds were 8-0 up with goals from Alun Evans (two), Chris Lawler, Tommy Smith (two), Bobby Graham, Alec Lindsay and Peter Thompson.

But they still weren't satisfied.

Supporters couldn't believe how easy this was and one lad commented, 'Dundalk couldn't even make a ripple in the "I Zingari" League,' a reference to a local amateur league in Liverpool, founded in 1895 and enduring until 2006. It seems cruel but, such was the Reds' dominance, who could argue?

Six minutes later it was nine, thanks to a 25-yard thunderbolt from Ian Callaghan. The Kop were now singing 'we want ten' and in the 82nd minute Bobby Graham dutifully obliged. Dundalk must have been delighted to hear the final whistle.

They left the pitch to a standing ovation from all four corners of the ground and a guard of honour from the Liverpool team. It was perfectly fine to destroy the opposition, but you didn't have to rub their noses in it.

The second leg was a formality with Liverpool cruising to a 4-0 scoreline on the night and a 14-0 aggregate win. Those were the days, my friends.

Chris Lawler, the 'Silent Knight', puts Blues to bed as Reds mount heroic derby fightback

It's 21 November 1970 and Liverpool are facing league champions Everton. Anfield is packed to the rafters, with more than 53,000 in attendance. Liverpool are rebuilding, with six members of the first team recently promoted from the reserves.

The Everton team is packed with Harry Catterick's so-called 'School of Science'. The likes of Brian Labone, Howard Kendall, Colin Harvey, Alan Ball and Joe Royle all run out for the Blues.

Yet they are a team struggling to live up to the standards they set in the previous season and are languishing in 13th place.

Liverpool, meanwhile, are up to eighth in the table having played a game less than their opponents. The Reds' problem is an inability to turn draws into victories; six wins so far, seven draws and only three defeats. They don't know it yet, but this is a problem they're about to overcome in spectacular fashion.

Bill Shankly is still reeling from the loss of his goalscoring youngster Alun Evans. The 21-year-old had notched six goals in 14 games before an injury against Bucharest in a European game put him out of the side.

In the team for only his second game is John Toshack, who signed from Cardiff for £112,000 just ten days earlier. The stage is set, the crowd are expectant, and the atmosphere is electric. Would the game live up to expectation?

This is how Horace Yates, of the *Liverpool Echo*, remembered it, 'For sheer, undiluted excitement, and nerve-shattering tension, with both sets of fans experiencing all the emotions, there is nothing to equal Liverpool's 3-2 Anfield victory on November 21, 1970.'

However, if it becomes possible to own this game on DVD, you'd be wise to start watching from the second half because the first was a war of attrition. Reports reveal a tense affair, with both teams simply cancelling each other out.

Forward to the second period and the unappetising gruel served up in the first 45 gives way to a sumptuous main course and dessert, all rolled into one. It would leave Liverpool supporters drooling and the Blues crying into their beer, as they drowned their sorrows at full time.

For the Reds there would be three heroes that day: Steve Heighway, who had only joined the side in the August, would find himself on the scoresheet, Toshack would grab his first for the club, but the man who would seal the game was Liverpool's goalscoring full-back Chris Lawler.

Lawler had burst into the Liverpool team in 1963 after a showdown with Shankly. He had joined the club under previous manager Phil Taylor and was struggling to make headway.

Another Scouse youngster, Tommy Smith, was having similar problems and when United's Matt Busby indicated he would take them both for £50,000, the pair went knocking on their manager's door. Shankly wasn't about to let two talented young players go and told them he'd look after them.

He would be as good as his word and both went on to be Anfield greats. Lawler played 316 consecutive games for the club between 1965 and 1971. He ended his career with 61 goals in 549 appearances, a statistic that made him the club's highest-scoring defender.

Lawler's knack of arriving unexpectedly in the box earned him the nickname the 'Silent Knight'. Some supporters called him 'the Ghost'. His goal would certainly haunt Everton fans after this game.

The Blues went two goals up with efforts from Alan Whittle in the 56th minute and Joe Royle in the 63rd. The Kop were stunned at first but immediately started to roar the Reds on. Six minutes later Steve Heighway pulled one back, then in the 76th minute Toshack levelled with his first for Liverpool.

The noise inside the ground reached epic proportions with the Kop in full fury. Evertonians, who had been jubilant just ten minutes earlier, were chewing fingernails to the bone.

Toshack would describe his equaliser as 'the greatest goal of my career', but it was upstaged by Lawler's winner, in the last minute of the game.

Here's how Yates saw the goal, 'Alec Lindsay, in his first derby match, dropped a centre on Toshack's head, who nodded wide of the defence. Running in was Liverpool's "Silent Knight", the player the fans swore wore carpet slippers – Chris Lawler. Realising that this was probably the last chance of the game, he picked his spot and the hit the winner.'

The Liverpool supporters went berserk and refused to leave the ground at the end of the game, singing incessantly. Deep within Anfield's inner sanctum a reporter asked, 'What are they waiting for, the other results?' Shankly replied, 'Why, was there any other game today?'

Toshack admitted afterwards that, not being a local, he hadn't been able to get himself worked up about the derby before the game. He soon changed his mind, saying, 'But afterwards I realised just how seriously people took it. I don't think it will take me long to get as fanatical as they are.'

Chris Lawler remembers the end of the game with some amusement, recalling, 'We were walking off the pitch. The scenes in the stands were incredible. Johnny Morrissey came over to me and said, "Thanks for that, I won't be able to go out tonight now."'

Alun Evans's triumphant return sees Bayern Munich crushed at Anfield

Alun Evans was one of the most exciting teenagers in football and, in 1968, Liverpool snapped him up for a record fee of £100,000. He exploded on to the scene at Anfield, managing to score on his debut and soon being tipped as a potential successor to Roger Hunt. Sadly for him he never fulfilled that promise and was far from lucky with injury. He left the club four years later, having scored 33 times in 111 appearances.

In 1970 he sustained a knee injury in a Fairs Cup match in Bucharest. It put him out of action for four months but glory awaited him in March 1971.

His return to match action came in the fourth round of the same competition. The opposition were European giants Bayern Munich, who boasted three World Cup stars; Sepp Maier, Gerd Muller and Franz Beckenbauer.

The Reds were struggling for goals and Shankly had boasted that the return of the youngster for the first leg would sort things out. He was right. Despite being out for four months, Evans managed to finish top scorer that season with 15 goals in all competitions.

Few gave much credence to Shanks's prophecies ahead of the game, though. Munich were heavy favourites. Muller had won the European Young Player of the Year and Golden Ball awards after scoring 38 goals the previous season.

He was also the first player to win both of those awards in the same season. In addition, he'd lit up Mexico '70 with ten goals in a World Cup that saw Germany finish third.

The game at Anfield refused to go to script though and it was Evans's name being sung to the rafters, not Muller's. He struck his first after 30 minutes following an assist from Steve Heighway.

Then four minutes into the second half the Reds won a free kick in a dangerous position. Alec Lindsay whipped it in and Toshack headed it down. The youngster was quickest to react and hooked the ball into the goal for his second.

Anfield was a cauldron of scarves and song, the Kop swaying, synchronous with the movement of the team. What a joy to behold Shankly's boys giving the mighty Munich a footballing lesson.

The Germans' humiliation would be complete in the 73rd minute when Evans grabbed his hat-trick. The imperious Beckenbauer had been reduced to ashes and Muller rendered anonymous thanks to Shankly and Liverpool's tactical prowess.

The German side's coach, Udo Latteck, would blame the result on rustiness as Munich hadn't played for three weeks due to frozen pitches back home. However, he acknowledged the Reds were a 'fine team' and gave his charges little hope in the second leg.

Evans was delighted with his comeback and the result. 'Those goals had been building up inside me since I went out of the game in November,' he said.

Shankly was brimming with pride after watching his side demolish European royalty. 'Our enterprise could have brought us six,' he growled. 'I was delighted with the way my lads built up and finished off their attacks.'

Sadly the Reds would crash out of the competition in the semi-final stages and the Fairs Cup would forever elude them. Of course, they would go on to collect more than their fair share of European honours in the years to come, but we'll save those tales for later.

Bill Shankly, Chairman Mao and Charlie George: the vanquished are afforded a heroes welcome

This defining moment in Liverpool's history takes us back to 1971, where the Reds had just lost the FA Cup Final to Arsenal, in front of 100,000 at Wembley. The game had gone into extra time and, after Steve Heighway had given them the lead in the 92nd minute, they had succumbed to an Eddie Kelly equaliser and the now-infamous winner by Charlie George.

Bill Shankly had been furious with the way George had celebrated his goal and famously said the player would have received a 'kicking' if the boss had been on the pitch. The great Scot hated defeat and the gloating Gunner must have added insult to injury.

The mood among the squad was a sombre one but the welcome the team would receive on their return to Liverpool will reverberate through the ages. Up to half a million people are said to have turned out to honour their heroes, despite the defeat.

There is a popular portrait of Shanks on sale in tourist shops in Liverpool and available from the club itself. You will have all have seen it, I'm sure. It's the one of Shankly in grainy black and white tones, arms outstretched on the steps of St George's Hall. Behind him was an enormous throng of adoring Liverpool fans. It bore all the hallmarks of a returning king, fresh from battle, carrying the spoils of conquest.

However, few realise that this image is one of Shankly after the 1971 FA Cup Final. Those supporters are toasting a man who had led his team to defeat. Such was the aura surrounding the manager, a mere cup final defeat could never come between him and the Liverpool supporters.

The manager and his players had been told there would be a civic reception for them at Lime Street, 24 hours after their cup final defeat. They couldn't have relished the prospect, but with suggestions that hundreds of thousands would turn up, Shankly knew he had to find some words of inspiration to lift the masses.

The story goes that as the bus weaved its way to the city centre, Shanks was in contemplative mood. Suddenly he turned to Brian Hall, who had been staring out the window, disconsolate. Hall was a university graduate and regarded, alongside Heighway, as being the brains of the outfit.

'Son,' said Shanks. 'You know about these things, who's that chairman with the red book, lots of sayings? The Chinaman, what's his name?'

Brian Hall replied, 'Do you mean Chairman Mao?' Shanks nodded, his face lighting up, 'Aye, that's him son, Chairman Mao, that's him.'

Hall was bemused and couldn't think why the boss had asked him such an obscure question. However, as the team stood on the steps of St George's Plateau, listening intently to their manager, all became clear.

The crowd chanted 'Shankly, Shankly!' The noise was deafening. Then the boss raised his arms aloft and gestured for them to cease. The crowd obediently fell silent – he had them in the palm of his hand.

Then in gravelly Scottish tones, he uttered the immortal words, 'It's questionable if Chairman Mao of China could have arranged such a show of red strength as you have shown yesterday and today.' That was the genius of Shankly. In victory or defeat, he could always lift and inspire the people.

Keegan greeted with a kiss as Bill Shankly unleashes his new superstar on Forest

The 1971/72 season saw Liverpool enter their sixth campaign without a trophy. The burning disappointment of the 1971 FA Cup Final lingered, but there was cause for hope.

Bill Shankly felt he'd secured the services of a future superstar who would transform the Reds into contenders once more. That man was Kevin Keegan.

Liverpool had paid Scunthorpe £25,000 for Keegan and Shanks was so pleased with his bargain he described it as 'robbery with violence'. And the boss couldn't wait to unleash his new protégé on Nottingham Forest in the opening game of the season.

The great manager said this of his new acquisition, 'I was just as sure of Keegan as I was of Denis Law and I never had cause to think again about Denis. These two players are so much alike in many ways. Keegan is an exciting boy all right.'

However, the youngster nearly incurred his boss's wrath by missing his debut. He'd been used to driving up to the game at the last minute during his Scunthorpe days. He hadn't banked on the huge Anfield crowds and his car got stuck in traffic. Fortunately, he made it in the nick of time and avoided a fine.

Keegan was afforded a hero's welcome as he took to the pitch, as a supporter leaped out of the Kop and ran on to the pitch to pay his respects to the new star. This was an accepted ritual at Anfield, whenever a new player arrived. Even the police turned a blind eye.

Keegan remembers the event with some amusement, 'The self-appointed representative of the Kop came on the field to greet me. He gave me a kiss, and the smell of booze on his breath almost knocked me off my feet. He needed a shave as well as his beard was rough ... This Kopite was a nice old fellow with no harm in him. He kissed me, then kissed the grass in front of the Kop and went back to join his mates in the crowd.'

It took the 20-year-old just 12 minutes to justify his welcome. The press unanimously declared that a star was born. A common word used to describe his performance was 'explosive'.

In front of an exultant crowd of over 51,000, Keegan would grab the first and create the second in a mesmerising three-minute spell. His debut strike came from a John Toshack cross and just moments later he was fouled in the box, grabbing a penalty. Tommy Smith smashed home the resultant spot-kick.

Forest hadn't even had time to settle but in the 40th minute they pulled one back thanks to a penalty gifted them by a Ray Clemence foul. Ian Storey-Moore stepped up and halved the deficit five minutes before half-time.

Liverpool weren't messing around, though, and Emlyn Hughes finished Forest off on 55 minutes. The Kop were in raptures and began singing 'we're going to win the league'.

Keegan admitted he hadn't been prepared for the power and pace of Anfield. 'I had to take the occasional two-minute breather,' he said.

Shankly was glowing at full time, saying, 'What wonderful entertainment this was for the fans. And what a performance by Keegan. This lad's got all the confidence in the world. With such a busy bee buzzing about, someone's bound to get stung.'

Keegan would go on to play 323 times for the Reds and scored 100 goals. He won three league titles, the FA Cup, two UEFA Cups and a European Cup before leaving for Hamburg in 1977. Not a bad return on a £25,000 outlay.

The night 55,000 supporters packed out Anfield for a testimonial

It's April 1972. A great army of Liverpool supporters march through the streets of Anfield. The turnstiles at the ground clatter and spin, as tens of thousands of Liverpool supporters pour into the ground. The weather is awful and torrential rain lashes the streets.

Some 55,214 people fill the stadium as the stewards close the gates, a full half an hour before kick-off. Thousands are left waiting, wet and bitterly disappointed, on the pavements around the ground.

This is no European night under the floodlights. Nor is it a derby match or a clash with a hated rival. Instead this is a testimonial for a beloved former player, and one who had left the club two years previously.

The man in question was the great 'Sir' Roger Hunt. He had received his honorific from the Kop, not the Queen, but it was no less deserved.

Hunt played for Liverpool from 1959 to 1969 before leaving for Bolton Wanderers. This meant he was entitled to a testimonial. However, the rules at the time stated that players could only be awarded such an honour once they had retired, so the Reds would have to wait until 1972 to pay their respects to one of the club's greatest strikers and a member of the 1966 England World Cup-winning squad.

Hunt played 492 times for Liverpool, scoring 285 times. He finished eight consecutive seasons as top scorer. In one of them he netted 41 times in 41 games, including five hat-tricks; a contribution that secured Liverpool promotion to the First Division.

His medal collection was equally impressive. In ten years he had collected two First Division titles and one Second Division championship. He was also key to securing the club's first FA Cup triumph in 1965.

It is, therefore, no wonder that the supporters turned out in such large numbers to honour their hero. The opposition on the night was an 'International XI' made up of veterans of the '66 World Cup-winning squad, including future Everton manager Howard Kendall.

The supporters were treated to a 14-goal thriller with Hunt's Reds winning 8-6. The result, though, wasn't important; this was a chance to say farewell to a star who had lit up Anfield for a decade.

Of course, Hunt scored a hat-trick, adding to an own goal by Martin Peters and strikes by Ian St John, Tommy Smith, Peter Thompson and a penalty scored by former goalkeeper Tommy Lawrence. All had played in the 1965 FA Cup Final.

Liverpool fans never forget their heroes and this game, on a rain-drenched night at Anfield, is a testament to the undying bond between players and supporters. It was also a fitting tribute to one of the greatest players to grace the game, during the formative years of the Bill Shankly era.

Bill Shankly's tactical genius, coupled with some stormy weather, hands Liverpool a first league and European trophy double

On Wednesday, 9 May 1973, Liverpool were attempting to become the first British side to win a league title and a European trophy in the same season. They had already secured the First Division championship and standing in the way of a historic double were a German outfit, Borussia Monchengladbach, in the final of the UEFA Cup.

The first leg of the contest took place in torrential rain at Anfield. The Germans put in a commanding performance and fielded a very strong team, featuring the likes Berti Vogts, Rainer Bonhof and Jupp Heynckes. Liverpool had recalled Brian Hall in place of John Toshack.

However, with the weather deteriorating, the referee abandoned the game after 27 minutes. It was a relief for Bill Shankly, who had watched his team struggle. He wouldn't waste his second chance.

The game went ahead the next night and more than 41,000 braved the howling wind to watch the Reds go again. Shankly had noticed that Monchengladbach had a small defence and opted to restore Toshack to the attack. It worked a treat.

Keegan opened the scoring in the 21st minute with a diving header that had the goalkeeper rooted to the spot.

Then four minutes later, the number seven had a golden opportunity to make it two from the spot.

Bonhof, terrorised by Toshack, handled in the area. Amazingly the striker, usually lethal from anywhere in the box, missed from 12 yards. Sensing their opportunity, Borussia went on the attack and almost punished the Reds with right-back Dietmar Danner hitting the post.

However, Liverpool were relentless and in the 33rd minute Emlyn Hughes headed the ball to Toshack, who flicked it backwards with his head for the waiting Keegan to slam it into the net. The crowd swayed and surged as they sensed glory was edging closer. The roar was enormous as the ball hit the net.

Liverpool continued to press and Toshack was giving the Germans nightmares. On the hour mark he forced a corner.

The Gladbach defence was in disarray by this stage and as Keegan floated the ball in, the unmarked Alec Lindsay headed home easily. Sixty minutes gone, and the Reds were 3-0 up and looking to take a hefty advantage to Germany for the return leg. They just had to avoid gifting their opponents an away goal.

Then disaster struck with the referee awarding a controversial penalty for a foul by Steve Heighway on Henning Jensen. Heynckes stepped up to take it and blasted the ball to Ray Clemence's right. However, the goalkeeper dived the right way, pulling off a spectacular save, and the Liverpool fans were in raptures.

The ground celebrated like it was the final whistle. Clemence had done his research and knew which way the striker would go. He explained, 'I watched Heynckes take a penalty in the semi-final on television and decided to dive the same way. The save was a reward for my homework.'

Liverpool held on and secured an invaluable first-leg lead. Shankly commented afterwards, 'It was an international-class game, really tremendous. I am not making predictions about the second leg, but we have a distinct advantage because we did not give away a goal.'

The German manager, Hennes Weisweiler, declared that Liverpool were 'a very attractive and powerful side, the best we have met in European competition'.

His defender, Gunter Netzer, would sum up the Reds' performance with just one word. He strolled out of his team's dressing room towards Shankly, who was waiting outside, shook the Scot by the hand and simply said 'brilliant!'

Borussia won the second leg 2-0, but Liverpool took the cup 3-2 on aggregate. They owed their first European trophy to the vagaries of the English weather, a barnstorming performance by Keegan, Clemence's homework and a canny tactical switch by their boss.

'Supermac' upstaged by Shankly's boys at Wembley

In the run-up to the 1974 FA Cup Final, Malcolm Macdonald attempted to get into the heads of the Liverpool players, claiming he would be the star of the show. In an act of hubris that was as ill-judged as it was inflammatory, he claimed he would use Wembley as a stage on which he could showcase his talents to the world. Liverpool would be his whipping boys.

Newcastle's manager Joe Harvey and club captain Bobby Moncur also joined in the pre-match barrage of boasts. The Magpies had never lost a cup final at Wembley, winning the competition three times in the 1950s. There was also a super-stition about teams in striped shirts always prevailing. They thought the game was a foregone conclusion. Big mistake.

Just imagine what Bill Shankly made of their 'trash talk'. The great Scot probably felt that the Geordies had written his team talk for him.

The Reds' Scouse contingent, Smith, Thompson, Heighway and Callaghan, would have been eager to shove those words right back down Newcastle's throats. Suffice it to say Macdonald barely got a kick of the ball for 90 minutes.

This was an eagerly anticipated game. Both teams were famed for their passionate support and for each, the final represented their only chance of silverware that season. 100,000 supporters packed into Wembley to witness the spectacle, with millions more watching on TVs around the world.

This was English football's showpiece event of the year and the biggest show in town. Playing for Newcastle that day were two men who would go on to greatness at Anfield. Alan Kennedy and Terry McDermott both went on to sign for Bob Paisley's Reds and would be pivotal to his success in the late 1970s and '80s.

Sadly for them, they would be utterly vanquished by Shankly's Liverpool in '74. As you might expect, the atmosphere was incredible. Wembley officials had banned flags and banners for the day, but they had underestimated the Liverpool supporters, who could smuggle a banner into a coffin at a state funeral.

The ground was awash with red and white and Shankly himself would drape himself in a red flag at full time. The *Liverpool Echo* described conditions for the game as 'perfect – an overcast sky, cool with very little wind'.

The first half was goalless, but the Reds were well in control, so much so that Shankly's team talk at half-time, according to Brian Hall, was simply, 'Keep it going.'

Writing in the *Mirror*, under the headline 'What a load of rubbish' and sub-header 'I wouldn't watch Newcastle if they were playing in my back garden', journalist Frank McGhee bemoaned the fact that the Reds took too long to realise that Newcastle were no good. This is what he said,

'Newcastle United should today be prosecuted under the Trades Descriptions Act for masquerading as a first-class football side, worthy cup final opponents for Liverpool.'

His verdict is damning and it's doubtful any United fans would disagree, but it does the Reds an injustice. In the second half, Shankly's boys served up a masterclass so ruthless that David Coleman, commentating for the BBC, said, 'Newcastle have been stripped bare by Liverpool.'

At one point, Shankly can be seen conducting his players from the bench. Hall recalled how they watched him and understood that he was saying 'pass and move, give and go'. It was poetry in motion.

Keegan opened the scoring in the 57th minute. A cross came in from the right and Hall dummied, allowing it to run through to the number seven who blasted it into the net.

Then in the 75th minute Alec Lindsay hit a long ball through the middle. It was headed on by Keegan to Heighway, who took it around a defender and shot low past the goalkeeper. The Reds were completely in command now.

The noise at this point was incredible, with the Red half of Wembley belting out 'oh Liverpool we love you', flags waving and banned banners being held high.

Newcastle tried to get back into it but they were totally outclassed. The *Echo* reported sarcastically, 'The menace of "Supermac" had been completely snuffed out by Liverpool's superb defence.'

Then Tommy Smith ran down the right, exchanging passes as he went, before delivering a low centre which Keegan stretched to poke home: 3-0 and the cup was Liverpool's. The Reds in the stands went mad.

At full time the Liverpool squad were running round Wembley with the cup. Hall remembers how he wore a scarf placed on him by a fan as he walked up the steps to get the trophy. He later passed it on to his son, who still wears it at cup finals today.

Shankly, though, cut a lonely figure. Leaving his players to celebrate, he walked to the tunnel and applauded the Liverpool supporters. With a red flag around him, he left the pitch for the dressing room.

Little did anyone know that he would retire months later, leaving behind broken hearts and an unrivalled legacy.

Shock and grief as Bill Shankly retires

'It was like going to the electric chair,' said Bill Shankly when he shocked the city by announcing his retirement in 1974 after 15 years in charge, creating a dynasty that still lives on today:

> 'Dear Sir,
> I would like to retire as Manager of Liverpool Football Club as soon as possible and I would be grateful if you could take the necessary steps for my pensions to commence.
> Yours faithfully
> W Shankly'

With these simple words, hand-typed by the man himself and addressed to the chairman of Liverpool FC, an era was ended on 12 July 1974.

Of course, the board tried their utmost to talk him out of it; they probably thought they could. He'd threatened to do this before but had always been persuaded to change his mind. This time it was different; he was really going.

Liverpool hastily convened a press conference and stunned the waiting media by announcing that the man who had rebuilt the club, from an average side in the Second

Division, playing in 'the biggest toilet in Liverpool', into First
Division champions, UEFA Cup and FA Cup winners, was
leaving.

Only a couple of months previously, Shankly's Liverpool
had 'stripped Newcastle United bare' in the FA Cup Final
according to one commentator.

Suddenly, inexplicably, Shankly was leaving the club
he had formed a symbiotic relationship with. This is how
chairman John Smith broke the news to the press, 'It is
with great regret that I as chairman of Liverpool Football
Club have to inform you that Mr Shankly has intimated
that he wishes to retire from active participation in league
football. And the board has with extreme reluctance accepted
his decision. I would like at this stage to place on record
the board's great appreciation of Shankly's magnificent
achievements over the period of his managership.'

Hearts were broken. Tony Wilson, a young journalist
working for Granada News, immediately took to the streets
of Liverpool to gauge the reaction of the people. What he
captured was stunned disbelief, deep sadness and something
bordering on grief.

The players too were devastated, and some wondered if
this was the end of Liverpool Football Club. Kevin Keegan
would later say that, for him, the club lost some of its lustre
that day. He left for Hamburg three years later.

Shankly's love of football was legendary, but managing
Liverpool and building not one, but two great sides, had had
an enormous effect on him. It had quite simply dominated
his every waking moment.

The legend would sit up for hours, replying to fans'
letters. He would work tirelessly to restore the club to the
pinnacle and on his days off he would play football on the
field in front of his house with the local kids.

That field is now named after the great man.

It was bound to eventually take its toll and he needed a break. In truth, Shankly lived to regret his decision and became a regular visitor to Melwood, the club's training ground, for a long time after his retirement. This soon turned out to be a problem with players deferring to Shanks instead of Bob Paisley at times – it couldn't go on.

In the end, Liverpool asked Shankly not to attend training but allowed him to train at Melwood when the first team weren't there. His love of the game was such that he missed being around the players and ended up watching Everton train.

It was a sad end for a man who had given so much to the club and who had once said of retirement, 'It's the most stupid word I've ever heard in all my life. It should be stricken from the record. You retire when they put the coffin lid down with your name on top. Until then nobody can retire.'

Nothing will ever erase Shankly's legacy. He built the foundations of the club we all love today. His philosophy and ethos are ingrained in the fabric at Anfield and his enduring spirit is still evident at Melwood. He left us with countless memories, three league titles, two FA Cups, and a UEFA Cup.

Above all of that though, he made the people happy.

Keegan and Bremner go to war – the 1974 Charity Shield sees sending-offs resulting in 11-game bans!

You may know it today as the Community Shield but years ago we called it the Charity Shield. This is a friendly game in which the winners of England's most prestigious domestic honours, the FA Cup and the First Division, come together in the spirit of sportsmanship to raise money for good causes.

For the first time, in 1974, the game was played at Wembley and featured two of the country's bitterest rivals.

Liverpool had vanquished Newcastle just a few months earlier in the FA Cup Final and Leeds United were league champions.

There was never any love lost between these two and they had vied with each other for dominance of English football for more than a decade. The Reds had famously beaten the Yorkshiremen in the 1965 FA Cup Final, ending the club's painful wait for success in that competition.

Leeds had a fierce reputation for what they called hard tackling. The rest of football just called them 'dirty Leeds'. And, on 10 August 1974 they did nothing to dispel that reputation, although Liverpool gave as good as they got.

Both sides were going through a transition. Billy Shankly had shocked Liverpool and the football world by announcing his retirement months earlier and Bob Paisley had succeeded him. Similarly, Don Revie was leaving Leeds to be replaced by Brian Clough.

Despite Shanks relinquishing the manager's job, Liverpool awarded him the honour of leading the team at Wembley in recognition of his services to the club. Apparently, Clough had a similar idea and wanted Revie to lead United out. Revie didn't fancy it so the young pretender would join Shanks, the master, at the front of the line-ups.

Clough admitted later he was in awe of the great Scot and had tried to engage him in small talk. Bill completely blanked him.

Behind the two managers walked two completely different teams: Liverpool, solid and united, and Leeds, who looked like a team with the weight of the world on their shoulders.

This was a game in which no quarter would be given, and none expected. Leeds were at it from the off and despite dire warnings from Clough to behave, they seemed unable to help themselves. Within 60 seconds of the kick-off Alan Clarke left Phil Thompson writhing on the turf. According to the *Daily Mirror*, Tommy Smith exacted brutal revenge by 'hacking Clarke off his feet' and Liverpool's Alec Lindsay joined in, leaving the Leeds man sprawled on the deck.

The tone was set for an encounter that would have more in common with a boxing match than a football game. Despite that Liverpool took the lead through Phil Boersma in the 19th minute and held on to their advantage until half-time.

United huffed and puffed while continuing their attempts to kick the Reds' house down but they couldn't break through Liverpool's rearguard. They did succeed in lighting a fuse under Kevin Keegan though and it led to an explosion in the 58th minute of the game.

Keegan was like a man possessed after the restart. He went charging into Billy Bremner and then Johnny Giles. From a resulting free kick, Bremner charged after Keegan and punched him in the kidneys. The red mist descended and the Liverpool man retaliated. The tussle ended with Keegan punching Bremner before ending up in a Norman Hunter headlock.

Keegan and Bremner were both sent off and according to the Leeds man, who was consoled in the tunnel by fellow Scot Shankly, Keegan and he shook on it and shared a beer after the game.

Clough, furious with his own players, had this to say about the incident, 'Keegan was a victim, not a culprit, that day at Wembley. The double dismissal was all down to Bremner. Keegan was an innocent party who had been pushed beyond the limit by an opponent who appeared determined to eliminate him from the match, one way or another. I told Bremner afterwards that he had been responsible for the confrontation. He should have been made to pay compensation for the lengthy period Keegan was suspended.'

However, the FA saw it differently and both players were suspended for 11 games and fined £500. There were calls from Fleet Street for both teams to be kicked out of the First Division, such was the hysteria around the incident. Thankfully calmer heads prevailed.

The drama didn't end in the 58th minute though. Leeds, against the run of play, equalised through Trevor Cherry, with 20 minutes left on the clock. The game was destined for a nail-biting shootout.

After five successful spot-kicks, the teams remained deadlocked. David Harvey missed Leeds's sixth and it was left to legend Ian Callaghan to bring the shield home. 'Cally' didn't disappoint, sending the travelling Kop home with smiles on their faces and plenty to talk about in the days and weeks to come.

Kings of Europe

Liverpool Football Club
1974–1990

**Eleven goals and nine scorers as Bob Paisley's
Liverpool set a club record against Stromsgodset**

One of the many gifts bestowed on the club by Bill Shankly,
after his resignation, was a place in the European Cup
Winners' Cup in 1974. The Reds had qualified for the
competition courtesy of their 4-0 victory over Newcastle
United in the FA Cup Final.

In the first round they were drawn against Norwegian
part-timers Stromsgodset. The tie, the first leg of which took
place on 17 September, hardly set Kopite pulses racing and
only 24,743 turned out.

They would prove to be the lucky ones, witnessing a
record-breaking avalanche of goals that remains unsurpassed
to this day.

Godset were founded in 1907 and by 1974 they were
three times winners of the Norwegian Football Cup. They
had won their first league championship just four years
earlier, in 1970. However, they were no match for Liverpool,
who hammered 11 goals past them at Anfield. It would beat

the previous record established by Shankly's team, who had previously crushed Dundalk 10-0.

Against Stromsgodset, nine different Reds players were on the scoresheet with only Ray Clemence and Brian Hall failing to get in on the act.

The Norwegians set the tone early when their goalkeeper conceded a penalty within three minutes. Alec Lindsay tucked the ball away and Liverpool were on their way. By half-time they were 5-0 up thanks to a Phil Boersma brace and goals from Phil Thompson and Steve Heighway.

Liverpool were so comfortable, they probably could have given much of the squad a rest after half-time. However, Paisley sent the same 11 out to destroy the opposition in the second half.

It was merciless, but that was Liverpool back then. The boss was almost apologetic at full time, saying, 'It's a bit embarrassing, but then if we had messed around people would have said they did not get value.'

The Reds initially toyed with their opponents after the restart and Godset managed a couple of attacks. But in the 65th minute Liverpool went up a gear.

Three goals in 11 minutes, from Peter Cormack, Phil Thompson and Emlyn Hughes, made it 8-0, but the Reds weren't finished yet.

With just five minutes left the Norwegians were chasing shadows and praying for full time.

Liverpool, on the other hand, would have been happy to play all night and simply went for the jugular. They fired three goals in three minutes through Tommy Smith (85), Ian Callaghan (87) and Ray Kennedy (88), to crown a monumental victory.

It was a chastening experienced for the Scandinavians and chairman Josef Mathison acknowledged, 'They are the best team we have played against ... better than Arsenal, who beat us years ago, and Leeds, who beat us last year. They were far too good for us amateurs.'

Thompson confessed that, in an Anfield without a scoreboard, it was difficult for the players to keep track of the score.

'In the second half I was confused about all the goals. I even had a chat with Emlyn Hughes to try to work out what the score was,' he said.

Amazingly Liverpool only won the second leg, at the Ullevaal Stadium, 1-0 thanks to a 17th-minute Kennedy strike. That meant Paisley's men had racked up a 12-0 aggregate victory.

Sadly though, the Reds would crash out of the cup in the second round, to Hungarian side Ferencvaros. Sometimes football makes no sense.

Barcelona fans hurl cushions in anger as Liverpool become first English team to win at the Nou Camp

The 1975/76 season was Bob Paisley's second in charge. His first had drawn a blank with the Reds finishing runners-up in the league, two points behind Derby County. They had also crashed out of the cup competitions early on.

The Reds had last won the title in 1973, under Bill Shankly. They also won the UEFA Cup the same year. In 1976 Paisley would repeat the feat with a league and European double, kick-starting his Anfield reign in earnest.

The Reds pipped QPR to the title by a single point and won an enthralling two-legged final against FC Bruges, involving an astonishing comeback at Anfield.

However, their route to the final was blocked by the mighty Barcelona and a certain Johan Cruyff. The Dutch master was arguably the best in the world at the time and the fixture would be a stern test. However, the game never went to script and Liverpool turned in a masterclass of European football.

The press reported that Barcelona afforded the Reds a lot of respect and played like the away side. Liverpool's reputation 'had clearly gone before them'.

Even when Cruyff and his team-mates ventured forward Phil Thompson and Emlyn Hughes shut the gate firmly, with Ray Clemence excellent as the last line of defence.

In the 13th minute the travelling Reds were in heaven as their team went a goal up. Clemence hit the ball long and Toshack was first to it, heading it backwards to Kevin Keegan. The number seven controlled it with his chest brilliantly and played a delightful one-two with his strike partner, who took his time and finished exquisitely past Pedro Mora.

With the Reds securing that all-important first goal, Barcelona had to come out and attack. Liverpool could sit back and hit them on the break.

The home side huffed and puffed but they couldn't knock down the Reds' rearguard and as the game wore on, the home crowd of 70,000 became increasingly frustrated.

The stadium began to empty with five minutes to go and the remaining fans hurled cushions on to the pitch, holding up the game.

Reports suggest that at full time the trickle became an avalanche as Barcelona supporters vented their anger.

Rod Helsby was there at the Nou Camp and describes the scene, 'I remember the thousands of cushions getting chucked on to the pitch and Joey Jones throwing them back.

'We played in all white [the same as Real Madrid] and the crowd went mad when the Redmen came on to the pitch in white. At the end of the game, we all had cushions, but the police took them off us. But I had two – one up my jumper and one to hand in.

'There was a bit of "bovver" outside but nothing we couldn't handle. Most fans went home with more luggage than they came with.'

As the Liverpool team ran to their own support they were greeted as heroes, with the remaining Catalans joining in sportingly. Keegan had put in such a good performance, some newspapers suggested he was bound for the Nou Camp at the end of the season. In a post-match interview, he wasted no time in gloating about their victory, 'We frustrated both their players and their fans. Every cushion that came down convinced us further that we had done what we came for.'

Liverpool drew the second leg at Anfield 1-1 and advanced to the final, with their European reputation massively enhanced. The English press swooned with one report stating, 'This was certainly a wonderful night for the Anfield team. They won well, worthily and cleanly and the reputation they had when they came to Spain is now even higher.'

In little over a year's time, it would climb to another level.

The remarkable Ray Kennedy inspires comeback to put Reds on the brink of second UEFA Cup, in 1976

Hopeless in the first half, a mountain to climb in the second and a heroic comeback inspired by one of Liverpool's truly great players – sound familiar?

No, this is not the miracle of Istanbul in 2005. It's 1976, we're at Anfield, our opponents are Club Bruges in the first leg of the UEFA Cup Final and the hero of the hour is Ray Kennedy. Kennedy signed for the Reds in 1974, just as Bill Shankly resigned.

The legendary manager was a big admirer of Ray and the player would turn out to be a great parting gift to his successor. He struggled at first, but Bob Paisley's decision to move him to the left wing proved to be an inspiration.

Steven Scragg, writing for *These Football Times*, described the triumphant and tragic aspects of Kennedy's career. Ray played 275 times for Liverpool, scoring 51 goals and winning 15 major honours, including three European Cups. However, he would later be diagnosed with a debilitating neurological condition.

Scragg puts Ray's monumental achievements into context, saying, 'I just think Kennedy is the most remarkable footballer Liverpool ever had. To do all he achieved while slowly being consumed by Parkinson's disease is truly startling. The most graceful and unassuming of footballers.'

Today Ray lives in relative obscurity, and is supported still by devoted fans who raise money so that he can maintain a degree of independence. He describes them as his 'ray of hope'. Those who know him say that he is genuinely shocked that the supporters still remember him at all. As if we could ever forget.

Liverpool had reached the final of the UEFA Cup in 1976 thanks to a magnificent semi-final triumph over Barcelona. The final was a two-legged affair back then, no neutral territory, and the Reds played Bruges at Anfield first.

The ground was packed with the official attendance put at almost 50,000. The first half was a disaster and the Belgian side were two up in 15 minutes through Raoul Lambert and Julien Cools. Liverpool went to pieces.

Bob Paisley was furious and, in his own inimitable style, he said, 'We were like a gang of schoolboys in the first half. We committed hara-kiri. We let our own mistakes upset us. We went berserk after their first goal and made childish mistakes.'

Paisley, a genius tactically, recognised that Liverpool had gone route one in an attempt to get their top scorer, John Toshack, into the game. It hadn't worked, and Bob took his striker off at the interval.

Tosh wasn't happy and left the ground before the rest of the team. The boss was unrepentant, simply saying, 'I made the change to get more movement in our attack.' It worked a treat.

In an utterly spellbinding five minutes, the Reds went 3-2 up. The man who inspired the fightback was Ray Kennedy. He scored the first, a stunning goal from the edge of the area, in the 59th minute. He hit it so hard and true that the goalkeeper didn't move.

Two minutes later he unleashed another rocket which struck the post. Jimmy Case scored the rebound. Here's how the legendary number eight tells it, 'I thought for a split second that the shot was going in, but suddenly the ball rebounded and was coming my way. It could have hit my thigh and run out of play, but I jumped instinctively and side-footed the ball into the net.'

Amazingly, Liverpool were level, but it was about to get a lot better. Just three minutes later they won a penalty.

Phil Neal would normally have taken it but he was struggling and asked Keegan to do the honours. The number seven didn't disappoint and put his side into the lead.

Journalist Derek Wallis, writing for the *Mirror*, described the response of the crowd. The images his words conjure are simply wonderful, 'The sustained roar assaulted the eardrums: the banners, the flags that had been stowed away were unfurled turning the jubilant Kop into a mass of colour.'

Case said, 'The Kop and the supporters were magnificent that night. Throats must have been red-raw with cheering. But you know what? I believe those fans liked to see us with our backs to the wall because they knew we could win.'

This was one of the greatest fightbacks in the club's history and many deserve credit; Paisley for his tactical nous, Case and Keegan, but journalists were united in declaring Kennedy the hero of the hour.

Horace Yates, in the *Liverpool Daily Post*, said this of Ray's contribution, 'There was no greater hero than Ray Kennedy. He has the reputation of being the most difficult man in the game to move off the ball. He did more, much more than that last night … He played the part of pathfinder for Liverpool, for his shooting on target lit a flare path for the rest of the team.'

Liverpool drew the second leg in Belgium 1-1 and Keegan would score the vital equaliser. However, there is no doubt that the 1976 UEFA Cup win belonged to Ray Kennedy.

The apprentice becomes the master as Paisley wins his first title as Reds boss

On Tuesday, 4 May 1976, Bob Paisley took his Liverpool side to Molineux. They were on the brink of winning their first title under the Englishman.

Paisley had assumed control in 1974 after Bill Shankly's resignation and led the Reds to a second-place finish in his first season. Liverpool went into the last game of 1975/76 just a single point clear of QPR, who lay in second spot. Only a victory would do. The game was also sandwiched between the first and second legs of the UEFA Cup Final, making this an epic week in the club's history.

Wolves desperately needed a win to avoid relegation. Even if they had secured that, their fate depended on other results going their way. This would be a desperate battle for both teams.

Official figures put the attendance at 48,900. However, it was certainly much higher than that. Tens of thousands of Liverpool supporters made the journey to the Midlands, hopeful of seeing the Reds lift the championship.

They would be met by scenes of utter chaos outside the ground before the game that illustrate just how dangerous going to the match could be back then.

One supporter who was there was a young Tony Lanigan. Here are his recollections of that incredible night, 'A mate got me a ticket at the last minute for the game. It was actually the first away game I'd been to. We went down by car and got to the ground fairly handy.

'Outside the away end, in what seemed like a really tight area, a crowd was building up gradually. I remember some people were being passed out over the crowd and it was all feeling a bit dangerous.

'Eventually one of the gates near the turnstiles gave way and loads of fans spilled into the ground. The press reported that the fans knocked the gate in, but I genuinely think it was just the sheer pressure of the crowd that forced it open. Something had to give in that packed space.

'As we entered the stadium, it was obvious that the vast majority inside were Liverpool fans. It was an incredible sight.

'Although there were a few nerves, I think everyone was pretty confident about the result. I remember Steve Kindon scoring for Wolves early in the game and although we were on top, nerves were fraying as time ticked away.

'Eventually, with 15 minutes to go, Keegan scored, and the place went mental. I got trapped against a barrier with the weight of the crowd behind me and I was pretty worried for a few seconds.

'At that point I lost sight of my mates, who I thought were just behind me. The pressure was just easing when Toshack scored the second. The crowd exploded again, and I was once more up against a barrier. I must have had ribs of steel back then. I'd learned my lesson by the time Ray Kennedy clinched it and avoided that barrier.

'I remember loads of fans on the pitch at full time and "You'll Never Walk Alone" being sung. Having lost my mates and the car, I decided to follow the crowd to the station and made my way home. I remember there were a few skirmishes along the way.'

Succeeding Shankly had been a tall order. However, Bob was only concerned with maintaining the standards set by the great man and making the supporters happy. At the end of an incredible season he could reflect upon how he had delivered on both of those ambitions.

Talking to Michael Charters in the *Liverpool Echo* later, Paisley said, 'When I took over the Liverpool management from Bill Shankly nearly two years ago, my philosophy was that if I could keep up the standards of success he had created, I would consider I had done my job.

'Now at the end of what I believe our fans will consider has been a fair old season of entertaining play and success, I will stand by the creed.'

That the boss could describe winning the title and the UEFA Cup in the same year as 'a fair old season' is a testament to his understated brilliance. This was an extraordinary achievement by an incredibly modest genius.

The King is gone, long live the King: Kenny replaces Kevin as hero of the Kop

When Kevin Keegan left Liverpool in 1977, many fans feared the worst. They needn't have worried.

In the summer of 1977, Liverpool announced the sale of their superstar striker to SV Hamburg for £500,000. There was widespread anger at the deal and fans couldn't believe their talisman had deserted them, with many calling him a mercenary.

Replacing Keegan looked like an impossible task but Bob Paisley was a master at identifying talent and immediately splashed a British record fee of £440,000 on Kenneth Mathieson Dalglish from Celtic.

According to an article in the *Daily Mirror*, the deal was clinched in dramatic fashion, just before midnight on 9 August 1977.

Celtic were about to travel to Dunfermline to play a league game when Paisley phoned Jock Stein and made the record offer for the player. Dalglish was in the team. The two managers made their way to Celtic Park and met with the club's directors to thrash out the deal.

Kenny was then summoned to the stadium and told, to his delight, that he had been sold to Liverpool. Paisley was overjoyed and described Dalglish as a 'great player', stating that he would 'do a great job for us'. How right he was.

Kenny was beaming, clearly delighted at his move south of the border. He is quoted as saying, 'It's a golden chance. I came to Celtic ten years ago, after they won the European Cup. Now I'm joining Liverpool after their European triumph and I am looking forward to playing in English football.'

Kenny had won four Scottish League titles, four Scottish Cups and one Scottish League Cup with the Glasgow giants, scoring 112 times in 204 appearances. He would prove to be the perfect replacement for Keegan and immediately established himself as a Kop favourite.

His first outing for the Reds came just a few days later, in the FA Charity Shield at Wembley. Liverpool and

Manchester United shared the silverware that day, drawing 0-0, and Dalglish was introduced to the hordes of Liverpool supporters.

The man who would be King then scored on his league debut, just a week later at Middlesbrough, and on his Anfield debut against Newcastle United.

Kenny's first season in English football was a baptism of fire. He scored the sixth goal in a 6-0 thrashing of Kevin Keegan's Hamburg in the European Super Cup and featured in the League Cup Final replay defeat to Nottingham Forest.

Brian Clough's Forest finished the season a full seven points clear of Liverpool to win the league title also. However, in May, Kenny was back at Wembley for the European Cup Final. Liverpool's opponents were Bruges.

In front of 92,000 supporters, Dalglish was crowned the new King of the Kop after scoring the goal that retained 'Old Big Ears' in the 65th minute. Who can forget him leaping over advertising boards and racing towards the Liverpool supporters behind the goal, arms in the air and that big grin on his face?

With typical modesty, Kenny credited the team performance for the win, but he added, 'It's just wonderful to get my first European Cup medal with a great club like Liverpool. I was thrilled to score the goal.'

Kenny scored a total of 172 goals in 515 appearances for the club. He won an astonishing array of medals too, including six league titles, one FA Cup, four League Cups and three European Cups.

He then went on to achieve glory as a manager in not one, but two spells in the club hot seat. Dalglish's relationship with Liverpool FC and its supporters now transcends football and he serves to this day as a director of the club. He was well worth the £440,000 Paisley paid for him in 1977.

That was surely the biggest bargain in the history of football.

Long live the King.

The Kop sings 'Allez Les Rouges' as David Fairclough writes his name in history in 1977

The night of 16 March 1977 is now forever etched into Liverpool history. It ranks alongside all the Reds' great cup final victories and league title wins for its significance. It is, of course, the night that David Fairclough emerged from the bench and sent Anfield wild with a goal that put Liverpool on their way to European glory.

The Reds were fighting for a place in the quarter-finals of the European Cup and had been drawn against French outfit Saint-Etienne. They lost the first leg 1-0, putting their progress in jeopardy.

Scousers were determined to see their team through though and the return match at Anfield was a seething cauldron of emotion and pride. Les Rouges would not be moved.

In the away end the French supporters were decked out in their colours, some wearing wigs.

They sang 'Allez Les Vertes' and the Kop responded with a chant that would later adorn banners and echo in history. 'Allez Les Rouges, Allez Les Rouges,' they sang.

Even before kick-off the stadium was rammed. More than 55,000 were inside Anfield, with 10,000 more locked out. The noise was incredible, the colour, the atmosphere. It was all electric.

The Spion Kop heaved and sagged as fans swayed forward and back and side to side. Supporters who started at the back would end up at the bottom of the famous old terrace by full time.

This was the pinnacle of Kopite fury, when the supporters could infect the players with their passion and vice versa; when away fans could only marvel at the spectacle and the power of the mighty stand on Walton Breck Road.

In the Main Stand, near the Anfield Road end, 12-year-old Keith Williams was sat with his older brother. To him the night was already special – he was celebrating his birthday. His dad had got him a ticket courtesy of Ronnie Moran.

Behind them were a row of Saint-Etienne supporters with green wigs and bottles of wine. Keith picks up the story, 'I remember Keegan scored after two minutes, from a short corner just to our left. We were off to a flyer. There was this fella to my left, he was probably in his 30s. He told me he had to leave at half-time to go on night shift – he was still there after 90 minutes.

'I'll never forget the Kop singing in French, to the delight of those wine-swilling Saint-Etienne supporters behind us. It was a packed steaming wall of noise, a picture.'

Liverpool had levelled the tie, on aggregate, and a party broke out inside Anfield. However, in the second half, disaster struck as the French equalised on the night through Dominique Bathenay.

The visiting supporters went wild and Liverpool needed two more to go through. Just eight minutes later Ray Kennedy got the Reds' second and the Kop sensed a miracle could happen. However, with time running out, Bob Paisley decided to make a change.

He took John Toshack off and put young Scouser David Fairclough on. It would prove to be a truly momentous switch.

With the atmosphere building to an incredible crescendo and only four minutes remaining, Kennedy picked the ball up in his own half. Fairclough would later tell how Kennedy had always told him where to run if he ever saw his team-mate get hold of the ball in an area like that. He duly obliged and glided between the Saint-Etienne defenders.

Then the ball was in the air and Fairclough was on to the pass and racing towards the Kop, which was roaring him home. With the defender on his shoulder and the goalkeeper rushing out at him, he held his nerve and slid the ball into the net.

The youngster with fiery red hair jumped in celebration and was immediately engulfed in a sort of volcanic noise, the likes of which Anfield had rarely witnessed.

Then he fell to the turf as he was set upon by his team-mates, finishing off under a pile of Liverpool players.

This is how Keith remembers the goal, 'It was total bedlam in the stadium. The night-shift worker is still there holding me in the air. The French wigs sat behind us, with their wine bottles in hand, are open-mouthed.

'I've never heard such an atmosphere in the stadium before or after. The final whistle went a few minutes later. The crowd started singing "we're gonna win the cup".

'After the game, I'm waiting for the bus and cars are going past with horns tooting. Amazing, brilliant night. The best atmosphere ever!'

French newspaper *Le Figaro* said that Saint-Etienne had been 'stabbed' by Fairclough's late winner. It was evocative language, but somehow it feels apt.

So, what did the youngster do to celebrate his history-defining moment? He would later tell LFCTV that he simply went for a pint in the Hare and Hounds, in West Derby village, not far from his home in the Cantril Farm housing estate.

Liverpool were in the quarter-finals of the European Cup but nobody who left Anfield that night was in any doubt that the Reds were going to Rome. *Allez Les Rouges*.

'Joey's Munching Gladbach' as Liverpool bring home the European Cup for the first time

In 1959, Bill Shankly breezed into Anfield claiming he would build a bastion of invincibility that no team in Europe would be able to resist. He went close to achieving his aim in 1965 but was undone by an allegedly corrupt official.

While he would claim European football's equivalent of the silver medal, the UEFA Cup, in 1973, Shanks never lifted the continent's premier trophy. That honour fell to Bob Paisley on 25 May 1977.

Liverpool were imperious that season. They began it with a Charity Shield victory over Southampton and ended it as First Division champions.

However, just four days before the European Cup Final against Borussia Monchengladbach, they were robbed of an opportunity to win a treble by Manchester United at Wembley.

Four crazy minutes saw three goals scored and United emerged 2-1 winners of the FA Cup. It was terrible preparation for a final in Europe. The mood in the city would have been grim, but for the promise of even greater riches in Rome.

Stories of how Liverpool fans cobbled together the money to travel across the continent are now legendary. Many sold furniture and appliances – some with, some without the permission of their wives. Others resorted to more 'entrepreneurial' methods to generate the necessary cash for their journey.

Tens of thousands made the journey, over land and sea. It was a Scouse invasion and many endured appalling conditions on a train ride across the continent.

They travelled carrying red and white chequered flags and returned with the finest sportswear Europe had to offer. Few in Liverpool had heard of Adidas or Sergio Tacchini

125

until those Kopites came home with armfuls of the stuff. But that's another story.

Their songs would echo around the squares of the Italian capital as they drank wine in the streets and danced with locals. Here's one song that filled the air that night:

'On the 25th of May,
All the Kopites will be singing,
Vatican Bells they will be ringing,
Liverpool boys they will be drinking,
When we win the European Cup.'

Liverpool had reached Rome after beating Saint-Etienne in the quarter-final and FC Zurich in the semi-final. Their navigation through the latter stages of the competition was inscribed on the greatest Liverpool banner of all time. On a giant red sheet, white letters had been stitched, spelling out a tribute to Reds defender Joey Jones:

'JOEY ATE THE FROGS LEGS
MADE THE SWISS ROLL
NOW HE'S MUNCHING GLADBACH'

The players hadn't expected many to make the expensive and difficult journey from Liverpool to Italy. Ian Callaghan described his feelings of wonder as he emerged from the tunnel to witness a sea of red. Liverpool supporters vastly outnumbered their German counterparts.

Filled with pride and feeling ten feet tall, Liverpool took the game to Monchengladbach, pressing relentlessly high up the pitch and forcing errors. The Germans were finding it difficult to build, but one breakaway, in the 22nd minute, resulted in a shot clipping the Liverpool post.

That was a let-off but in the 27th minute the Reds were in front through Terry McDermott. What followed was wild euphoria in the stands and jubilant celebration on the pitch.

In the second half, Monchengladbach poured forward in search of an equaliser.

Sadly, it would take an unforced error by Jimmy Case to gift them a goal. The Scouser played a careless ball back to his goalkeeper but Danish striker Allan Simonsen was on to it quickly and scored.

It was a disaster and things could have got even worse but for a brilliant save by Ray Clemence, denying Uli Stielike. Liverpool were rocking and Simonsen almost added his second, but his header went wide.

Liverpool needed a hero and fortunately they had Tommy Smith. The veteran defender was playing his 600th and last game for the club. However, he would leave the Reds one last gift.

From a corner, taken by Steve Heighway, Smith rose magnificently to head home. Liverpool were back in front on 64 minutes. They then had to face a tense 20-minute spell, relying heavily on the brilliance of their goalkeeper, before Phil Neal sealed the deal from the penalty spot in the 87th minute.

That made the score 3-1 and, as the TV commentator said, 'With such simplicity, the European Cup was won.'

Michael Charters, writing in the *Liverpool Echo*, saw it like this, 'Liverpool are the masters of Europe – and the masters of how to play European football with style and efficiency, class combined with effort, individual brilliance with superb teamwork.

'On an unforgettable night in Rome, a night to live forever as the highlight of a thousand sporting memories, this magnificent team completed the greatest season in the history of any English club by adding the European Cup to their league championship.'

The night Ian Callaghan played his 857th and last game for Liverpool

On 29 March 1978, in front of a crowd of 67,000 people in the Rheinstadion in Germany, a Liverpool legend brought his career to an end. That man was Ian Callaghan, a Scouser born and bred and a stalwart of the Shankly and Paisley eras.

He was playing his 857th match for Liverpool Football Club, a record that will surely never be surpassed. The Reds lost the European Cup semi-final first leg 2-1.

They would triumph in the return fixture at Anfield, but for the purposes of this moment in the club's history, that's irrelevant.

Cally made his Liverpool debut at home to Bristol Rovers, in the Second Division, on 16 April 1960.

The Reds won 4-0. However, it was a young player, Ian Callaghan, who caught the eye of the media.

This is how the *Express* reported his first game, 'Liverpool seem to have at last solved one of their most pressing problems, that of outside right. Eight men of experience have been tried there this season without giving complete satisfaction.

'So Anfield manager Bill Shankly introduced 17-year-old local boy Ian Callaghan who signed professional only six weeks ago.

'And what a debut the boy had. So good in fact that at the final whistle Peter Hooper dashed up to shake Ian by the hand, referee Reg Leafe ran over to give the lad a word of praise, and the 27,000 people stood and cheered him. And Callaghan deserved it, for he had a part in three of the goals.'

Toxteth-born Callaghan had already been singled out as a future star by none other than the great Billy Liddell. Upon his retirement, the old master was asked if there was anyone at the club who could take his place. He replied, 'There is a 17-year-old called Ian Callaghan who looks like taking over from me. I played with him twice, watched his progress and I believe he'll be a credit to his club, the game and his country.'

His words could not have been more prophetic. Callaghan would go on to win five First Division titles, one Second Division title, two FA Cups, two European Cups and two UEFA Cups. He was capped four times for England and scored 68 goals for Liverpool.

Cally's debut goal came in a 3-1 victory over Preston North End in 1961, in the second tier of English football. He scored his last against the mighty Benfica in a 2-1 European Cup third-round victory en route to the Reds' second European Cup in as many years.

There is no better illustration of the rise of an Anfield great. In the 18 years that he was a Liverpool player he was only booked once. That came, agonisingly, in the penultimate game of his career.

The sanction, which was hotly disputed, came in a 1-0 defeat to Nottingham Forest on 22 March 22 1978, during a replay of the League Cup Final at Old Trafford.

It must be seen as but a mere blemish on a career any player would be immensely proud of. In truth, few could ever dream of getting close to such a record.

In summing up his achievements in the game, there can be no higher praise than that offered sincerely by his manager and mentor, the legendary Bill Shankly, 'Ian Callaghan is everything good that a man can be. No praise is too high for him. He is a model professional, and a model human being. If there were 11 Callaghans at Anfield there would never be any need to put up a team sheet. You could stake your life on Ian.

'Words cannot do justice to the amount he has contributed to the game. Ian Callaghan will go down as one of the game's truly great players.'

He would leave the club as he had found it, on the brink of making history. As he trudged off the field in Germany he had kicked his last ball for the Reds. However, he had been a pivotal member of the team for almost two decades.

And as he walked out the door, Liverpool Football Club was in a much better place than when he found it.

Thank you, Cally.

Emlyn Hughes sets the benchmark as Paisley's Scots wizards cast spell over Europe

In the glorious aftermath of Liverpool's 1977 European triumph in Rome, Emlyn Hughes was asked how the Reds could ever top such a feat. His reply, accompanied by that trademark grin, was simply to say, 'Go out and win it again.'

One year later in 1978, in front of a Wembley crowd which topped 92,000, he would once more lift the famous trophy before a throng of jubilant supporters. Liverpool had achieved what no other British club had ever done; they had retained the European Cup. Bob Paisley had delivered Shankly's dream of invincibility.

This was the crowning moment of a mixed season. It had started with a 7-1 aggregate trouncing of Kevin Keegan's Hamburg to lift the European Super Cup. They would also end up sharing the Charity Shield with Manchester United.

However, in the league, Paisley's men finished runners-up to Brian Clough's Nottingham Forest. The outspoken boss would also pip Liverpool to the League Cup in a controversial final that featured a penalty for Forest and a disallowed goal for Liverpool's Terry McDermott.

However, nobody could stop the Reds in Europe. Liverpool had overcome Dynamo Dresden, Benfica and Borussia Monchengladbach en route to Wembley, with aggregate scores of 6-3, 6-2 and 4-2 respectively. The final was to be against Club Bruges, of Belgium.

Liverpool had, of course, replaced one icon, Kevin Keegan, with another, Kenny Dalglish, for the 1977/78 season.

The former Celtic striker had settled in well to his new home, scoring 31 goals in all competitions in his first season. However, he had managed just two in Europe – turns out he was keeping his powder dry for the final.

Also joining the Reds that season were two other Scots, Alan Hansen and Graeme Souness, who along with Dalglish would form the most powerful triumvirate of Scottish players in modern football history.

Bill Shankly, speaking about the potency of players hailing from north of the border, once said, 'If you've got three Scots in your side, you've got a chance of winning something. If you've got any more, you're in trouble.'

Dalglish will always get the plaudits for scoring the winning goal in the game, but Souness was also instrumental and delivered the pass that set Kenny on his way. Horace Yates, writing in the *Liverpool Daily Post*, named the future Reds captain as man of the match, declaring that the player was 'a veritable box of tricks and with his wide array of passing and subtle midfield manoeuvres, it was apt he should be the man to provide Liverpool's winner'.

It seemed Paisley had been consulting Shanks's book of spells as he set about finding the missing Scottish ingredients, allowing him to enchant all of Europe. His sorcery would ultimately win him three European Cups, but it was the capture of his second that set Liverpool's most successful manager apart from all the rest.

To be the first of your kind to achieve something so magnificent guarantees him immortality, within the hallowed walls of Anfield and far beyond. The Liverpool supporters had already begun chanting 'Why are we so great?' before the Reds grabbed their winner in the 65th minute. In truth, it was starting to seem like they may never get the breakthrough.

An earlier defensive lapse by new boy Hansen almost let in Sorenson for a Bruges opener. Fortunately, Clemence was up to the task on that occasion. Then Phil Thompson scooped one from Simoen off the line when a goal seemed a certainty.

However, Liverpool were not to be denied their place in history. After all, a street party of enormous proportions awaited them back home. The goal came eventually and it created delirium at Wembley.

This is how Yates described it, 'A Dalglish overhead kick was pushed out by goalkeeper Jensen and from a Belgian point of view it could not have been a more ill-directed punch. The ball flew to Souness and another brilliant pass sent Dalglish racing on to the ball.

'Although angled and covered by Jensen, Dalglish, with commendable calm, flipped the ball over the goalkeeper and into the net. It was a magnificent exhibition of the striker's art.'

Liverpool saw the game out and the celebrations would last long into the night. Here is the *Daily Post*'s take, 'The scenes of jubilation surpassed those in Rome last year simply because nine-tenths of the crowd were sporting Liverpool favours.'

At full time, Bob Paisley gave an interview to the waiting press. He was clearly irritated with the tactics employed by Bruges, who he felt had come to 'park the bus', to coin a modern phrase. He said, 'It takes two teams to make a game into a spectacle and Bruges only seemed to be concerned with keeping the score down. Bruges didn't come at us much – apart from one mistake in our defence, they never looked like scoring.'

Apparently, the Belgian side's manager, Ernst Happel, was less than enchanted with the Reds, 'Liverpool seemed only a shadow of the side we played in the UEFA Cup Final two seasons ago. I was disappointed with them.'

Not to worry, Ernst lad. History will record that in 1978 a 'disappointing' Liverpool became the first British side to retain Europe's top prize. You may have been disappointed, but at Wembley the cup belonged to the Reds.

The greatest goal ever scored at Anfield

It's 1978. Liverpool are champions of Europe and they're getting ready to face Tottenham at Anfield. All talk in the build-up is of Spurs' two new signings – the stuff of Panini sticker album fantasy, Osvaldo Ardiles and Ricky Villa.

Tottenham had just been promoted to the top flight and had caused a bit of a sensation by signing the two Argentine World Cup winners. This was now becoming a trend, with several foreign players gracing the English league. For the Reds, foreign signings were of the Scots, Welsh or Irish variety.

Spurs hadn't beaten Liverpool at Anfield since the year the *Titanic* sank, 1912. They were going to have to wait a while longer too as within half an hour the home side were three goals up.

Two from Kenny Dalglish in the eighth and 20th minutes had set them on their way. A third from the great Ray Kennedy had them coasting by half-time. The Kop was as cruel as it was witty and immediately rubbed salt in the Londoners' wounds.

'What a waste of money!' is a cliché chant these days. Back then it was fairly new, at least to me, and filled with cruel irony. Who knew what the two Argentines were thinking, but as far as Reds fans were concerned, they had joined the wrong club.

Liverpool brought on local lad David Johnson in the second half. He had come to Liverpool from Ipswich Town, after starting out as an Everton player. He enjoyed his best days playing for Liverpool and averaged a goal every three games, before rejoining the Blues in the early 1980s.

As the game restarted the men in red moved up a gear. Tottenham, still reeling from the first 45 minutes, were like lambs to the slaughter and Johnson made it four almost immediately. He grabbed the fifth ten minutes later.

This was sublime stuff and the Kop were in raptures, singing 'London Bridge is falling down'. Poor old Tottenham.

No sooner had they finished celebrating the fifth goal than the players were winning a penalty. Phil Neal, stood over the ball, hands on his hips and, as he waited for the okay from the referee, young fans like me were stood, hands clasped in prayer over their mouths. There was no need for appeals to a higher power, 'Zico' never missed; 6-0.

Michael Charters, writing for the *Liverpool Echo*, summed up the sumptuous quality on display perfectly, 'Have you ever heard 50,000 people purr with pleasure? Well, the Anfield spectators were doing that constantly as Liverpool stroked the ball around with one-touch moves of staggering accuracy. This display confirmed for me, particularly after the splendour of their wins at Ipswich and City the previous week, that the current Liverpool team is playing better, more exciting, attacking football than any side I've seen since the war.'

If the whistle had gone at that moment, it would have still gone down as one of the greatest games in Liverpool history. However, the Reds weren't finished there. They were about to cap off a mesmerising display by scoring the greatest goal Anfield has ever seen. That's how Bob Paisley described it and he had seen quite a few.

The ball broke on the left-hand side of the pitch, facing the Anfield Road end. Steve Heighway was on to it in a flash. The Kop swayed, and, in the Main Stand, an expectant crowd rose from their seats, sensing something was about to happen. The noise levels began to rise as Terry McDermott raced from his own half and crossed the halfway line. Heighway motored down the wing and looked up, spotting McDermott's run.

The pace of the Reds' attack caught the Spurs defence out and they looked ill-prepared to defend the onslaught. Heighway swept the ball towards the penalty spot. At the precise moment the ball arrived, so too did McDermott. The ball and his head aligned like planets in some cosmic dance and in an instant, it was in the net.

It was a goal of sheer wonder, amazement and unadulterated joy. How did they do that? Surely these men must be magicians. That's how supporters like me saw it. The timing of it was sublime, the precision and then, bang – goal, 7-0. Game over! But then, in truth, this Liverpool team were so good, Spurs were probably beaten before they set foot on the pitch.

Wembley bakes, as on-fire Terry McDermott shoots down the Gunners: the story of the 1979 Charity Shield

It's 11 August 1979. We're at Wembley for the Charity Shield and the pitched is bathed in the glorious summer sun. In the stands, 92,000 supporters bake in the heat. The new season is upon them but Liverpool supporters can still taste last season's title win. For Arsenal fans the memories of their FA Cup Final triumph over Manchester United still linger.

Bob Paisley had played down the significance of the tie, stating that his focus would be entirely on the opening game of the league season, against Bolton at Anfield. He may have been telling the truth but the press wasn't listening and ran with the headline 'Liverpool in no mood for Charity'.

The season before, the Reds had conceded just 16 goals, only four of them at home. In a 42-game season, Ray Clemence had kept 28 clean sheets. In attack, Liverpool were deadly, scoring 85 times. By contrast the Gunners had finished a distant seventh, 20 points behind Paisley's men.

The gulf in class doesn't always show in the Wembley sunshine, but it did on this day. The Reds looked every inch the champions they were, with an impressive demolition of their opponents.

Wielding the sledgehammer that day was Terry McDermott with a brace. The Scouser was utterly devastating for Liverpool with his trademark late runs into the box. He would score an impressive 81 goals in 329 appearances in midfield.

Terry had a reputation, though. He worked hard, and he played hard. Bob Paisley summed this up perfectly, saying, 'Off the field he was one of the biggest jokers we have had and a man who enjoyed a pint or two. But no matter how well he celebrated he was always in at training the following morning and that is all that mattered to Liverpool Football Club.'

He was a man of the people, too, and frequently shunned the high life. In 1980 he won the Sports Writers' Player of the Year award but didn't show up. Later he would explain, 'I'd sooner go and have a pint and a pie in the pub rather than go to a big function like that.'

For all his modesty off the pitch, he was ruthless on it. And Arsenal felt the full force of his wrath at Wembley as the Reds blew them away to lift the Shield that day.

His first goal was a 25-yard thunderbolt that gave Pat Jennings no chance. Kenny Dalglish hit the second just past the hour mark with a trademark finish and Terry rounded off the win just two minutes later.

Arsenal grabbed a goal through Alan Sunderland, but it was a miserable afternoon for them and their fans. They had been thoroughly outclassed and it was Scouser Terry who tore them to shreds. He'd have partied hard that night, you'd imagine.

McDermott has always been held in the highest regard by Liverpool fans, who voted him at 37 in 'The 100 Players Who Shook the Kop'. He would respond with typical Scouse cheek, 'Who voted for that, by the way? Some of the players who got in front of me … I thought … Stevie Wonder must have voted … I should have been number 20, not 37.'

Carefree conquest and the loss of a hero: the tale of Liverpool's two ties against Oulun Palloseura

Oulun Palloseura is a Finnish team from the town of Oulu. They play in the third tier of Finnish football at the Raatti Stadium, with a capacity of 5,000. It's doubtful many of the current generation of Reds will have heard of them.

However, in 1980 and 1981 they competed with Liverpool in the first round of the European Cup, the sides facing each other four times over two ties. Each time Bob Paisley's men would labour in the first leg only to crush their opponents in the return game at Anfield. In all, Liverpool would score 19 times and concede just once.

I remember both ties for very different reasons. The first evokes amusement and laughter while the second recalls an emotional farewell to a legend and an icon of the club.

On 1 October 1980 I travelled to Anfield by taxi to see Liverpool take on Oulun. I was with my father, my uncle and cousin. The cabby asked us for our predictions for the game. We were all a bit non-committal – the Reds had drawn the first leg 1-1 and we had no idea what to expect from the visitors.

The driver was full of scorn. 'Yer joking aren't yer lads?' he laughed. 'These are rubbish. I'm tellin' yer, if Liverpool gets four by half-time, it'll be double figures by the end.'

I remember turning to my cousin and rolling my eyes. The Reds were invincible heroes to me, but double figures in the European Cup? Nah, I wasn't having that.

At half-time, as the players traipsed off the pitch 4-0 up thanks to a brace each from Graeme Souness and Terry McDermott, my cousin and I were thinking this guy might be from the future or something.

In the second half the Reds scored another six. Souness and McDermott completed their hat-tricks, David Fairclough got two and Ray Kennedy and Sammy Lee made up the numbers.

This was a total demolition job, it had rained goals, but all we could think about was the time-travelling cabby who took us to the game.

Liverpool, as the taxi driver probably could have foretold had we asked him, won their third European Cup that season. They would beat Real Madrid in Paris.

The following season, as they began their defence of the trophy in 1981, they would again be drawn against Oulun in the first round. They won the first leg thanks to a goal by Kenny Dalglish and returned to Anfield for another potential drubbing.

Sadly, the day before the game, Liverpool Football Club lost the man who laid the foundations for all of our European conquests.

Bill Shankly had died, following a heart attack, on 29 September 1981. I remember a few of us had gone to school wearing our Liverpool scarves in tribute. The teachers turned a blind eye, even though we kept them on in lessons.

The atmosphere in the ground that night was sombre. It was described as the saddest night on the Kop and emotions were understandably raw.

Liverpool were two up at half-time. The result was no longer in question and, as the action resumed, the Kop delivered its own heartfelt tribute to the man they adored.

For the whole 45 minutes of the second half, they sang 'Shankly, Shankly, Shankly' to the tune of the great man's favourite song, 'Amazing Grace'. Many grown men and women had tears streaming down their cheeks. They just couldn't believe the man was gone.

Liverpool won 7-0 (triumphing 8-0 on aggregate). Never could such a rout have felt so hollow.

These are two very different tales, one of carefree conquest and the other of grief and loss. And for the briefest of moments in the early 1980s, a small team from Finland, called Oulun Palloseura, became inextricably linked with both.

In the belly of the beast: Howard Gayle silences 70,000 in West Germany

This is the story of how Howard Gayle, Liverpool's first black player, produced a statement display in adversity as he turned out in a furious Munich atmosphere in 1981. Back in the spring of that year, Liverpool faced Bayern in the second leg of the European Cup semi-final at the Olympiastadion in West Germany.

After a goalless draw at Anfield, in which Bob Paisley's men had been lucky to get zero, the manager was faced with an injury crisis. Kenny Dalglish was struggling but he would at least make the starting line-up. However, it was a team packed with reserves that flew out of Liverpool to face the German giants. Richard Money, Colin Irwin and Sammy Lee joined a young Gayle on that flight – they were hardly names likely to set their rivals' pulses racing.

In the case of Gayle, that would prove to be their fatal mistake. Paisley had watched the youngster blast a hat-trick against Blackburn in a Central League fixture on the Saturday before. He calculated that Bayern would have studied every one of Liverpool's first-team players, but they would know nothing of Howard.

Still he wasn't underestimating the scale of the task facing his team. Only Real Madrid had escaped defeat at Munich in European competition. He described the encounter as 'one of the hardest tests we have ever had', adding, 'Any score draw will do me.'

With Dalglish declaring himself fit, Gayle took a place on the bench. He had to wait just seven minutes to take his bow though, as Kenny limped off with the game barely under way.

The atmosphere inside the stadium was later described as horrific by Gayle, who was no stranger to racist abuse at English grounds. So when he was subjected to Nazi salutes and monkey chants from sections of the German support, it just made him even more determined to be better, faster and stronger than his opponents.

He ran his opponents ragged and soon they resorted to hacking him down. Liverpool should have had a penalty after one such incident. He burst into the penalty area and was pulled down by German international Wolfgang Dremmler, but the referee saw nothing.

Fearful that the youngster might retaliate and get sent off, Paisley took him off in the 70th minute, bringing on Jimmy Case in his place. The manager had spoken to Gayle previously, after he had punched an opponent who had racially abused him and spat in his face, receiving a red card for his troubles.

The boss had told him that his opponent had resorted to abusing him because he couldn't compete with Gayle as a player. 'You're no use to us off the pitch,' Paisley had said. The youngster had learned a lot from that experience and had been determined not to allow Bayern to goad him into retaliating, so he was bitterly disappointed to be subbed.

The boss explained his reasoning, 'We should have had a penalty when Howard Gayle was pulled down. Later on, Howie ran out of steam and started retaliating but he did tremendously. We thought his pace would surprise them which it did.'

The boss had been desperate to avoid playing extra time with ten men against superior opposition. However, teams were only allowed two substitutions and bringing on Case was the last throw of the dice for Paisley. It almost backfired immediately. Gayle had just left the pitch when David Johnson started limping. The boss was livid and is reported to have shouted at a nearby policeman, 'Give me that gun, I'll bloody shoot him!'

He needn't have worried though, as it was Johnson who set up Ray Kennedy to score a priceless and decisive away goal in the 83rd minute. Karl-Heinz Rummenigge levelled just four minutes later, setting up a nervy finish. The Reds hung on though and Gayle described the moment the whistle blew as the greatest feeling of his life.

Liverpool had given a great account of themselves and stunned their opponents, becoming only the second team ever to avoid defeat at the Olympiastadion. They were through to their third European Cup Final and would face Real Madrid in Paris.

Gayle's performance had been inspirational, especially given the abuse he had received. He was the Reds' secret weapon that night and will forever have a place in Liverpool's glorious history.

Kopites drinking wine on the Seine, as 'Barney' turns Madrid to rubble

In 1981, Liverpool supporters descended on Paris for the European Cup Final against Real Madrid. It would be the club's third final and not even the spectre of mass unemployment could deter an army of Scousers from invading France.

In typical fashion, as they strolled along the banks of the Seine, they would mock their situation and poke fun at the rest of the country, singing 'on the dole in Paree, drinking wine!'

Just as in 1977, football was a way out of the struggles of everyday life for many Liverpudlians. If it wasn't for Liverpool Football Club, many Scousers would never have experienced life on the continent. For some, following the club was an education, as well as an act of pilgrimage – not to mention the greatest 'shopping spree' of all time.

The final was to take place in the Parc des Princes, which only held around 50,000 supporters. Fans were angry at the way tickets were allocated, with many season-ticket holders losing out.

A comment in the *Liverpool Echo*, from a Mr D. Tootell of Ellesmere Port, raged, 'May I express my disgust at the way in which tickets for the European Cup Final have been allocated. It seems quite clear that Liverpool Football Club have handed over all responsibility to the tour companies who after all, are only in it for profit.'

The *Echo* was filled with stories of supporters struggling with travel arrangements and affordability. These issues are still being raised by modern fans. It seems the more things change, the more they stay the same.

Still, tens of thousands of Reds made the journey and as the game got under way, a total of 48,360 were inside the stadium. The Reds' opponents were Spanish giants Real Madrid, themselves European royalty.

Liverpool had started the season with a Charity Shield win over West Ham. They would meet the Hammers again in the League Cup Final, eventually overcoming them in a replay at Villa Park to win the first of four League Cups in a row.

Sadly though, the Reds' defence of their league title had faltered and they finished a disappointing fifth.

The European Cup therefore offered a real chance to add some polish to an atypically underachieving season, at least by Bob Paisley's standards.

Liverpool were led out that night by Kirkby-born Phil Thompson, who would become the first Scouser to captain the Reds to European Cup glory – a feat not repeated until 2005, when Steven Gerrard would have that honour in Istanbul.

The team was filled with legends of Liverpool's history, names long since immortalised, such as Clemence, Neal, Hansen, Souness, McDermott, Dalglish, Johnson, Lee and the two Kennedys, Alan and Ray.

On the bench the great Jimmy Case and Howard Gayle joined Colin Irwin and Richard Money. Steve Ogrizovic was the goalkeeping backup.

However, for all the riches of Paisley's European kings, it would be an unlikely hero who delivered glory for the Reds that night.

With the game deadlocked and seemingly heading for extra time, Alan Kennedy, a left-back signed from Newcastle

United in 1978, burst into the box to score the winner with barely eight minutes to go.

Kopites thought he looked like a character from a famous cartoon, *The Flintstones*. As a result, they had nicknamed him Barney Rubble and in their thousands, they would sing 'Barney, Barney' as the ball hit the net.

This is how the *Echo* reported the goal that gave the Reds their third European Cup, under the headline 'Goal of a lifetime sinks Real', 'It was just after 9.50 in the stylish bowl of Parc des Princes last night when Alan Kennedy earned himself instant immortality. What the assembled masses from all corners of Europe made of the 'Barney, Barney' chant that rose from the Red sections of the arena, as Kennedy's clubbing left footer hit the Real Madrid net, no one knows.'

The player's celebration tells the story of a man who is every bit as astonished as everybody else that he had scored. It was a spectacular moment.

The young lad from the north-east of England had smashed European aristocracy and turned Madrid to rubble. Perhaps his feats were the perfect metaphor for the struggling Scousers who had made it to the French capital, despite their meagre means and the obstacles placed before them by the club's ticketing system, finally tasting the most exquisite of glories available to any supporter.

To crown this great victory, it would be a lad from Kirkby who once stood on the world famous Kop, the terrace he once described as his 'pride and joy', who would lift the great trophy aloft at the end of the night.

He would take that cup all the way to his local pub, where locals would drink pints of beer in its honour, as youngsters peered through the windows to catch a glimpse.

They would never forget how, on 27 May 1981, they had been 'on the dole in Paree, drinking wine'.

Ian Rush on fire as Reds hammer five past the Blues

Liverpool supporters are blessed to have witnessed some amazing games down the years. Some of them have passed into legend and others are immortalised in song. The day we played the Toffees for a laugh and left them feeling blue is one such game.

Scratch beneath the surface of any Scouser, red or blue, and it still evokes a response. For Reds it's the Ian Rush derby. For Blues it's synonymous with Glenn Keeley, the hapless rookie they blame for the rout.

The game kicked off at three o'clock on a Saturday afternoon in November 1982. Liverpool were top of the league but only on goal difference over West Ham. Everton lay four points behind the Reds in 11th place and would finish the day in 13th.

Goodison was packed with almost 53,000 crammed into the old ground. Reds and Blues mixed freely throughout the stadium. Lining up against Liverpool was Steve McMahon, a player who would go on to be a Liverpool great. However, on this day, he would leave Goodison with his tail between his legs.

Everton fielded former Reds hero David Johnson, who had yo-yoed between the clubs; first playing for the Toffees, before winning trophies with the Reds and then returning to the Blues.

Kevin Sheedy would also make a substitute appearance for the home team, having previously worn the Liver Bird on his chest. That made three players in a Merseyside derby who had played for both teams – a quiz question if ever there was one.

Ian Rush scored four that day, etching his name into derby folklore. He ended that season as a league champion and with 30 goals to his name.

Rush opened the scoring after just 11 minutes. Alan Hansen delivered a slide-rule pass which Rush slotted past the onrushing Neville Southall.

Kenny Dalglish then went close to a second, before having a perfectly good goal ruled out for offside. The referee gave the goal, but was overruled by the linesman. Evertonians celebrated like they had won the league and Dalglish went nuts. Already this was shaping up to be a classic.

Disaster struck for Everton though on 37 minutes. Dalglish, sent through again by Hansen, was pulled back by debutant Glenn Keeley; handing every Blue in the ground their excuse for defeat. He saw red and actually never kicked a ball for the Blues again.

Somehow Everton survived until half-time, going in at the interval down by only one goal. However, they wouldn't be able to stem the red tide in the second half. Rush scored his second just six minutes after the restart with a deflected shot, after another Hansen assist. Then the floodgates opened and swept the home side away.

Dalglish broke free on the right four minutes later and swept the ball across the box. Everton's defence crumbled, and Mark Lawrenson popped up at the far post to poke the ball home. The scenes in the Park End were incredible, as jubilant Liverpool fans went wild.

Then it got even worse for Evertonians.

Dalglish, who had been imperious all game, sent Rush through again with a pass from his own half. Everton's line was high, and Rush's pace got the better of John Bailey. He raced away and with only the goalkeeper to beat crashed his shot off the post.

The Blues' relief was short-lived though as he pounced to score the rebound from a tight angle. It was the first hat-trick in a Merseyside derby, in the league, since 1935, the last one coming in a 6-0 hammering of the Blues at Anfield, in which Fred Howe plundered three – two of them coming in the last five minutes.

In one of those convenient historic symmetries that people like me love, Rush would score his fourth and Liverpool's fifth in the 85th minute.

Sammy Lee grabbed the ball in the middle of the park. Full of energy, he burst forward, before spotting Rush playing just off the defender's shoulder. He sent an inch-perfect pass upfield to the Welsh wizard.

Rush was on to it. This time he elected to go around the keeper and finished superbly; 5-0. Blue weekends lay in tatters. History had been made and Kopites would go home with dreams and songs to sing.

Phil Neal overcomes pain and injury to notch up record run

With the great Chris Lawler coming to the end of his career at Liverpool, Bob Paisley signed a right-back, Phil Neal, for £66,000 from Northampton Town. The boss had even paid to watch the player from the terraces, so that he could ask the supporters what they thought of him. They must have sung his praises because the Reds snapped him up straight away, on 9 October 1974.

Neal, who would go on to be nicknamed 'Zico' by the Kop, became the club's most decorated player. Neal was particularly proud of his nickname, saying, 'I'd like to thank the fans for the nickname they gave me ... Zico! He was a great Brazilian player and they started calling me by his name at a time when I was playing particularly well I guess and scoring goals – 11 I think in one season. But it was down to them that I was roaring along because they gave me so much support and confidence.'

In all the defender would compete in five European Cup finals, winning four of them. He also won eight league titles, four League Cups, one UEFA Cup, one UEFA Super Cup and four FA Charity Shields.

Only the FA Cup and the World Club Championship would elude him. He would finish runner-up in the latter, in 1981 and 1984.

While he has to cede the record appearance honour to the legendary Ian Callaghan, Neal made an astonishing 650 appearances for the Reds. This was a feat made even more impressive by the fact that it included a 417-game run of consecutive appearances over nine seasons.

Neal was eventually forced out through injury in 1983, missing three games, before returning to play a further 127 times on the spin. In all, he scored 59 goals for the Reds.

Neal played in arguably the most successful and dominant Liverpool side of all time. The team rarely changed and if you lost your place for any reason, you faced a real battle to win it back.

Phil was acutely aware of this and so desperate was he to play for the Reds, he played with a fractured cheekbone on one occasion and a broken toe on another. Phil still speaks of his record today and at one event at Anfield told supporters, gathered for a 'Legends Day' event, about how he had played through the pain barrier on two occasions, 'My first big scare was when I had a fractured cheekbone. It was in a game against Derby and their centre-forward, Davis, elbowed me in the face. I had to have an operation to fix it.

'The specialist told me I couldn't play for a month, but I told Bob Paisley I was okay. We got away with it.'

Then there was the story of his heroics with a broken toe. It's hard to imagine, in these days of multi-million-pound players carrying huge insurance premiums, that any club today could countenance the decisions made by Ronnie Moran and Phil Neal to keep the player in the team.

However, football was a different world back then and when they discovered Neal had broken his toe they moved heaven and earth to avoid a spell on the sidelines.

Phil tells it like this, 'I played for six weeks with a broken toe once. I had to play with a size eight-and-a-half on one foot and size seven on the other. Ronnie Moran made me a plaster cast for my toe. I had to pack the bigger boot with newspaper, but still needed injections to get me through a game.'

Neal never missed a day's training, saying he wouldn't even phone in with a cold. Such dedication to the cause is a rare commodity, but when allied with skill and ability you get a legend of the game. You get Phil Neal.

Ronnie Whelan the hero as Reds come from behind to lift their second League Cup

It's 13 March 1982. Liverpool are lining up against Tottenham Hotspur in the League Cup Final at Wembley. This is the Reds' second visit to the capital in successive seasons and they do so this time as European champions.

It had taken Liverpool extra time and a replay to clinch their first League Cup, against West Ham, the season before. With the emergence of Ronnie Whelan and Ian Rush, they now hoped they had the necessary firepower to clinch the cup in normal time.

The match was given added significance because arguably our greatest ever goalkeeper, Ray Clemence, was lining up for the opposition this time. Liverpool now had Bruce Grobbelaar between the sticks and, after a shaky start, he was proving a decent replacement.

Liverpool were on their way to a 13th league championship in what was Bob Paisley's penultimate season. These were the club's glory days but this game would get off to a bad start.

Steve Archibald put the Londoners in front with a goal in the 11th minute and Spurs hung on doggedly until the 87th minute. With Tottenham fans already dancing in the stands, Ronnie Whelan broke their hearts by equalising and taking the game into extra time for the second year running.

Spurs had put so much into keeping the Reds out that they were on their knees at full-time. Neal described how they looked knackered, many of them down with cramp. However, Liverpool's legendary boss wouldn't tolerate his players taking a break, explained Neal, 'Paisley would not let us sit down before extra time started. He was bellowing, "Get up on your feet, don't let them see you are tired." It stemmed from Shankly, who would never let an opponent see that you were weak. After that, we felt we had it in the bag.'

Clemence would later say he knew the game was up at this point. He had been there so many times and knew exactly what Liverpool were capable of. His team had come so close but he felt sure the Reds would go on to finish the job.

He was right and in the second period of added time, Whelan and Rush put Spurs to the sword. The goals came in the 111th and 119th minutes. There was no need for a replay; Liverpool had won their second League Cup in two years.

Whelan recalled how he hadn't slept the night before. It was his first taste of Wembley and a cup final. He had fantasised about scoring the winner and had achieved his dream. Here's how he described the day, 'Tottenham had a great side with players like Glenn Hoddle, Micky Hazard and Ossie Ardiles. They looked like they had the game won until I squeezed a shot past Ray Clemence towards the end and we got stronger in extra time.

'I was so over the moon after getting my second that I ran over the running track to celebrate with our fans. Only when I got there did I realise it was such a long way back to the pitch and I was so tired that I barely made it. It was a magical day, and special as it was my first major medal.'

It would prove to be just the beginning for the young boy from Home Farm, Ireland.

Whelan wonder-strike clinches the Milk Cup as Bob Paisley bows out in 1983

By 1983, Bob Paisley had transformed Liverpool Football Club into the undisputed kings of the English and European game. Bill Shankly's vision of the Reds as a 'bastion of invincibility' had been achieved. It had taken Bob just nine years, during which he had achieved things other managers could only dream of.

Paisley had tasted success at the highest levels of the game, but had initially derided the League Cup, a trophy he hadn't won, describing it as a 'bit of a Mickey Mouse competition'.

Then his team went on to win it three times in a row. The third in this cup hat-trick came in 1983, with a victory over arch-rivals Manchester United.

This would be the great man's last season in charge and the last time he would lead a team out at Wembley. The trophy was sponsored by the Milk Marketing Board, meaning it was now referred to as the Milk Cup.

The game took place on 26 March 1983 in front of 99,303 supporters. Liverpool were runaway leaders of the First Division and United were the underdogs, but cup finals often serve up a shock and this one was no different.

In the 12th minute United took the lead through 17-year-old Norman Whiteside. For a long time, it looked as though that would prove decisive and Ron Atkinson's side were about to stage an upset, denying Paisley a League Cup treble in successive years.

However, deep into the second half and with United flagging, Alan Kennedy brought the tie level in the 75th minute. Recalling his goal, he would talk of how his team-mates were laughing as it went in. They couldn't believe he had got his shot on target.

The Reds would take the game into extra time and their rivals looked shattered. Paisley said he felt like a bullfighter and described United as a bull with '40 arrows in its back'.

Nevertheless there was one more scare for the Reds, as Bruce Grobbelaar appeared to foul Gordon McQueen, who was through on goal.

The referee booked the goalkeeper, with United fans screaming for him to be sent off. It was a huge escape and one which Liverpool wouldn't squander. Just eight minutes into the 30, Ronnie Whelan would score the decisive goal and return the cup to Anfield.

It was an absolute beauty, curled in from the edge of the area and over Gary Bailey, truly one of the greatest goals scored by a Liverpool player in a cup final. All that remained was for Liverpool to collect the silverware.

What followed was a genuinely emotional moment. As the players got ready to collect the cup, Graeme Souness stepped aside and urged his manager to lead the team up the steps and lift the trophy first.

Alan Kennedy, scorer of Liverpool's first, recalls the moment, 'I remember a fantastic game between two closely matched sides. It was only in extra time that we got on top when Ronnie Whelan settled it with a fantastic goal.

'As we had won it the previous two years, it had become a special competition and the gloss was applied when Graeme Souness insisted that Bob Paisley go up to collect the cup, as he was retiring at the end of the season. It was a fitting tribute to a legend.'

However, it had been a young Whelan who had stunned United with a sublime finish – he would go on to become Liverpool's big-game player. This was a fact not lost on his boss, who would say this in an interview with Clive Tyldesley, 'And when those special matches come round and there are medals to be won and the pundits are asking whether the match winner will be Rushy or Kenny or Brucey.

'Then I look past them all towards Ronnie Whelan and think to myself, "There's our man for the big occasion."'

Paisley calls time at Anfield in 1983

Bob Paisley retired as Liverpool manager in 1983. In just nine years he had amassed six league titles, three European Cups, a UEFA Cup and three League Cups. He was also named Manager of the Year six times.

It was quite a haul for a man who famously didn't want the job. This is what former club chief executive, Peter Robinson, said of the day they offered Bob the job, 'It was definitely a crisis time when Bill left. It was a bombshell and Bob was very reluctant to take the position as manager. When we approached him, he said no. In the end the chairman, directors and I had to gang up on him.'

Paisley was a genius, but his modesty and self-doubt meant he thought carefully about every decision. In that way he was the polar opposite to Shankly, who famously said that 'if a man can't make decisions, he's a bloody menace.'

Bob preferred to take his time, worried about tripping up or making a mistake. He once said that in the early years of his managerial career, he would count to ten before reaching a conclusion on any issue. By 1979, he said, he only needed to count to two.

This methodical approach would serve Paisley well and his ability to spot talent and build a team is probably unrivalled in football. Tommy Smith once remarked, 'If Shankly was the Anfield foreman, Paisley was the brickie, ready to build an empire with his own hands.'

Many speculated on the secret of Liverpool's success during the 1970s. Some thought the club must have employed revolutionary, top-secret training methods. Not so, said Brian Clough, it's down to sheer talent. He argued, 'Bob is the Frank Sinatra in his field.'

In truth the magic ingredient that drove Liverpool to 13 trophies in under a decade was a vision based on appreciating the simplicity of the game. Joe Fagan sums it up here, 'Keep it simple, don't complicate things. He loathed all soccerspeak; he wouldn't have recognised a Christmas-tree formation if it had toppled on to him.'

He once said, 'What does getting round the back mean? We're not talking about burglars, are we?'

Bob saw it slightly differently and preferred to talk in terms of honest football. He had grown up as a player and coach in the city of Liverpool. He knew the people he served and had fought alongside them through thick and thin.

When asked about his relationship with the Kop, Paisley said, 'The whole of my life, what they wanted was honesty. They were not concerned with cultured football, but with triers who gave 100 per cent.'

That's exactly what Paisley gave: 100 per cent effort to the club, his players and the supporters. The return on his investment was a legacy of untold riches. He is fondly remembered by all who came into contact with him down the years, as much for his sense of humour as his footballing genius. Take this story from Alan Kennedy, for example, 'My first game was against Queens Park Rangers at Anfield early on and I mis-kicked with my right foot – the one I use for standing on – and knocked a policeman's helmet off. I also conceded a couple of corners and made a few errors. I just wanted half-time to come to get some reassurance from the manager but when I got back to the dressing room, Bob said to me, "I think that they shot the wrong Kennedy!"'

Beneath the quiet exterior was a razor-sharp mind and the sort of ruthless streak you see in all great leaders. Make no mistake; although he was clearly different from his predecessor, Paisley was a consummate leader of men.

It is often said that a great leader never asks a subordinate to do something they wouldn't do themselves. So, perhaps this quote from Kevin Keegan gives us the greatest insight into the man's leadership style, 'Bob was so down to earth. A common phrase of his was, "If the floor needs sweeping, I'll pick up a brush and do it."'

We were truly blessed to have had him as our manager and football was all the better for his reign. Many Reds are annoyed that Bob never received a knighthood. In reality such a trinket would have been meaningless to a man whose career had amassed so much silverware. He probably wouldn't have wanted it anyway.

Of course Paisley was driven by success and a fierce desire to win, but ultimately, he did it all for the love of the game. Therefore, let's end this moment in Liverpool's history with Bob's own reflections on his career.

'Some may have made more money in the game, but no one has enjoyed it more than me.'

Fagan's Reds immortalised in the eternal city

The 1983/84 season saw Liverpool lift the league title, League Cup, and European Cup – not bad for a debut season as manager for Joe Fagan.

When Bob Paisley announced he was going to step down, the board simply opened the door to the Anfield boot room and called for Fagan to step forward. It may have been the easiest decision they had made since, well, the day they replaced Bill Shankly with Paisley.

Fagan had given everything to the club he joined as a coach in 1958. He nurtured players like Roger Hunt, Ian Callaghan, Kevin Keegan and Tommy Smith, all of whom went on to greatness.

It was Joe who created the boot room ethos, established the routine in which the players met at Anfield and travelled together to Melwood and of course, he won a historic trophy treble in his first season in charge.

It was a stunning achievement on a personal level, but it also proved that the greatest brains in world football, between 1959 and 1984, were on the payroll at Anfield.

The season didn't exactly get off to a flying start though, with the Reds going down to a 2-0 defeat to Manchester United in the Charity Shield in August 1983. There was worse to come too, as they would crash out of the FA Cup to Brighton and Hove Albion in January 1984.

However, there was more than enough consolation to go around. Fagan's Liverpool were now five points clear at the top of the table, in the semi-finals of the League Cup and were still in the European Cup thanks to victory over Athletic Bilbao.

And in Ian Rush, the Reds possessed a goal machine who would end the season on 47 goals in all competitions, 32 of them in the league.

In March, Fagan and Liverpool secured the first part of their treble, when a Graeme Souness goal saw off Everton in the League Cup Final. It was the first of three cup final duels against the Blues that decade and even though they took us to a replay at Manchester City's Maine Road ground, victory was no less sweet.

With his first trophy in the bag and Liverpool maintaining a ruthless efficiency in the league, Fagan turned his attention to Europe. A 5-1 aggregate win over Benfica was followed up by a bitter confrontation with Dinamo Bucharest, from which the Reds emerged 3-1 winners over two legs.

Liverpool had reached their fourth European Cup Final. They would face Roma in their own backyard a month later.

There was still plenty of time to sew up the league title, or so they thought. The Reds must have had Rome on their minds because they drew three out of their last four matches, the win coming in a 5-0 demolition of Coventry City at Anfield. It was the perfect revenge for a 4-0 drubbing they had endured in the earlier away fixture.

That meant Liverpool were on the brink of a third title in a row and a goalless draw at Notts County, on 12 May, would seal it.

Manchester United, who had ensured Fagan's managerial career started with a defeat, would finish third. After being in second place they were pipped by Southampton to the runners-up spot, on goal difference in the final game of the season, allowing Kopites to joke that they were the only team to finish third in a two-horse race.

All that remained was a trip to Rome, a Phil Neal penalty, a Roberto Pruzzo leveller, a Steve Nicol penalty miss, Bruce Grobbelaar's spaghetti legs, Alan Kennedy's crazy celebration and a fourth European Cup in eight years. It was a remarkable season that crowned an unbelievable career in football for Joe Fagan.

Ian Rush's 47 goals in a single season: the high point of a stellar Liverpool career

Ian Rush is the greatest striker in the history of Liverpool Football Club. To those lucky enough to have seen him play, he was simply the most lethal finisher they had ever seen.

But in his early days, he struggled to cope with the dressing room at Liverpool.

The club he joined in 1980 was full of established stars and born winners, the banter in training could be merciless and Kenny Dalglish, in his autobiography, would talk about how he had no idea how much the youngster was struggling.

Somehow though the young kid from Flint, in Wales, would overcome these early tribulations and become a legend in his own right. His record at Anfield is second to none and may never be beaten.

Rushy scored 346 goals in 660 games for Liverpool, 222 of them in the First Division. He managed 30 goals or more in five out of his first six seasons at the club.

The highlight of his Liverpool career, from a scoring point of view, was the 1983/84 season, under manager Joe Fagan. His 47 goals in 65 appearances would propel Liverpool to an astonishing treble.

Thirty-two of Rush's goals came in the league, two in the FA Cup, eight in the League Cup and five in the European Cup. His predatory instincts in the First Division saw him score five in a 6-0 win over Luton Town, four in a 5-0 victory over Coventry City and a hat-trick against Aston Villa. He grabbed a brace against four other teams.

In the game against Luton, Rush became one of only five players in Liverpool history to score five goals in a single game.

It was a scoring masterclass that had supporters and journalists drooling. The 'Welsh Wizard' would inspire admiration in legends of the past and future alike. The great Roger Hunt, who saw his record fall after Rushy had burst on to the scene, said this of the man who stole his crown, 'Records are there to be broken. I thought it'd last a bit longer when he went to Italy but then he came back! I wasn't gutted when he re-signed – if anyone had to break my record I'm glad it was Ian Rush.'

In 2005, one of Europe's greatest strikers, Andriy Shevchenko, talked of the day he met his idol, 'I was just 13 when I went with Dynamo Kiev boys' team to play in a tournament in Wales. We won the tournament and I was named the best player. What made it special was that Ian Rush was there to give me my prize. I treasured those boots for years.

'It meant such a lot because everyone in Ukraine knew about Ian Rush, the legendary Liverpool player. Funnily enough, the boots were too small for me, but I still tried to play in them – until my big toes poked through.'

He left Liverpool in 1996 on a free transfer to Leeds United. In his last game for the Reds, against Middlesbrough, both teams formed a guard of honour for the striker and at full time he threw his number nine shirt into the Kop as the away fans also chanted his name.

It was a final act of communion with supporters, who had witnessed him win 14 major honours, including five First Division titles, three FA Cups, five League Cups and a European Cup.

In his parting interview with the press, Rush said this of his last game, 'It was an emotional day but also a fantastic day for me. I had no idea of the reception I was going to get until Roy Evans told me before the game. It was a great surprise … I wanted to stay on the pitch forever.'

If only you could, Ian.

Rome 1984: Liverpool become kings of Europe thanks to Bruce Grobbelaar's 'spaghetti legs'

On 30 May 1984, Joe Fagan's Liverpool were preparing to take on AS Roma in the European Cup Final. The game would be contested at the Stadio Olimpico, Roma's home ground.

The Reds travelled as English league champions and League Cup winners and Fagan was on the brink of a historic treble in his first season in charge. For Liverpool fans it was a case of 'here we go gathering cups in May'.

Many Reds would have felt a little apprehensive about the reception awaiting them in Italy.

The Mayor of Rome's assurances that the red carpet would be rolled out for them did little to comfort the travelling Liverpool supporters.

A riot involving Roma fans had broken out during a queue for tickets days earlier, but despite all of these issues 10,000 Liverpool supporters still made the journey.

They would receive a hostile and intimidating 'welcome', with the Italian media condemning the Roma fans who had 'carried out a concerted campaign of violence against Liverpool supporters'.

Several fans suffered stab wounds and riot police had to deal with scenes of chaos and violence by the home fans on the night. This was the backdrop to the game some felt should have been moved to a neutral venue.

Frank McGhee, writing in the *Mirror*, pointed out the injustice of forcing a team to play an opponent on their home turf in a cup final, saying, 'Liverpool had surmounted the terribly unfair challenge, which UEFA will now ensure will never happen again, of having to beat opponents in their own hot and hostile backyard to win Europe's most prestigious trophy.'

Liverpool's 'team of Macs' – John Houlding's Liverpool in 1892.

Liverpool FC, 1905/06, league champions for the first time. Back row, L-R: S. Hardy, H. Griffiths, M. Parry, R. Blanthorn, C. Wilson, P. Saul, J. Bradley, Middle row, L-R: W. Connell, (Trainer), S. Raybould, A. Raisbeck, (captain), J. Hewitt, J. Hughes, (Sheriff of London Charity Shield) J. Gorman, R. Robinson, W. Dunlop, F. Brown, J.E. Doig, Front row, L-R: G. Lathom, (League Cup) T. Chorlton, J. Carlin, (Liverpool Cup) J. Parkinson.

Liverpool FC won their second title in as many years in 1922/1923, Back row, left-right, H. Chambers, J. McNabb, E. Scott, W. Wadsworth, T. Bromilow, R. Forshaw, Front row, left-right, W. Lacy, E. Longworth, D. McKinley, T. Lucas, F. Hopkin, G. Patterson (Secretary), On ground, left-right, D. Shone, H. Lewis.

November 1949: Billy Liddell races down the wing, as his adoring fans look on. Allsport Hulton/Archive

March 1952: Bob Paisley leads Liverpool out as team captain. He would go on to become the most successful manager in the English game.

Liverpool fans at Euston Station, London, 1 May 1965. They are on their way to see their team play Leeds United in the FA Cup Final at Wembley. A woman (centre) is holding a copy of the Evening Standard newspaper with the headline 'Liverpool trying for cup double'. Liverpool later won the final 2-1.

1965, Liverpool FC's Gerry Byrne (left) and Gordon Milne show the FA Cup trophy to the Kop, Byrne broke his collarbone during the final at Wembley during the 2-1 victory over Leeds United.

Bill Shankly testimonial, Anfield, May 1975. The great man looks overcome with emotion as he salutes the Kop faithful.

Bob Paisley completes the quest started by Shankly. Liverpool have conquered Europe and plundered its top prize for the first time in 1977. Jubilant Liverpudlians turn out to welcome home their team and the trophy.

27 May 1981: Liverpool's Scottish kings; Graeme Souness (left), Kenny Dalglish (centre) and Alan Hansen (right) after conquering Madrid in Paris. *Allsport UK /Allsport*

Joe Fagan with the European Cup after his team beat Roma 4-2 on penalties in the final, 1984. Fagan led Liverpool to the league championship, the European Cup and the League Cup in his first season in charge.

Kenny Dalglish's double winning team victory parade. Reds and Blues turned out to welcome home the conquering heroes.

John Barnes terrorises Everton in an FA Cup fifth round tie, at Goodison Park in 1988. Liverpool won 1-0.

Anfield becomes a shrine to those lost and suffering as a result of the Hillsborough stadium disaster on 15 April 1989.

Gerrard Houllier revived Liverpool, after a barren spell in the 1990s. After securing a historic treble of League Cup, FA Cup and UEFA Cup in 2001, the team were welcomed home by huge crowds in Liverpool.

Steven Gerrard and Rafa Benitez step off the plane at Liverpool John Lennon Airport, with the club's fifth European Cup, in 2005.

Kenny Dalglish returned as Liverpool manager, after the sacking of Roy Hodgson. He is pictured here with Jamie Carragher and his son, after leading the Reds back to Wembley in his first full season, and restoring pride to a club in turmoil.

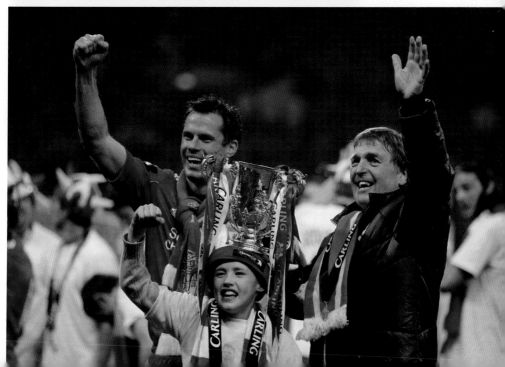

The Kop salutes Brendan Rodgers, as his Reds side fall short against Chelsea in the 2014 title run-in.

Liverpool's Hong Kong supporters pay tribute to manager Jurgen Klopp during the 2017 Asia Trophy.

It would take a heroic performance on the pitch to win the European Cup for the fourth time and that's exactly what the Reds would deliver, with the *Liverpool Echo* describing it as the club's finest hour.

Just 14 minutes into the game, Liverpool fans were in heaven when Phil Neal poked the ball home to put their side 1-0 up. The goal stunned the Roma crowd, who vastly outnumbered their English counterparts.

However, with just a minute to go in the half, Roberto Pruzzo levelled for the Italians. It was a horrible time to concede and it set up a terribly nerve-wracking second half. Roma initially took the game to Liverpool but they soon ran out of steam and the Reds dominated the last 25.

Fagan pushed on Steve Nicol and the Scot almost grabbed the winner with four minutes to go after being sent through by Kenny Dalglish, but Roma goalkeeper Franco Tancredi blocked the shot.

Extra time finished goalless and the referee signalled penalties. The home crowd certainly seemed the happier of the two sets of supporters. For Liverpool's fans it was a tense time: the Reds hadn't yet established themselves as penalty kings.

Sensing the trepidation among the ranks of Liverpool players, Fagan gathered his charges around him and said, 'I am proud of every one of you this evening. Whatever happens now, nothing will change that.'

First up was Nicol, who sent his kick sailing over the bar. It seemed disastrous and there were wild cheers from the Italians. Then Agostino Di Bartolomei and Neal scored to tie the shootout.

The tension was unbearable as Bruno Conti walked towards the spot. Grobbelaar decided to add to the player's pain and began clowning around on the line. His wobbly legs act is now the stuff of legend and it would inspire Jerzy Dudek in Istanbul in 2005 but back then it seemed remarkable behaviour.

Clearly it put the player off because Conti missed and suddenly the pressure seemed to lift from Liverpool's shoulders. Up stepped club captain Graeme Souness to put the Reds 2-1 up. Roma levelled and Ian Rush dispatched his kick with ease, making it 3-2.

Then Bruce was at it again, his 'spaghetti legs' causing Francesco Graziani to miss his chance to level. That meant that if Liverpool scored the next penalty, the European Cup was coming home for the fourth time.

Up stepped Alan Kennedy, the hero of Paris in 1981. In truth, Liverpool supporters would probably have preferred anyone else, but 'Barney' looked confident and put the ball away with ease.

His goal had once again secured Europe's greatest prize for the Reds. His celebration may have been just as crazy as Bruce's antics on the goal line.

As much as Kennedy deserves praise for his coolness from the spot, it has to be said that the contribution of Grobbelaar, who undoubtedly unnerved the Roma penalty takers, was genuinely significant.

The Reds had won four European Cups in just seven years. Only Real Madrid had won more, with six in ten years from 1956 to 1966. Now, thanks to Bob Paisley and Joe Fagan, Liverpool were the undisputed kings of Europe.

The Heysel Stadium disaster

When I think of Heysel, I see images of a crumbling stadium barely fit to host an amateur football match, let alone the champions of Europe. Scenes of carnage and destruction and of chaos and insanity come to mind. I can visualise it still, being played out on a grainy television set in my parents' home, a commentator's sombre tones providing the soundtrack. It was meant to be a pageant; a celebration of football and our lads were supposed to be holding the silverware aloft by the end of the night. The Juventus fans would have thought the same. It all seems so pointless now.

I remember how the people on TV were saying that supporters had died. How could that even be true, I was thinking. It's a fucking game of footy. People don't die watching a game of footy. That's bollocks.

But it wasn't, was it?

Then I could see the police hitting supporters with batons. There's a guy holding what looks like a gun and a banner screams 'Reds Animals'. I'm thinking the lads holding that banner must have brought it with them. Why would they do that? Then I see a lad in a Liverpool shirt getting battered by uniformed men.

This was horror, it was unbearable, and I couldn't bear to watch it. But I did. I was transfixed. I remember Phil Neal on the speaker system, appealing for calm. I had clearly gone way beyond that by then. Calm had left the building an hour earlier. In its place was shock and pain and, as we now know only too well, death, so much death.

This is still where I go, in my head, when I hear the word Heysel. To my mother and father's living room, to that old colour telly and to the horrified expressions we all wore as the madness unfolded. I also remember the shame, the gnawing, sickening shame in the aftermath of the tragedy.

There are many accounts of the events of 29 May 1985. Some say they started it, others argue our supporters did. I've been through all of that in my head over the years. No doubt the facilities were shocking, the stadium dreadful and the policing totally inadequate.

It's clear both sets of supporters were involved in a confrontation. Missiles were thrown in either direction and at one point a group of Reds fans charged. This caused a crush down at the front of the stand where many people were suffocated before the wall finally gave way.

The courts in Belgium agreed with all the above. They brought charges against several officials, including the police captain responsible for security that night. They also sentenced 14 Liverpool supporters for their involvement in events that led to the deaths of 39 people, mostly Italian, and saw 600 supporters injured.

All those injured or killed were guilty of nothing except indulging in a pastime we all love and took for granted until that night. They just went to a football match, that's all. They should have been having the time of their lives, eating, drinking, laughing and joking – like we all do on away days and at cup finals. They were supporters, just like us. They loved their team, just like us. Now they will never see them again.

That's Heysel; the senseless, avoidable death of mothers, fathers, sons and daughters, brothers and sisters, taken from their loved ones far too soon. Quite simply no one should send their loved ones to a game of footy and never see them return. Nobody should meet their end in a grubby decaying concrete stadium while following their team.

Finally, no game of football is worth the loss of so much humanity. So, this moment is dedicated to all of them; *nella memoria e nell'amicizia.*

Grobbelaar and Beglin set Liverpool on their way as Reds overcome Blues to win 1986 FA Cup

Liverpool had already met their rivals Everton at Wembley, in the 1984 Milk Cup Final, so the FA Cup Final of 1986 wasn't the first time they had faced off at the national stadium. The earlier game had gone to a replay, with the Reds coming out on top thanks to a Graeme Souness strike.

The FA Cup was bigger though, much bigger. Liverpool had just pipped Everton to the league title by two points and a historic double was now possible.

The Mersey giants had gone toe-to-toe all season and the title went down to the last game, with Liverpool needing to beat Chelsea at Stamford Bridge to clinch their 16th championship.

They did it thanks to a sublime finish by Kenny Dalglish. Everton were devastated, having assembled a formidable team capable of going on to win a double of their own.

They were therefore desperate not to hand the Reds a double at Wembley and at least salvage a trophy from their season.

The whole of Liverpool descended on the capital for the game. The official attendance was just shy of 100,000, but it was certainly higher. Both sets of supporters were chanting this little number:

'Scousers here,
Scousers there,
Scousers every-fucking-where!
Nah nah, nah nah, nah nah nah, nah nah.'

Reds and Blues mixed freely on Wembley Way and inside the ground, without a hint of trouble. This was still regarded as the 'friendly derby', with families and friendships split down the middle.

The *Liverpool Echo* would declare 'MERSEYPRIDE WINS A DAY IN SOCCER HISTORY'. Ian Hargreaves wrote, 'Football has waited the best part of a century for the first all-Merseyside FA Cup Final. I am pleased to say that when the day finally arrived the men of Liverpool and Everton did us proud.'

Liverpool had gone on an amazing run to clinch the title and were full of confidence going into the game. However, they served up a tepid first half in which Everton took the lead through Gary Lineker. The Blues went in at the interval deservedly in front.

The men in red looked dejected. However, when they reached the dressing room, they were met by a coaching staff who were coolness personified. Ronnie Moran would tell them not to worry, because they hadn't even started playing yet. They would improve in the second half, but it would take two key moments, both involving Bruce Grobbelaar, to turn the game around.

The first involved a bust-up between Bruce and Reds left-back Jim Beglin. Recalling the incident, Beglin told the *Echo*, 'Bruce was telling me to let the ball run through, but I put my foot on it. I was trying to shield it from Trevor Steven and ended up getting into a bit of a muddle.

'Bruce got excited and called me something, I called him something back and then he hit me. I was about to hit him back when it flashed through my mind that my friends and family were in the stand and there were millions on TV watching.'

The incident ended with Grobbelaar rolling the ball to Beglin, who tapped it back. It seemed to calm the pair down and many have said that this was a turning point in the game. Hargreaves wrote, 'It was at that very moment that Liverpool's fortunes were at their lowest, that the players reached down into that remarkable reserve of fighting spirit that puts them apart from any other club in the modern game.'

In the space of six minutes Liverpool went 2-1 up. Rush equalised in the 57th minute and Craig Johnston added the second in the 63rd. However, it might have all been different had it not been for a stunning save by Grobbelaar, from a Graeme Sharp shot.

With the tie level, Everton went in search of an immediate goal. Bruce was way off his line and Sharp saw his chance, unleashing a powerful drive. Somehow, miraculously, the Reds goalkeeper got back and tipped it over. It was a huge let-off. There then followed an emotional moment as Johnston grabbed his goal and Liverpool's second. He can clearly be seen shouting 'I've done it, I've done it!' as he is mobbed by his team-mates.

He would later speak passionately on LFCTV about what that goal meant to him. He had always regarded himself as the 'worst player in the best team in the world' and to score a goal in the FA Cup Final was priceless to him.

The game would remain finely balanced, though, until the 84th minute. Ian Rush would seal the final with a wonderful strike. The cup and the double were Liverpool's. It could easily have gone to Everton.

The scenes of celebration at full time were remarkable. However, this final is notable for the unbelievable sports-manship demonstrated by the Everton players and supporters. The sight of the Blues, socks rolled down, dejected expressions on their faces, dragging themselves around the pitch to applaud both sets of supporters, will live long in the memory.

The whole stadium would respond in solidarity with shouts of 'Merseyside, Merseyside!'

That's how you do rivalry.

King Kenny seals the double as Liverpool's first ever player-manager in 1986

Out of the ashes of the 1984/85 season, a hero stepped forward and led Liverpool to new levels of glory. That man was Kenny

Dalglish. It wasn't the first time his genius had elevated the club to greatness; it wouldn't be the last. However, in 1986, the King showed he was more than a great player, he was an accomplished manager, too.

As the season got under way, Europe was still reeling from the trauma of the Heysel Stadium disaster. English clubs were banned from continental football and the city of Liverpool was in a soul-searching mood.

Joe Fagan, the man who had delivered the treble in 1984, was gone. Everton were resurgent and had won the league the season before by a convincing 13 points.

Liverpool were still a great club but to some they had lost some of their lustre. The club needed a hero and it would reach into the dressing room and ask one of its greatest players, Kenny Dalglish, to step into the breach. As he would do time and again in the future, he said yes.

The club's most successful manager, Bob Paisley, would act as his mentor. It's hard to underestimate the task facing the 34-year-old Dalglish; Liverpool's reputation was in tatters. The financial loss of missing out on Europe was enormous.

Somehow though, the legend swept all of that aside and rebuilt the Reds into the most feared and respected team in England once more.

The side Kenny inherited was full of players coming to the end of their Liverpool careers. This was a reconstruction job of epic proportions and the team would struggle to find its feet until the halfway stage.

In fact, after a defeat to the Blues at Anfield, Liverpool were 13 points off first place. However, they kept plugging away and after a 2-2 draw with Sheffield Wednesday at home on New Year's Day, Liverpool lay in third, five points behind leaders Manchester United.

Everton were ahead of the Reds on goal difference only. They then won 12 out of their last 13 games to clinch the title.

The drama reached its peak on an incredible Wednesday night at the end of April. With three games remaining, Liverpool went to Leicester City. They were two points clear of Everton at the top of the table.

On the same night, the Blues were home to Oxford United and simply could not afford to lose. They would endure a miserable night of missed opportunities and conceded a late goal that silenced Goodison. Their dreams of retaining the title lay in tatters.

Liverpool beat Leicester 2-0 and were on the brink. A win in their next game, at Stamford Bridge, would hand them the title. Howard Kendall infamously declared himself a Chelsea supporter in his post-match interview, following his side's defeat to Oxford. It drew scorn from the red half of the city.

So the scene was set for one of the most memorable moments in Liverpool history as the man who would be King delivered the killer goal and secured Liverpool's 16th title.

This is how captain Alan Hansen recalled Kenny's moment of brilliance, 'That was one of the great days. We had a horrific away record at Chelsea and when the fixtures came out at the start of that season everybody was saying, "Imagine us having to go to Chelsea on the final day and win the championship", which of course is what happened.

'We went to Chelsea and our confidence was high. It was typical Dalglish, taking the ball on his chest and the next thing it's in the back of the net.

'To win the championship in his first season as player-manager, especially after being so many points behind at one stage, was terrific.'

Liverpool and Everton had gone toe-to-toe all season. The Reds had taken their championship back and now all that remained was to beat the Blues in the FA Cup Final. That they did, with an emphatic 3-1 victory. Kenny had secured a historic first double of the First Division title and FA Cup in his first season in charge, at the age of 34. He was the first player-manager to achieve such a feat and forever cemented his place in the annals of football history.

Liverpool sign Barnes and Beardsley in 1987 and take the league by storm

In the summer of 1987, Liverpool signed two players who would form the cornerstone of arguably the most exciting Reds team of all time, John Barnes and Peter Beardsley. Barnesy had joined from Watford for the ridiculously low figure of £900,000 and Beardsley from Newcastle United, for £1.9m.

The then England manager, Bobby Robson, thought Liverpool had secured a bargain for the 'little wizard' Beardsley, saying of him, 'He's already just about the best player in England at the moment. Add 20 goals a season at Liverpool and he will become a megastar ... a name to bracket alongside Maradona and Cruyff.'

Of John Barnes, George Best said, 'John Barnes can be the greatest. He was described by the England boss Bobby Robson as the black Best, and I reckon he is right.

'Barnes has the ability to become the best, the most exciting winger in British soccer since me. His transfer to Liverpool was the perfect move for a man who was born with stunning talent.

'The Anfield academy will take that natural ability, harness it with consistency, and produce a truly world-class performer.'

It's hard to put into words the excitement and buzz that surrounded Anfield, after the capture of these two stars. Both players had an explosive impact on the league, firing Liverpool to the top of the table as early as October following a mesmerising 4-0 demolition of the then league leaders QPR. They would remain there until the end of the season.

From their first victory against Arsenal on the opening day, Liverpool had gone on an astonishing 29-game unbeaten run. The Reds were simply irresistible during this period, soaring 14 points clear at the top of the table with two games in hand over their nearest rivals, Manchester United.

Going into the Merseyside derby, in March 1988, they stood on the brink of setting a new league record. Liverpool had equalled the previous best for an unbeaten run, set by Nottingham Forest, and a victory over their neighbours, at Goodison, would set a new benchmark. Infuriatingly though the Blues won 1-0.

Everton supporters were desperate to stop Liverpool. They had been enraged by the fact that street stalls in the city centre had started selling 'Liverpool FC 1987-88 Champions' pendants halfway through the season. They would, therefore, celebrate denying the Reds their record with much glee.

It would prove to be their only high point that year though. The Toffees finished without a trophy, in fourth place and fully 20 points behind the Reds.

Liverpool guaranteed their 17th league championship on 23 April 1988 against Tottenham at Anfield, thanks to a Beardsley strike in the 34th minute. Spurs would be the Reds' 25th victims of the season with four games still remaining.

With the title in the bag though, Liverpool players looked like they had gone on an early summer holiday. They drew three of the remaining four fixtures 1-1, winning the other

5-1 away to Sheffield Wednesday. Of course, Barnes and Beardsley would be on the scoresheet that day too.

Sadly and unexpectedly the Reds ended the season with a shock FA Cup defeat to Wimbledon, robbing them of a deserved double. Few could believe what they had witnessed that day at Wembley, least of all the so-called 'Crazy Gang'.

In all, Barnes and Beardsley scored 35 goals between them in the 1987/88 season. However, it was the flamboyance of their play that had Kopites in raptures. Liverpool seemed invincible that season.

Alan Hansen thought they still had a long way to go before they could rival the great side of 1978/79. He should know.

However, for many Reds, lucky enough to watch both sides from the stands, the Barnes and Beardsley team were the most exciting ever to grace Anfield.

Liverpool hit Forest for five in 'finest exhibition' in the world of football

At one time, Nottingham Forest, under the stewardship of Brian Clough, were Liverpool's arch-rivals. Forest won back-to-back European Cups in the late 1970s and won the league in the same period. In 1979 they had also beaten Bob Paisley's Liverpool to lift the League Cup.

In the 1980s they began to fade as a force, but by 1987/88 there were signs of a new team emerging under Clough. Forest would finish third that season, but at Anfield on 13 April 1988 they were simply destroyed.

Liverpool had travelled to the City Ground just 11 days earlier and lost 2-1, meaning nobody went into the game expecting a walkover. Victory would put the Reds on the brink of the title, defeat might give second-placed United a faint glimmer of hope. In the context of a title run-in there was no room for error.

Kenny Dalglish fielded an experienced side with an average age of 27, with the likes of John Barnes, Peter Beardsley, Ray Houghton and John Aldridge in attack and Steve McMahon as the midfield general.

They proved more than a match for Clough's young pretenders, which included Steve Sutton in goal, Stuart Pearce and Des Walker at the back, Neil Webb in midfield and Nigel Clough up front.

The Reds started slowly, perhaps sizing up their opponents, but soon got into their stride. Their opening goal, on 18 minutes, was breathtaking. Hansen intercepted the ball in Liverpool's half and fed Houghton, who burst through the middle. There was a brilliant one-two with Barnes before he stroked the ball home.

It had seemed effortless and Forest didn't seem to know what had hit them. Aldridge added a second 20 minutes later, with a delightful chip, and just before half-time Beardsley crashed one on to the bar. Clough's men were living dangerously.

The Reds went in at half-time 2-0 up and it probably should have been more. The Kop were drooling and so were the watching media. Their first-half performance drew comparisons with the Real Madrid sides of the 1950s.

They thought it couldn't get any better, they were wrong. Just on the hour mark Gary Gillespie crashed in a volley for the third and Beardsley made it four with ten minutes to go. The Kop began chanting 'we want five' and Aldridge duly obliged with just two minutes remaining. It was Aldo's 24th of the season.

After the game, the plaudits poured in. Hansen, a veteran of so many great Liverpool performances, hailed this as the best since he had arrived at the club. Alan Green, reporting for the BBC, was left spellbound and gushed, 'That was simply the best display of an exceptional season from Liverpool. Reporters are often accused, rightly, of being too glib using words like brilliant, fantastic, fabulous. Liverpool deserved all these adjectives tonight.

'They were, after all, playing a quality side that had beaten them in the league just 11 days ago. They were two up at half-time through Houghton and Aldridge. They'd also hit the woodwork twice, and Sutton had made three tremendous saves.'

Maurice Roworth, the Forest chairman, conceded that 'no one could have competed against them' and declared Liverpool were 'too good' for the rest of Europe.

The Reds' goal difference was now so good that a single point from their next game would all but hand them their tenth league title in 15 years. This was a golden period to watch Liverpool Football Club, a time when their ruthless efficiency simply blew teams away.

Don't believe me though; listen to the legendary Sir Tom Finney, 'It was the finest exhibition I've seen the whole time I've played and watched the game. You couldn't see it bettered anywhere, not even in Brazil. The moves they put together were fantastic.'

Hillsborough: A tale of heroism, love and solidarity

So much has been written about Hillsborough, such is its impact on football and on society generally. Perhaps more than any other moment in the club's history, it has come to define Liverpool as a club and a city.

We would have chosen something, anything else, if we could. However, the story of that terrible day and all the days since continues to envelop Liverpool Football Club and probably always will.

So too does the spirit of solidarity, camaraderie and dignity that has endured for so long. And, as time passes, this will become the true and lasting legacy of the 96 and the countless survivors whose struggle goes on.

There is much still to say but, as the wheels of justice trundle on, we must leave all of that for another day. Instead, it seems fitting to tell the story of Hillsborough from a different perspective, that of heroism, defiance and a will to survive, so that others would know the truth.

This moment then, is as much for the survivors as it is for the 96.

The tragedy that unfolded in the Leppings Lane End on 15 April 1989 has broken the trust many people had placed in the institutions of society. For some, the burden of Hillsborough has been harder to carry than for others, but we have all had to shoulder it to a degree.

The families of those we lost have not only lived with the immeasurable pain of grief, but also the daily fight for truth and justice. It must have seemed intolerable for even the strongest among their ranks.

There is, though, an army of people who have suffered alongside the bereaved. Their story is a less well-known one but it deserves to be heard.

Imagine enduring the guilt of survival for more than a quarter of a century, watching helplessly as some among you can bear it no more. We may never know their number, but we can be sure they are legion.

Every mocking chant of 'Murderers', often sung by those too young to know the horror of Hillsborough, cuts deep into the hearts of those who came home. It reinforces their own sense of guilt and continues their trauma.

Those callous newspaper headlines and the throwaway lines, erroneously linking the disaster with hooliganism, perpetuate feelings of anxiety, self-doubt and depression. These, of course, are but a few of the many demons spawned by the Hillsborough disaster, but there are thousands fighting them every day.

If only we could grant them the peace they so richly deserve. Of course, that's easier to write than it is to achieve. Instead, we can only offer our thanks.

Thanks for staying in that hell and fighting for the lives of your fellow supporters. Thanks for standing by the bereaved through the decades of poisonous lies and calumny. Thanks for giving everything you had in the fight for truth and justice and for bearing witness, when the pain of retelling must have been enormous.

Most of all thank you for being the helpers. A 1950s children's TV host, in America, once talked of how his mother would comfort him when terrible things happened in the news. Mr Rogers would explain, 'When I was a boy and I would see scary things in the news, my mother would say to me, 'look for the helpers. You will always find people who are helping.'

Amidst the darkness of Hillsborough, many of us looked for the helpers and they were there. You were there.

It was the survivors who carried the fallen to safety and fought to preserve life where they could. They are heroes.

Though they won't know it, they have helped countless people find a sense of hope and peace since that day in 1989. Whenever my mind's eye is drawn to despair, I see them. They're helping.

They are the best of us.

So too are those whose struggle on that day was simply to survive, the ones trapped in the hell of the Leppings Lane pens. They could not get out and couldn't help. They would have, if they could. We all know that.

Their story is as much a source of pride to us as the efforts of other supporters to rescue their stricken comrades. Had they not lived, the post-Hillsborough landscape would have felt even more barren in that terrible aftermath. Thanks to them, hope now grows where once only pain could flourish.

When we, who did not have to endure that horror first hand, struggle to rationalise the insanity of Hillsborough, we look for them, the survivors, the helpers. They are always there and they restore our faith in humanity and decency.

May they never walk alone.

Reds edge emotional 1989 FA Cup Final as the city of Liverpool unites in grief

The 1989 FA Cup Final between Liverpool and Everton took place against the backdrop of a city in grief. After the horror of Hillsborough, football seemed irrelevant to many and the club debated whether they should withdraw from the FA Cup altogether.

The semi-final against Brian Clough's Nottingham Forest in Sheffield eventually cost 96 Liverpool fans their lives. Ultimately a decision was made that the team should return to the competition and the Reds would overcome Forest to reach the final.

Somehow, after the trauma of that season, it seemed only right and proper that the two Merseyside giants would be contesting a final in the nation's capital.

Everton, the club and its supporters, had shown tremendous solidarity to their neighbours and the final was an opportunity for the whole city to immerse itself in a great sporting occasion.

Merseyside boasted two of the best teams in the country throughout the 1980s. It was a period when the league title would preside at Anfield on seven occasions and twice at Goodison Park. The teams would also contest two FA Cup finals, in 1986 and '89, and a League Cup Final in 1984.

No game, not even a cup final, could ever erase the pain of grief, but the camaraderie associated with this one helped bind the supporters and the city together, even more tightly than before. And, for at least 90 minutes, watching football felt almost normal again.

Just like the survivors and the families of those lost, many of the players had struggled emotionally, they had attended funerals, and some had counselled those affected. They were footballers, not healthcare workers and for some, the responsibility was taking its toll. Players like John Aldridge even thought about quitting the game altogether although thankfully that didn't happen, and he would return to play a pivotal role for the remainder of the season.

As the final got under way, with his head bursting and mind racing, Aldo flew out of the traps and put the Reds in front after just four minutes.

They briefly entertained thoughts that this may not be as tricky as they anticipated. Not so. Everton made it a tough game and as it wore on the emotion of the occasion and the inevitable fatigue of a long painful season got to both sides.

Still, the Blues managed to summon enough energy in the final seconds to hit a brilliant equaliser. It completely deflated the Liverpool support, who had been on the brink of celebrating their third cup final victory over Everton.

Understandably the mood among the Blues was the opposite. They had been quiet for most of the second half and perhaps sensed a famous victory was at last on the cards.

Extra time now beckoned and there was every chance they could snatch victory from the jaws of defeat.

The late leveller could so easily have crushed the Liverpool players. The season had been arduous, and the energy expended in this game must have shattered them physically and emotionally. To have come so close to victory and then have it snatched from their grasp would have been heartbreaking.

Somehow though, they found what it takes to go again. Ian Rush restored the lead on 94 minutes and the sense of relief was all around. Then Stuart McCall scored an absolute cracker to level once more.

The drama was becoming hard to bear, but perhaps this was the game the occasion deserved. It was certainly shaping up to be a classic. Thoughts of a penalty shootout began to cross minds. That would have been a cruel way to settle such a great game though.

Thankfully Rush had other ideas, responding immediately with a deft header to grab Liverpool's third and clinch the cup in the 103rd minute. Liverpool had won, but Everton had pushed them all the way. Both teams had delivered a cup final to be proud of and once more the city of Liverpool gave the world a lesson in passion, sportsmanship and brotherhood.

Aldridge the hero says farewell as Reds demolish Palace 9-0 at Anfield

The Reds are facing Crystal Palace under Anfield's floodlights. It's 12 September 1989 and we're in the 66th minute of the game with Liverpool already 5-0 up. Striker John Aldridge is sitting on the bench.

Liverpool have just won a penalty after Andy Gray brought down Ronnie Whelan and Aldo is itching to get on and take it. This is his last chance to score in front of a stand he once stood on as a boy, as he has already been sold to Real Sociedad for £1.1m.

Aldridge had been deemed surplus to requirements despite netting an incredible 63 times in 104 appearances.

Kenny Dalglish had decided to go with Ian Rush as his main man up front and Aldo would either have to play second fiddle or find pastures new. He would go on to score 33 goals in 63 games for the Spanish side.

Thoughts must have raced through the player's mind, as the referee pointed to the spot and he gazed towards the Kop, more in hope than expectation. Perhaps he was reflecting on an emotional two years at the club that had seen him scale the heights of joy and then plummet the depths of despair, after the Hillsborough disaster.

He had, after all, given everything for the club and now it was coming to a sad end, on the substitutes' bench, on an autumn night in Liverpool 4. Then, in a moment of pure theatre, the boss turned to him and told him to get on there and take the penalty. It was to prove a most bittersweet moment for the Garston-born goal machine. The Kop roared their approval at the sight of their hero running on to the pitch. Few could believe that the Reds were about to part company with such a prolific striker.

The player recalled, 'Emotions were running high. I knew I was leaving and I wanted to take that penalty. I went about it in my usual way with a split-second glance at the keeper to see how he was shaping.'

Aldo was deadly from the spot and missed only once, in the 1988 FA Cup Final against Wimbledon. He didn't fail this time.

In a moment of perfection, the net rippled as the ball sailed past the goalkeeper and the Kop signalled its delight with an almighty roar. Aldridge had got his moment and had ensured he had signed off with a goal in his last game.

Liverpool were now 6-0 up and coasting, with Aldo joining Steve Nicol, Steve McMahon, Ian Rush, Gary Gillespie and Peter Beardsley on the scoresheet.

Palace simply crumbled from this point on and the Reds punished them severely with three more goals thanks to John Barnes, a debut strike from Glen Hysen and Nicol grabbing his second.

The 9-0 tally didn't flatter Liverpool at all and people joked that Crystal Palace were lucky to get zero, such was the Reds' dominance.

The London side's Scouse manager Steve Coppell, an ex-Manchester United player, later described how he was haunted by the team's worst ever defeat. Their agony was actually made worse by the fact that they missed a penalty of their own. Hysen had brought down a future Palace boss, Alan Pardew, in the box and Geoff Thomas put the ball high over the bar.

At full time the emotion of the occasion spilled over and, in a memorable communion with the Kop, Aldridge threw his shirt and his boots into the famous old stand, before running off to rapturous applause, with tears in his eyes and wearing just his shorts.

Kenny Dalglish told a reporter from *The Times*, 'Obviously the evening is tinged with sadness as it looks as if Aldridge is on his way and he's our most popular player. He's achieved a lifetime's ambition by playing for the club and contributing so much to it. No one deserved to come off but we're only selling him because we can't give him what he deserves.'

Aldridge summed up a heart-rending farewell by saying, 'I had to fight away the tears. I will remember it my whole life. My heart will always be at Anfield.'

Many of us think Aldo should never have been allowed to leave. The player never wanted to leave. However, he will forever a be a most welcome part of the club's illustrious history and this moment will live forever in the memories of those lucky enough to witness it.

Alan Hansen's 600th game is an eight-goal thriller as Reds legend winds down an astonishing career

Alan Hansen is, for Reds of a certain generation, the greatest centre-back ever to wear the shirt. 'Jockey', as he was known, racked up 620 appearances for Liverpool and collected a fantastic array of honours. He won eight league titles, two FA Cups, three League Cups and three European Cups.

That's not a bad record for a player Bob Paisley signed from Partick Thistle for just £100,000. Hansen would form a legendary partnership with Mark Lawrenson, creating an impregnable Reds defence.

In January 1990, Hansen played his 600th game for the Reds and wore the captain's armband. It was an FA Cup third-round tie against Swansea City, at Anfield.

The Swans had given Liverpool a bit of a shock three days earlier at their Vetch Field, holding them to a goalless draw. They wouldn't be so lucky away. Just over 29,000 attended the game and King Kenny was in the dugout. Hansen could scarcely have hoped for an easier ride for his milestone.

Swansea's defensive solidity in the first encounter was completely blown away and their attack, when it could muster anything at all, just ran into a brick wall.

Liverpool were 3-0 up by half-time thanks to two goals from John Barnes and another from Peter Beardsley. The second half would be no different for the rampant hosts.

Barnes and Ian Rush terrorised the Swans from the off and Beardsley and Steve McMahon might have made it five between them before Rush notched the fourth seven minutes after the restart, then the Kop had barely finished celebrating when Beardsley scored the fifth almost immediately. The ball was loose in midfield and nobody in a Swansea shirt seemed to want it. Beardsley did though, and drove through three defenders before tucking his shot into the back of the net.

The opposition simply vanished at this point, but not before the away end staged an embarrassing pitch invasion. It would have been kinder had the referee just blown up and led the teams off the pitch. Sadly, for them, there is no such mercy in football and they were about to be thoroughly humiliated.

Rush would cap another blistering performance with a hat-trick, scoring the sixth and seventh in a six-minute spell, before Steve Nicol sealed the eight-goal demolition job in the 86th minute.

Swansea striker Alan Curtis remembered the two games against Liverpool and in particular an encounter with the Welsh Wizard at the end of the first leg, 'At the end of the first game between the two sides, I went over to him at the final whistle and said, "You never looked like scoring." It was meant to be tongue-in-cheek.

'Anyway, Ian just shook my hand, winked and replied, "I'll see you at Anfield in a few days, Al." I always remember him saying it because Rushie went on to score a hat-trick. In fairness, he could have scored five or six.'

For Hansen, this was to be his last full season with the Reds. He would finish it by holding aloft the First Division title as the club's captain.

It was a fitting end to an astonishing career, that probably should have continued into the dugout. Jockey, however, had other ideas, 'In my last season as captain, I wasn't getting any sleep at night, worrying about three points here and three points there. And at 2.15pm on a Saturday I used to go back and forth to the toilet 45 times. So, I knew management wasn't for me.'

It's a great shame, because his knowledge of the game and exposure to the greats, such as Paisley, Fagan, Moran and Dalglish, would surely have stood him in good stead. In the end, like Jamie Carragher years later, a career in the media beckoned.

It was fitting, however, that the great defender would finish his spell at the Reds as he had started it, by winning titles and marshalling one of the meanest defences in club history.

The Fall and Rise of a Sporting Empire

Liverpool Football Club
1990–2017

Kenny Dalglish rocks the Reds as exhausted hero bows out at Anfield

To those on the Kop he was simply King Kenny. The bedroom walls of Kopites everywhere were like shrines to the man. As a player he could do no wrong, as manager he conquered all before him and as a man he carried a city through not one, but two tragedies. Then on 22 February 1991, he broke our hearts.

Dalglish left Liverpool three points clear at the top of the table and still in the FA Cup. His team had just fought a titanic battle against Everton in one of the craziest derbies ever witnessed.

Four times the Reds had gone ahead, only to be pegged back each time. The game ended 4-4. As a performance it was unrecognisable and so too was the man sat in the Reds dugout.

As he sat in the press conference in which he dropped the bombshell, he had the look of a broken man. History had caught up with him. The pressure of carrying the club and city for so long had proven to be unbearable.

We now know the full extent of the mental turmoil he was suffering but at the time many of us just didn't see it coming. We should have. I was at work when the news broke. I remember my boss took a call and I heard her say, 'You're joking!' She looked stunned, hung up the phone and announced to the whole office, 'Dalglish has resigned.'

We were all gobsmacked. Even the Blues looked genuinely dumbfounded. As we left work we passed *Echo* billboards and shook our heads in disbelief. It was so difficult to process.

Kenny later admitted he just needed a break. Had the club asked him to come back in the summer, he would have. Instead, they approached Graeme Souness. How many more trophies and cups might Liverpool have won if they had called Kenny instead? We'll never know.

There are some who point to the fact that Kenny made some mistakes in the transfer market before he left, that Liverpool were running out of steam and they needed to rebuild. Maybe so, but I'd have backed a fully fit and refreshed Dalglish to sort things out over anyone else.

It's hard to pick one moment that epitomises Kenny's contribution to this club. Would it be his goal in the 1978 European Cup Final, or the one that clinched the championship at Stamford Bridge? Maybe it's winning the double or helping to defeat Everton in two FA Cup finals.

His contributions to the club are legendary. He created perhaps the most flamboyant and entertaining Liverpool side in modern history, with the likes of Barnes, Beardsley and Aldridge lighting up the footballing world. They were a joy to watch and at times simply unbeatable.

However, it is perhaps his service to the city of Liverpool itself, in the aftermath of Hillsborough, which marks him out as someone special. It is for this and so many other reasons that his decision to resign devastated so many people.

Thankfully he couldn't stay away forever and will always be part of this club and its history.

Mark Walters the hero as Anfield hosts historic European comeback

In 1991 Liverpool were still reeling from the shock departure of Kenny Dalglish as manager. After a brief caretaker role, club stalwart Ronnie Moran gave way for Graeme Souness.

This was also Liverpool's first season back in Europe after the ban on English teams, which had been imposed following the Heysel Stadium disaster, was lifted. Liverpool entered the UEFA Cup in 1991 as the previous season's First Division runners-up.

After crushing Kuuysisi Lahti of Finland 7-2 on aggregate in the first round, the Reds faced French outfit Auxerre. The first leg ended badly with Liverpool going down 2-0.

A young Jamie Redknapp made his debut that night. Despite the defeat he described it as the game of his life. He would later explain how he played through the pain barrier for the last 20 minutes, with cramp in both legs, and he found himself back on the bench for the second leg.

Few will have given Liverpool any chance of recovering from such a setback. Maybe this explains the low turnout. An attendance of 23,094 in a European game would be unthinkable these days, but as the Reds emerged from the tunnel, vast swathes of Anfield were empty. The Kop, however, was full and in great voice, roaring the team on.

If it is true to say the stadium was threadbare, then so too was the squad. Liverpool were decimated by injury and

Souness could only muster four substitutes for the game. On the pitch was a mix of experience and youth. The likes of Bruce Grobbelaar, Jan Molby, Steve McMahon and Ian Rush rubbed shoulders with Mike Marsh, Nicky Tanner and Steve McManaman. Accompanying Redknapp on the bench were goalkeeper Robbie Holcroft, Steve Harkness and Barry Jones. Not exactly strength in depth.

As the whistle signalled kick-off, the Reds flew at the opposition and soon had them rattled. The French began wasting time almost from the start, something that angered the crowd. One report in *The Times* described the noise as deafening. How might it have been if the ground was full?

In any case it took just four minutes for Auxerre to wilt under the pressure. McManaman broke into the box and was eventually upended as his trickery got the better of Mahe in the French defence.

Molby stepped up and placed the ball on the spot. The great Dane was a specialist from 12 yards and he planted the ball effortlessly past goalkeeper Martini. Auxerre were both shaken and stirred.

Perhaps sensing a historic fightback, Anfield reached boiling point. The Reds mounted a relentless attack but were almost caught on the break as Grobbelaar saved one effort with his feet.

Then on the half-hour mark, there was more magic, as young Mike Marsh rose to head home a Ray Houghton cross. It was his first goal for the club. The sides went in at half-time with the score at 2-2 on aggregate; game on.

The second half never lived up to the first with Liverpool and the crowd growing a little frustrated, but with extra time beckoning the French side pressed self-destruct. Darras, who had been cautioned already for time wasting, was sent off for a second bookable offence after a trip on Walters. With

Auxerre down to ten men, Liverpool sensed their opportunity and pushed forward. The French were beginning to tire and perhaps intimidated by the crowd they lost their nerve.

With just six minutes remaining Molby hit a magnificent long pass that split the visitors' defence wide open. Mark Walters ran on to the ball and clipped it into the far corner, past the despairing goalkeeper.

Anfield erupted in joy. Liverpool were through after a historic comeback. No Reds side had overcome a two goal first-leg deficit in 27 years of competing in Europe.

Souness summed up what the game meant for the fans and for the future of the club, 'It was a wonderful night for the supporters and the players. We will know in four or five years' time if this was also a historic night.'

Graeme Souness has to be restrained as Reds secure their fifth FA Cup in 1992

Two years on from the shock resignation of Kenny Dalglish, Liverpool, under new manager Graeme Souness, were back in the trophy business. The Reds, having reached the final of the 1992 FA Cup, were set to take on Sunderland at Wembley.

The former Reds captain had undergone open heart surgery just 32 days earlier and was under orders not to indulge in any excessive emotional outbursts. He wasn't deemed fit enough to resume full duties and Ronnie Moran led the team out.

It was a great moment for the stalwart, who had served the club for so many years. This is how he would recall it, 'I marched out with the side and it was a very proud moment for me. I've still got the video at home and it will be something for my grandchildren to watch in years to come.'

Liverpool were having an otherwise indifferent season. They had finished sixth in the table, the first time outside the top two since 1981. They had also crashed out of the League Cup in the fourth round and the UEFA Cup in the quarter-finals. The FA Cup was their last hope of silverware.

The Reds' top scorer was Dean Saunders with ten goals in the league and 23 in all competitions. Promising youngsters like Rob Jones and Steve McManaman offered hope, alongside a sprinkling of legends such as Bruce Grobbelaar, Steve Nicol, Jan Molby and Ian Rush.

In truth, though, these heroes of the 1980s were coming to the end of their careers and it was clear that Liverpool needed rebuilding. But all of that could wait as supporters got ready to enjoy yet another day in the Wembley sunshine.

As is often the case they outnumbered their opponents massively. Of the near 80,000 spectators present, only 17,800 were there backing Second Division Sunderland.

What none of us realised though was that, so worried were they about Souness's health, the Liverpool hierarchy had assigned club doctor Bill Reid to shadow the manager throughout the day. He had to physically restrain the boss on four occasions.

Reid was unable to prevent a dressing-room broadside from Souness at half-time, though. Liverpool were poor in the opening stages of the final and as they walked off the pitch they knew they had been second best to Sunderland.

The fiery Scot was waiting for them and let rip, letting them know, in no uncertain terms, that they had to improve. Mark Wright, who captained the Reds on the day, told the *Mirror* what happened, 'He had a major dig at us and rightly so. He couldn't believe how we played in that first half ... you could say he had some choice words for us.'

Wright would have some of his own when he was presented with the trophy by the Duchess of Kent, but more of that later.

With their manager's stinging rebuke still ringing in their ears, Liverpool flew out of the traps in the second half. It took them just two minutes to go in front.

A tactical switch had been instrumental according to *The Times*, where a report said that moving McManaman to the left wing had led directly to Liverpool's opener. This is how it was described, 'Sunderland were penetrated on the left, a flank guarded by Anton Rogan, a defender more suited to patrolling the central area. Liverpool recognised the flaw, McManaman exposed it.

'Though surrounded, he scooped the ball into the path of Thomas, who specialises in deep and unexpected runs. Nobody was accompanying him as he swivelled and volleyed in a goal.'

Souness was a boiling cauldron on the bench and couldn't help himself as the Reds celebrated on the pitch. He had to be held back in 'a gentle headlock' to prevent him from getting too carried away. Just 20 minutes later, Rush made it two with a low angled drive that gave the goalkeeper no chance. From that moment on the tie wasn't in doubt, according to *The Times*, 'It was now a frolic, counting the Liverpool passes as they played keep-ball ... Liverpool are back, Europe beckons, and there was no equality at the end of our cup final.'

All that remained was for Wright to collect the cup. As he held it aloft, in full earshot of royalty, he shouted, 'You fucking beauty!'

He apologised, apparently, but there wasn't a single Liverpool supporter on Earth who wouldn't have done the same.

A new hero rises: Robbie Fowler hits five in demolition of Fulham

Five of Robbie Fowler's 183 goals for Liverpool were scored in one game against Fulham in 1993, on a night the Kop witnessed the birth of God. In the autumn of 1993, Graeme Souness's Liverpool side were struggling. They had recently crashed to a humiliating 2-0 derby day defeat to Everton at Goodison, and followed that up with a defeat to Chelsea and a goalless draw with Arsenal. Despite a forward line of Ian Rush and Nigel Clough, the Reds were firing blanks.

Souness's men had been drawn against Fulham in the second round of the League Cup. This gave the beleaguered boss a chance to hand a debut to a young striker who was making waves in the reserves by the name of Robbie Fowler.

The 18-year-old repaid his manager's faith, scoring a late goal to seal a 3-1 win at Craven Cottage in the first leg. The return game took place on 5 October, setting the scene for a historic night under the Anfield floodlights.

Sadly only 12,541 were there to witness what turned out be a goalscoring masterclass. Such was the gloom surrounding the club, a second leg against Fulham simply failed to set the pulses racing.

The lucky few who did turn up that night certainly got their money's worth as the youngster simply destroyed the Cottagers with a display of predatory marksmanship.

Liverpool fielded a very attacking line-up with Fowler, wearing the number 23 shirt, joining Rush and Clough up front. However, the two senior forwards were merely a supporting cast to a rising star.

Fulham made a spirited start but it took Robbie, the self-styled 'cheeky kid from Toxteth', just 13 minutes to score his first in front of a home crowd.

He followed that up only eight minutes later, handing the Reds a 2-0 lead they would take into the break. Both strikes had been typical poacher's goals and it was already becoming clear that Liverpool had unearthed yet another lethal striker.

In the second half the teenager struck three more times, in the 47th, 55th and the 70th minutes, to become only the fifth player in Reds history to score five in a single game. He had netted three with his left foot, one with his right and another with his head. It was a consummate performance.

The press went overboard, as they usually do when a promising young talent bursts on to the scene.

British Soccer Weekly predicted that Fowler had 'the ability to become the best England striker since Gary Lineker'. Few disagreed.

Fowler would go on to net 18 times in all competitions for the Reds that season (12 in the league). Sadly, it would not be enough to earn silverware for Liverpool, nor would it save Souness, with the manager getting the sack after a disastrous FA Cup defeat to Bristol City in January 1994.

The Kop's last stand

The Spion Kop at Anfield is perhaps the most famous terrace in world football. It earned its reputation as far back as 1905, but it reached its heyday in the 60s and 70s. During that period football fused with music and working-class culture to produce a uniquely anarchic and creative force of nature.

So potent was the Kop during this era that the BBC's *Panorama* documentary programme sent a team to study it. The programme's presenter stood in front of a swaying singing mass of people, as if he was an anthropologist discussing a newly discovered tribe, and said, 'I don't know what they do to the enemy, but by God they frighten the life out of me.'

Kopites hadn't read the script though, because at that moment they started singing Cilla Black's 'Anyone Who Had A Heart' in perfect harmony and in unison. The camera pans back and the reporter can only watch in amazement, speechless.

Ian St John once told a reporter that he would 'willingly die for these people and I know they would die for me'. Kevin Keegan also spoke of his devotion, saying, 'The only thing I fear is missing an open goal in front of the Kop. I would die if that were to happen. When they start singing "You'll Never Walk Alone" my eyes start to water. There have been times when I've actually been crying while I've been playing.'

If the Kop was inspired by the 1960s music scene, they would return the favour in the 70s. A recording of them singing 'You'll Never Walk Alone' can be clearly heard on a Pink Floyd album.

In 1977 against French giants Saint-Etienne they would reach new levels of support and, some believe, sucked in David Fairclough's winning goal to help the Reds on their way to a first European Cup. Sadly though, that version of the Kop would come to an end in 1994.

It would coincide with the demise of the team in a forgettable decade for the club. However, the fate of the famous old terrace was sealed with the publication of the Taylor Report into the Hillsborough disaster in 1989, which recommended the introduction of all-seater stadiums.

The last game in front of a standing Kop came on 30 April 1994. Norwich City were the opponents and with both teams not in contention for honours, the result mattered little.

Liverpool lost 1-0 thanks to a stunning strike by Jeremy Goss in the first half. It was a goal that received thunderous applause from the Kop.

However, the Reds' inability to reply and reward the fans left a bittersweet taste for manager Roy Evans, who said, 'Just imagine what they would have been like today if we had been challenging for the championship. It was a taste for some of the younger players of what this crowd is like. I think they are the best crowd in the world. It was about the Kop today and all our fans, and I thought they were magnificent. It's a pity we weren't in the same class.'

The historic occasion was marked with all the pomp and ceremony of a state funeral, with the Kop centre stage. *The Times* captured the mood perfectly, 'The Kop was awash with flags unseen since Liverpool dominated Europe. Appropriately enough, a succession of Anfield heroes were brought out to the centre circle ... But the day was about the people of Liverpool and one moment stood above all others. At the end of the heroes' parade, and as the teams stood in the centre circle, respectfully facing the Kop, Bill Shankly's widow, Nellie, walked slowly on to the pitch, on the arm of Joe Fagan ... On Fagan's other arm was Bob Paisley's wife. The applause from the fans was thunderous and the rest of the ground stood in stunned respect as the Kop chanted, "Shankly, Shankly."'

John Stulberg was one of those supporters. His memories today are as vivid as they were back then. He recalls, 'Long after the game had finished the Kop remained full and in full voice. Nobody wanted to leave because they knew it would be for the last time, never to be repeated.

'When we eventually left the ground the smiles and laughter continued back to the pub and long into the night. The buzz lasted well after the day itself, so did the sore throats. When I think back, I am filled with that same joy, but also a sense of sadness for what we lost. Having said that, I still think it's a price worth paying for the safety of the fans.'

The Kop would never be the same again. Yes, on a European night it gets close, but the much smaller and sedentary incarnation we witness today will always struggle to emulate that seething mass of humanity that roared Liverpool teams of old to glory. That's why many supporters did all they could to grab a last precious souvenir.

Ian Golder, a Kopite who left the ground at full time because he was working the taxis, explains what happened, 'I was driving down Walton Breck Road late on. I wanted to grab a last glimpse of the Kop before home. Next minute I'm pissing myself laughing at the sight of all these lads stripping the place of any piece of memorabilia they could lay their hands on.'

Some things are so precious, you simply can't let them go.

Robbie Fowler's record-breaking hat-trick against Arsenal in 1994

In 1994, Liverpool began a season of transition. This was Roy Evans's first full year in charge and there was a renewed sense of optimism at Anfield. The season before had seen the departure of Graeme Souness and a disappointing eighth-place finish.

Ian Rush's Liverpool career was beginning to wane. During the 1993/94 season he managed 19 goals in all competitions – it was a decent return but not by the stellar standards he had set at Anfield.

Realising they would soon need a goalscorer to take Rushie's place, the club had signed Nigel Clough in 1993 for £2.75m. However, they would soon realise that they had the perfect solution playing in the reserves. That man was Robbie Fowler.

Fowler would cement his place in the Liverpool line-up at the start of the 1994/95 season, which Liverpool began with a glut of goals. In their first game they obliterated Crystal Palace 6-1 at Selhurst Park and the youngster had scored, of course.

Eight days later they faced Arsenal at Anfield. The Gunners, under George Graham, were known as 'boring Arsenal' and were famed for their defensive solidity.

Their back five of David Seaman, Lee Dixon, Nigel Winterburn, Martin Keown and Tony Adams were a formidable force.

However, Fowler would go through them like a hot knife through butter that day. He opened the scoring in the 26th minute and within 276 seconds the game was over thanks to the fastest hat-trick in Liverpool's history.

It would also stand as a Premier League record until Sadio Mane smashed it by scoring three in just two minutes and 56 seconds in May 2015 when with Southampton.

The press went wild for the new kid on the Kop. Under a banner headline 'KOPS AND ROB-BERS', the *Mirror* celebrated the arrival of a new Anfield god. Liverpool knew they were in possession of a priceless gem and had offered the youngster a four-year contract worth a cool £1m.

The supporters were in 'ecstasy', with the *Mail* crowing, 'The goals were lapped up by a Liverpool crowd driven to ecstasy and quite forgetting the first sight of Anfield without a standing Kop.'

The famous old terrace had enjoyed its last stand at the end of the 1993/94 season. This was the first time in the club's history that supporters on the Kop would have watched the game sitting down.

Fowler was a bit more circumspect about his exploits, saying he thought the goals were 15 minutes apart and declaring, 'I didn't think I played that well.'

Evans couldn't believe his luck, telling the waiting press he would have been happy with any sort of win. He had good reason: Arsenal had boasted the meanest defence in the league just a few months earlier.

Fowler had the world at his feet and supporters were confident they had witnessed the heir apparent to Rush, who was now in his penultimate season. The legendary striker felt the same way.

As he left Liverpool, he could pay the youngster from Toxteth no greater compliment than this, saying, 'I leave it in good hands; Robbie will probably eclipse all that I have achieved at Liverpool.'

McManaman provides the fizz as Reds lift the Coca-Cola Cup

In April 1995 Liverpool reached their sixth League Cup Final and were looking to secure a record fifth success. Ian Rush, who captained the side on the day, had featured in the previous four wins and was hoping to make history with a fifth success in the competition.

This was Roy Evans's first season in charge of Liverpool and a chance for him to open his account with silverware. A young Robbie Fowler had burst on to the scene at Anfield and would go on to score 31 goals in all competitions. This was a chance for him to display his talents on the biggest stage in English football.

For Bolton, a young Jason McAteer, a lifelong Red, dreamed of one day playing for Liverpool and hoped to earn a move to his boyhood team. There were so many personal stories and opportunities for players to sparkle.

However, it was left to a youngster from Kirkdale to steal the show in the 1995 Coca-Cola Cup Final with a display of sheer effervescence. Steve McManaman destroyed Bolton with a goal in either half of the game.

But his overall performance drew high praise from one of the true greats of the game, Sir Stanley Matthews. Sir Stanley was guest of honour at Wembley and was hypnotised by the youngster's display. 'He reminds me of me, when I was playing,' said the former England hero.

The game was an even affair until the 37th minute when Liverpool opened the scoring. Here's McManaman's description of the goal, 'I picked the ball up from John Barnes's pass and went past a couple of players before shooting towards the goal. It wasn't the best shot I've ever hit but the goalkeeper couldn't keep it out and it was a brilliant feeling to see the ball hit the net.'

The Reds were in front but Bolton hadn't surrendered and Liverpool would need a second to put the game to bed. It came in the 68th minute and again it was McManaman who delivered.

This time he cut in from the left and glided effortlessly past a series of challenges by the Bolton defence, curling a delightful effort into the corner of the net. Liverpool fans celebrated all around the stadium.

'THANK EVANS' declared one banner, but it was McManaman who'd earned their gratitude.

All Liverpool had to do now was shut the game down. Sadly, this was a quality all Evans's sides lacked. Bolton hit back instantly thanks to a stunning shot from Alan Thompson. David James had no chance but the Reds had fallen for a sucker punch.

Liverpool held on, though, and Rush claimed a historic fifth winners' medal, Fowler put in another mature performance, Evans christened his managerial debut season with a trophy and McAteer eventually got his move to L4. However, all the plaudits would go to McManaman.

Sadly it would prove to be the last trophy he secured for the Reds and he would leave Anfield to join Real Madrid in 1999 on a 'Bosman' free transfer. He missed out on the famous Houllier treble of 2001 but he made up for that with two La Liga titles, two Champions Leagues, one UEFA Cup and two Spanish Super Cups.

McManaman should forever be viewed as one of the finest talents to pull on the red shirt. However, it's an eternal shame that he had his best years away from Anfield.

Cream suits at Wembley – the 1996 FA Cup Final

After feasting on the sumptuous banquets that were the 1960s, 70s and 80s, the 90s were nothing short of a famine for Liverpool supporters. The period coincided with the re-emergence of our bitter rivals from the other end of the M62, adding to the pain.

Liverpool had not won the league since 1990 and had only managed one FA Cup under Graeme Souness and a League Cup under the man who succeeded him, Roy Evans.

As the Reds lined up against United at Wembley on 11 May 1996, it was only their third final of the decade. However, it did represent a great opportunity for Evans's exciting young team to kick on. All they had to do was want it more than their enemy.

By now the likes of John Barnes and Ian Rush were starting to wane. Goal machine Rush started on the bench and Barnes, who lined up in the middle, captained the side.

New stars were beginning to shine. Rob Jones, Stan Collymore, Jamie Redknapp, Steve McManaman and of course Robbie Fowler promised much on the pitch.

Unfortunately, it was their escapades off it that seemed to be holding them back. This was a team later dubbed the 'Spice Boys' and it seemed David James, a sometimes-calamitous goalkeeper with an ambition to become a model, was fixated more on their sartorial qualities than on winning the final.

In the run up to the game, James had apparently used his contacts at Armani to secure the squad some unforgettable suits. As the teams took to the turf for the traditional pre-match stroll, their attire was anything but traditional. Looking like refugees from *Saturday Night Fever*, they drew a bemused reaction from those watching inside and outside the stadium.

United, by contrast, were ruled by a stern disciplinarian, Alex Ferguson, who wasn't afraid of hurling boots, teacups and hairdryers at his charges whenever he felt they needed it. Maybe that's why they maintained their concentration levels throughout a terrible final.

The Liverpool side may have sought to bring a little flair to the occasion, but the game itself never lived up to that. *The Sunday Times* described it as 'deadlocked mediocrity'.

United took care of Liverpool's most creative player, McManaman, and Evans couldn't find a solution. Barnes did little to rekindle his past glories and the game descended into a dull, tense affair that seemed to be heading for extra time.

However, in the 85th minute disaster struck. United won a corner and Beckham flashed the ball into the box. James struggled from set pieces and instead of collecting the ball, he elected to punch. At first, he seemed to have cleared the danger, but the ball fell to Cantona. From roughly 20 yards out he struck it low and hard into the net.

In the stands, Liverpool hearts sank. There were only minutes left and the Reds, devoid of ideas for much of the match, didn't look like they had the nous or the inclination to get them out of this mess. The seconds evaporated, and the cup was United's.

James had been beaten by a sucker-punch and so had Liverpool. Evans's side never reached another final after that and the club saw further decline before the arrival of Gerard Houllier in 1999.

It was said that the cream-suited 'Spice Boys' lacked the discipline to mount a serious challenge to their rivals. It was a deficiency the Frenchman would set about rectifying as he restored the Reds' pride at the turn of the century. As for those Armani suits, I hope I never see their likes again.

The kids were all right: the 1996 FA Youth Cup Final

No matter how much success you taste, the first one is always the sweetest.

Older heads will recall the first time Liverpool won the European Cup in 1977. Even older ones will remember '65 when Shankly's Reds ended decades of pain by ramming the words of Evertonians right back down their throats, lifting their first FA Cup.

For Reds of a much younger vintage, maybe recollections of the FA Youth Cup Final in 1996 will linger longest in the mind. Steve Heighway's young guns promised great things and oozed talent. Although only two of them, Jamie Carragher and Michael Owen, would go on to play at the highest level in the game, the rest will be immortalised for clinching that first FA Youth Cup in the club's history.

Liverpool had lost the FA Cup to Manchester United just a week earlier. The pain lingered long in the city. Not just because of the Eric Cantona pile driver that settled an ultimately dull encounter, but mainly because the senior team had done little to dispel most supporters' views that football was beset with overpaid prima donnas.

David James had used his contacts in the modelling industry to secure each of his team-mates a white Armani suit. They stood out in the pre-match stroll on the Wembley turf but they were anonymous for the 90 minutes that followed. By contrast their youth team counterparts were full of ambition and desire.

Carragher personified the grit that was missing in the first team and in Owen, it seemed, Liverpool had unearthed yet another prolific scorer.

It's a testament to the hope placed in those young players that a combined 35,000 supporters watched both legs of the final, with 20,000 attending the second leg at Anfield.

Our opponents were West Ham, who had beaten the Reds in the final three decades earlier. Their 1996 incarnation boasted the likes of Frank Lampard and Rio Ferdinand.

Liverpool, though, were in ominous form and had crushed Manchester United 3-0 en route to a semi-final with Crystal Palace, which ended 7-5 on aggregate.

Owen, aged just 16, had notched two hat-tricks along the way and his contribution would also be telling in the final.

The Reds had won the first leg 2-0, with goals from John Newby and David Larmour, and headed to Anfield for the return fixture brimming with confidence.

Owen started on the bench but came on to put the Reds in front. Lampard netted for West Ham but Liverpool won 2-1 on the night, wrapping up a 4-1 aggregate victory to lift the cup. Carragher would go on to achieve legendary status for Liverpool. The epitome of a one-club man, he devoted his life to the club and tasted great success. Sadly, despite helping Liverpool to trophies and scoring some sublime goals, Owen is remembered far less fondly by supporters.

Keegan and Dalglish witness horror show as last-gasp Reds down Newcastle in successive seasons

In 1996 and 1997 Liverpool and Newcastle played out two remarkable games at Anfield. They will live long in the memories of all those who were there to witness them. Both ended 4-3 to the Reds and on each occasion Roy Evans's Liverpool had beaten Newcastle with a last-gasp goal in front of the Kop.

Sky Sports's Martin Tyler regards the game in '96 as his all-time favourite. He recalls, 'I get goosebumps every time I hear it because it was such a special time. Poor Kevin Keegan slumped over the advertising hoardings at the end is one of the iconic shots of the game, perhaps the iconic shot. Whatever makes us so addicted to football it was the drug. I think if you take all the elements of why we all love football they all happened in this particular game.'

In the run up to the game Liverpool, Newcastle and Manchester United were locked in a three-way tussle for the Premier League title. Neither the Reds nor the Magpies could afford to lose.

Keegan had built an attacking team in his own image, but they couldn't defend to save their lives. Roy Evans's Reds suffered from a similar affliction. On 3 April 1996, the two sides served up an explosive encounter that had the Kop and the watching media drooling.

Like two punch-drunk boxers, the teams traded blows throughout the game. Fowler put Liverpool in front after just two minutes. Then Newcastle raced into the lead through Les Ferdinand and David Ginola.

At half-time the Reds had done enough to convince their boss they could grab all three points. He told them to just keep going and they would win. They would take his words to heart.

Fowler equalised in the 57th minute, before Faustino Asprilla put Newcastle back in front two minutes later. The Kop had barely had time to celebrate their hero's leveller and they were behind once more.

Eleven minutes later the Reds were level again, this time through Stan Collymore. Anfield was rocking and the realisation that either side could press self-destruct at any moment added to the nervous tension.

Then deep into injury time, Barnes and Collymore exchanged passes in the penalty area and the latter drove a low shot into the far corner to send the Kop wild. The scorer would later tell the waiting media, 'We left it late. It was such an open game and there were chances galore. Both sides went for the win but fortunately we got it.'

Evans bemoaned his side's defensive qualities, saying, 'I didn't get much time to relax. It was a fantastic effort from both teams and a great game. But to be fair, it was kamikaze defending. Managers would be dead within six months if every game was like that.'

Keegan somehow found it in his heart to praise his former team. 'Liverpool are made of pretty stern stuff. In the last five or ten minutes they came on strong. It reminded me of the Liverpool side 20 years ago,' he said.

Neither manager could have imagined that just a year later, Anfield would witness another classic encounter resulting in the same scoreline.

In a sort of cock-eyed symmetry, the man in the Newcastle dugout in March 1997 was the legend who had replaced Keegan at Anfield 20 years earlier, Kenny Dalglish. Again, the Reds were in a title race, but this time Newcastle were fourth.

By half-time the game looked as good as over with the Reds racing into a three-goal lead through Steve McManaman, Robbie Fowler and Patrick Berger. However, lightning was about to strike in the same place for the second time in successive seasons.

With just 20 minutes remaining Newcastle drove their supporters crazy and sent the Kop into the depths of despair by mounting a heroic fightback. Keith Gillespie and Faustino Asprilla set up a tense finale, scoring in the 71st and 87th minutes to make it 3-2.

Liverpool's defence was rocking and Anfield was a portrait of nervous tension. Then disaster struck in the 88th minute when Warren Barton levelled for the Magpies. Kopites were incandescent with rage; how could Liverpool surrender a three-goal lead like that?

A Press Association report describes the drama that followed, 'Then Stig Bjornebye raced down the left and pumped a high ball into the middle. Little Fowler out-jumped everyone to steer his second goal of the game past a stunned Shaka Hislop and history had repeated itself.'

The scenes of jubilation at full time were incredible. To think that a trio of Liverpool greats could preside over such a pair of amazing games and in the space of just one year; it was truly amazing.

However, the defensive frailties of both sides would ultimately cancel out their attacking prowess, robbing them of any chance of a league championship. Still, they were incredible to watch.

Roy Evans calls time on distinguished Anfield career as Gerard Houllier becomes sole manager

Towards the end of the 1990s all was not well at Liverpool. The initial optimism that had surrounded the club's decision to part ways with Graeme Souness and go back to the boot room, with Roy Evans, had evaporated. Liverpool were a team full of attacking flair, but suspect defensively.

The epitome of this, what Evans himself would call 'kamikaze football', were the two monumental 4-3 victories over Kevin Keegan's Newcastle United.

In both games the Reds had surrendered leads through poor defensive play before eventually emerging with the three points. Liverpool were a team struggling on the pitch and with alleged disciplinary and attitude problems off it.

Evans, though, was a club stalwart and much loved. He represented a golden thread that ran all the way back to Bill Shankly. Chairman David Moores couldn't summon the ruthlessness he had shown Souness years earlier.

Instead of another parting of the ways, the club embarked on an ultimately doomed experiment. In 1998 they asked Frenchman Gerard Houllier to join Evans as joint manager. It was quickly seized upon as a risky gamble and journalists and supporters alike pointed out the obvious flaws in the plan.

'What happens if Roy wants to select one player and you want another?' asked one reporter at a press conference.

'We'll pick both,' was the reply.

It didn't fool anyone and sure enough, just three months later, Evans resigned. It was described as the kindest sacking in football. I'm not sure Roy would agree, but the move left Houllier in sole charge.

The Frenchman, who had worked in Liverpool as a teacher in the 1960s and who had stood on the Kop, quickly endeared himself to the supporters.

He immediately identified the club's problems and can be credited with modernising training methods and improving discipline off the pitch. Mobile phones were banned from Melwood and players were given strict diets to follow.

Gerard was as quotable as Shankly, too. He talked of the need for unity in the squad, 'We don't have any splits here. The players' country is Liverpool Football Club and their language is football.'

The Frenchman had a profound understanding of the supporters and what the game means to them. He also got the Scouse humour – as shown by his famous quote, 'Our job is to make the fans happy. When we win, 45,000 people go home happy. When we lose, it not only affects them, it affects their cats.'

Houllier restored the club's pride after a barren decade. The 1990s saw Liverpool slip down football's pecking order and the return of just two trophies wasn't good enough for a club that had previously won everything. All that changed at the turn of the century and with the arrival of Gerard Houllier.

He will be best known for the glorious treble season of 2001 when Liverpool lifted the League Cup, FA Cup and UEFA Cup. He would later go on to survive a major heart problem, returning triumphantly in a Champions League encounter with Roma at Anfield.

Houllier also gave rise to the careers of two players who would go on to become legends in their own right, Steven Gerrard and Jamie Carragher.

However, for Houllier, the highlight of his Liverpool reign would surely be that magical 2000/01 season, when he unleashed a rampant Reds team on the Premier League and secured Champions League football for the first time in a generation.

Jamie Carragher's 'longest penalty run-up in history' seals his first major trophy for Liverpool

In February 2001 Liverpool reached the League Cup Final. For Jamie Carragher, it was an opportunity to win the first trophy of his Reds career. The opponents were Birmingham City and the game, at Cardiff's Millennium Stadium, represented a chance for the club to secure their first piece of silverware since 1995.

Carragher had burst on to the scene in the FA Youth Cup Final of 1996 when he and Michael Owen had been among the team that won the cup.

He broke in to the first team soon afterwards but the Reds struggled under Roy Evans and eventually Gerard Houllier took charge of the team in 1998.

Thanks to the Frenchman, Carragher, who had not seen a winners' medal in five years, bagged three in 2001. The first came in the League Cup and Jamie played a key part in the team's success.

Over 73,000 people were in Cardiff with most cheering on Liverpool.

Houllier's rebuilding job was well under way. In goal was Sander Westerveld and in front of him was Sami Hyypia and Stephane Henchoz, while Carragher was right-back.

Didi Hamann had joined Steven Gerrard in the heart of midfield and Emile Heskey was club captain Robbie Fowler's strike partner.

The pair combined brilliantly on the half-hour mark to create the Reds' opener. Westerveld cleared downfield and Heskey flicked the ball on to Fowler, who cracked a brilliant shot from fully 25 yards.

The game was far from a walkover for Liverpool, though, with Birmingham going toe-to-toe with the Reds throughout. Still, it looked like Houllier's men would hold on for that all-important first trophy when in the 92nd minute disaster struck.

Henchoz brought down Martin O'Connor in the penalty area. The referee immediately pointed to the spot. It was a crushing blow for Reds supporters, who were getting ready to party. To add to their agony the spot-kick was delayed as the player received treatment for an injury. He was eventually stretchered off.

Up stepped 24-year-old Darren Purse who showed no signs of nerves and beat Westerveld easily with his penalty. The final went into extra time and it would prove a real test of the nerves.

Both sides had chances. For Liverpool, Fowler went close and Hamann hit the woodwork. Birmingham probably should have had another penalty.

However, the deadlock could not be broken and, as is so often the case with Liverpool, the final went to penalties. After five spot-kicks each the shootout was tied at 4-4. Hamann had missed for the Reds, as did Martin Grainger for Birmingham.

It was now sudden death and walking from the halfway line was the last player Liverpool supporters wanted to see: Jamie Carragher. There was no doubting his versatility, or his grit and determination, but Carragher was not a goalscorer and certainly not someone you wanted to take a crucial penalty.

TV cameras panning the crowd revealed images of supporters chewing what was left of their fingernails as the player shaped up to take the kick. His run-up looked huge. Surely he would give the goalkeeper ample opportunity to guess which way he was going to shoot.

Didn't it also mean there would be time for Carragher himself to second-guess himself and change his mind as he approached the ball?

We needn't have worried though, because the lad from Bootle had nerves of steel. Here's how Carragher recalled it, 'People remind me about my run-up for the penalty I took in the shootout and how it must go down as the longest in history. It was sudden death, but I didn't have any nerves. I knew where I wanted to put it and thankfully it went in.

'It was my first trophy with the senior Liverpool team and it was the catalyst for us to go on and win the cup treble.'

The goal put Liverpool in the driving seat and a miss by Andy Johnson, who would later go on to play for Everton, handed the cup to the Reds.

Liverpool fans were jubilant but on the pitch, Birmingham manager Trevor Francis was devastated. Cameras caught him crying as he attempted to console his players.

Houllier urged his team to use the feeling of victory to drive them to ever greater glory. They did and it proved to be a case of one down, two to go in what turned out to be a historic and memorable season.

Gary McAllister cements his place in Mersey derby folklore with last-gasp winner

Gary McAllister played a key role in Liverpool's cup treble campaign of 2000/01 but his match-winning goal in the Premier League encounter at Goodison Park is the one that Kopites will always remember most fondly.

In 2001, Liverpool were a team reborn and competing for a lucrative place in the Champions League. After six long years without a trophy they had won the League Cup with a victory over Birmingham City. They were still in the FA Cup and the UEFA Cup. If they were to live their dream, and qualify for Europe's top competition, they would need to finish at least third as England only had three places that season.

As they reached the business end of the season there was no room for error; every point counted. In April they faced Everton at Goodison Park. The Blues, with nothing to play for, were eager to put a dent in Liverpool's quest for glory.

The Reds took the lead early on through Emile Heskey, but Duncan Ferguson levelled for the Blues two minutes into the second half. Markus Babbel looked to have won it, putting Liverpool back in front ten minutes later, but maddeningly Everton won a penalty in the 83rd minute.

David Unsworth scored from the spot and Liverpool were staring down the barrel of two dropped points. The Gwladys Street end was delirious. They had won a point against Liverpool at home, or so they thought.

With all hope lost, young French defender Gregory Vignal picked up the ball in his own half. Houllier's teams were famous for shutting up shop in such situations. 'Keep the result' was the mantra. A draw wasn't a disaster. However, this was a derby and the Reds needed the win.

Instead of playing it safe and seeing the ball back to Sander Westerweld in goal, Vignal chose to surge forward, drawing a foul fully 50 yards from goal. By the time McAllister placed the ball and got ready to take the free kick, it was 44 yards out.

Time was up. This was the last kick of the game.

He had floated one into the box earlier in the game and he gestured to his team-mates again, indicating he would do the same this time. It was a ploy and the Blues defence fell for it.

Only he knows if he has ever hit a sweeter shot, but instead of delivering the obvious cross to heads he hit it hard and low. The keeper scrambled to his right but got nowhere near it and the ball crept into the bottom corner.

The sight of Blue faces behind the goal was a joy. So too were images of a dancing Sammy Lee and a disbelieving Houllier on the touchline.

Gerard looked as astonished by the goal as anyone in the stadium. McAllister will doubtless remember that moment for the rest of his life, as will every Red lucky enough to witness it. The final whistle went, and Liverpool supporters danced in the away end. Everton fans went home to lick their wounds.

Michael Owen grabs a brace as the Reds say arrivederci Roma on road to 2001 treble

En route to winning the UEFA Cup in Dortmund in 2001, Gerard Houllier's Liverpool stopped off at the Stadio Olimpico in Rome. This was a fourth-round tie and the opponents were, of course, Roma.

The Reds had won two European Cups on this ground already. In 1977 they defeated Borussia Monchengladbach to lift their first and, in 1984, they triumphed over Roma on penalties to clinch their fourth.

On each occasion the locals had given the Liverpool supporters a torrid time and this night would be no different.

Nevertheless, the Reds took a healthy contingent to the Italian capital. Thousands of Reds filled the bars and cafes around the stadium before kick-off. The Eternal City was awash with banners and the streets echoed to Scouse song:

'When Robbie Fowler scores a goal
You can stick your Totti up yer hole
And we'll all get blind drunk
When Liverpool win the cup'

In truth, most Liverpool supporters would have been nervous prior to the game. The Reds were a team in development and although they would win the first of their three trophies that year in just a few weeks, on paper at least they were no match for the Italians. Fortunately, football is played on grass, not on paper.

Roma were running away with Serie A. They were six points clear and boasted the likes of Cafu, Gabriel Batistuta and Francesco Totti. However, Batistuta started on the bench and Totti didn't figure in the squad at all, a fact that must have given Liverpool a lift prior to kick-off.

A tense first half ended goalless with Roma going closest with a wayward header from club captain Marco Delvecchio. It was a case of so far so good for Liverpool, who would have happily taken a 0-0 draw back to Anfield. Instead they did much better than that.

With the second half just two minutes old, Michael Owen cut out a poor pass from Alessandro Rinaldi and thumped the ball past goalkeeper Francesco Antonioli. The home support was stunned into silence. The Italians flickered briefly into life after that, testing Westerweld with a shot from sub Marcos Assuncao. Then they introduced Batistuta, which must have sent ripples of anxiety through the away support. But no sooner had the Argentine entered the fray than Owen doubled Liverpool's lead with a header.

Liverpool saw the game out for a famous win and almost added a third through Nicky Barmby in the 89th minute. However, his shot was saved. Gerard Houllier was beaming after the game and with good cause. 'The whole team was superb,' he grinned. 'I was worried because we had players missing through injury and others cup-tied, while there were several playing who were only just back from injury. But Michael's goals gave us confidence and the defence were outstanding.'

All that remained was for the Liverpool supporters to negotiate the chaos outside the ground as they made their way home. Little did they know, they were on the brink of one of the most memorable seasons in the club's history.

The 2001 FA Cup triumph: revenge for Liverpool in the first final played outside England

Liverpool faced Arsenal in the FA Cup Final at Cardiff's Millennium Stadium in May 2001. It was the first time the final had been contested outside of England. Liverpool had a few scores to settle with the Gunners that day. Many will recall the bitter disappointment of the 1989 title decider at Anfield, when Michael Thomas broke Kopite hearts in the 90th minute to clinch the league from under Liverpool's noses.

The Reds had also suffered cup final defeats to Arsenal in 1950, 1971 and 1987.

This would also be the first of two games in five days that would decide a historic cup treble. Liverpool had already beaten Birmingham City to lift the League Cup in February and were due to face Alaves, in Dortmund, in the UEFA Cup Final on 16 May.

With so much at stake, the atmosphere surrounding the game was one of nervous anticipation as 72,000 people made the trip to Wales to witness a dramatic late comeback in the sweltering heat.

Arsenal were strong, boasting the likes of Thierry Henry, Freddie Ljungberg, Robert Pires and Sylvain Wiltord. Their defence was reliable but, crucially, it was an ageing one.

Gerard Houllier had assembled a great cup team with a solid spine. In defence, Stephane Henchoz and Sami Hyypia were rock solid, Didi Hamann and Steven Gerrard were formidable in midfield and with the pace and power of Emile Heskey and Michael Owen up front there was always a chance of goals.

For all the hype and fanfare, though, the first half failed to live up to its billing. It wasn't until the 17th minute that the game saw its first chance. Henry burst into the box and took the ball around Sander Westerveld.

Fortunately Henchoz raced back to narrow the angle and the Frenchman shot into the side netting. It was a let-off but Liverpool continued to look nervous, giving the ball away often and sitting deep. Houllier's tactic was to allow Arsenal to come at Liverpool and try to use the pace of Owen to hit them on the break.

As a result any Liverpool supporter watching the DVD can probably just fast-forward to the 72nd minute: the moment the game erupted into life. A bad clearance from Westerveld saw the ball at Pires's feet. He sent Ljungberg through on goal and the Swedish international calmly rounded Westerweld to score. The Arsenal fans went wild. In the Liverpool end, there was despair.

Liverpool looked so anaemic that it was hard to see them getting back into it. Then Henry wasted two further opportunities in quick succession, giving the Reds a glimmer of hope. And in the 83rd minute they were right back in it.

Owen grabbed the equaliser from a free kick which the Gunners failed to clear. From the resultant scramble the ball fell to Owen, who turned sharply and fired a low drive into the bottom corner.

Game on! Though most Reds were just praying their team could hang on for extra time and maybe even penalties. They couldn't, in their wildest dreams, have predicted what would happen next.

With time almost up, in the 88th minute, Patrik Berger hit a long ball forward for Owen to chase. Berger was probably trying to ease the pressure on his back four, but the youngster latched on to it and sprinted towards goal.

Lee Dixon, looking tired, couldn't keep pace with him. David Seaman came off his line to try and narrow the angle but Owen fired his shot across the goal and managed to hit the only spot that the goalkeeper couldn't reach.

It was a magnificent finish and with virtually no time left, it was the perfect moment to score. At the final whistle the Liverpool contingent were ecstatic while the Arsenal supporters headed home. All that remained was the trophy presentation, which took place on the pitch.

Jamie Redknapp was club captain but had been out injured for a while. Some of the players had asked him to receive the cup anyway but he refused.

However, he then had a dramatic change of heart which led to him and Robbie Fowler lifting the cup together, despite Sami Hyypia being captain on the day.

Here, in Redknapp's own words, as recounted on TV's *A League of Their Own*, is what changed his mind, 'Out of the corner of my eye I could see Gerard Houllier going to Sami Hyypia, "You go. You are the captain. You go up there." I thought, "Oh, really? I think I will do this!" That's a true story. I thought, "Houllier, you wanker! Have some of that!"'

Does that say more about Jamie than it does Houllier? You decide.

Liverpool edge out plucky Alaves in the greatest UEFA Cup Final of all time

The 2001 UEFA Cup Final is one of the greatest European finals there has been. It had everything; a resurgent Liverpool under Gerard Houllier, a plucky underdog in Alaves and a victory for the Reds, courtesy of a golden goal, in the depths of extra time.

The game took place at Borussia Dortmund's Westfalen stadion on 16 May 2001. Just as in 1976, the last time the Reds had won the trophy, Liverpool had overcome Barcelona to reach the final.

With two trophies already in the bag, the Reds were confident of clinching a treble. The stadium was packed with Liverpool fans, who must have outnumbered their Spanish counterparts two to one. This was the Reds' first European final in 16 years.

Alaves, on the other hand, were in their first European final. They were clearly overawed in the opening stages and Liverpool took just three minutes to take the lead through a header from the completely unmarked Markus Babbel.

On the quarter-hour mark they were two up through Steven Gerrard and it was starting to look like a stroll in the park. Alaves were rocking and the manager decided to make a bold early substitution in the 22nd minute, replacing defender Dan Eggen with a striker, Ivan Alonso.

It paid off almost immediately with the Spaniards grabbing a goal back on 26 minutes through Alonso. Not even half an hour gone and three goals scored in a major European final. The scene was set for an absolute classic.

Alaves were no pub team, as Alan Hansen would suggest in commentary, and the goal gave them a huge lift. They were now on the front foot and were giving Liverpool a stern examination. But for a brilliant double save by Sander Westerweld, first from Javi Moreno and then from Ivan Tomic, the Spaniards would have drawn level on 35 minutes.

To the relief of the supporters, Liverpool grabbed a third just five minutes later thanks to a penalty scored by Gary McAllister. At half-time the score looked comfortable but in reality this game was just getting started.

Within five minutes of the restart Alaves were level thanks to two goals from Javi Moreno. This was turning into an epic encounter with supporters unable to believe what they were seeing.

Houllier decided to throw the dice on 64 minutes, bringing on Robbie Fowler for Emile Heskey. It took Fowler just eight minutes to put Liverpool back in front. Surely now the Reds would see it out.

Alaves weren't lying down and laid siege to Liverpool's goal. They even had a penalty appeal waved away. With just two minutes left on the clock, Houllier's men looked to have done enough when the Spaniards served up another twist.

From a corner, Jordi Cruyff, son of former Barcelona great and Dutch international Johan, headed home the equaliser. With commentators searching the record books to see if this was the greatest ever UEFA Cup Final, the referee blew for full time to signal 30 minutes of extra time.

A new rule had been introduced into the competition, meaning that the first team to score in extra time won the game. This was referred to as the 'golden goal' rule and ironically Houllier had been a critic of the change.

Anything could happen in the next half-hour and the tension inside the stadium was palpable. Neither side gave any quarter as they traded blows, both desperately seeking the knockout punch.

Ivan Alonso had a goal disallowed. Then Fowler had an effort ruled out for offside. This could have gone either way, but perhaps the Spaniards' inexperience was the decisive factor. They had a player sent off in each period of extra time, reducing them to nine men.

The drama reached its peak as the teams were three minutes away from a penalty shootout. Liverpool won a free kick out wide, to the left of Alaves's goal, and McAllister stood over it. He swung it in and defender Delfi Geli headed into his own net.

Liverpool had gone 5-4 up and thanks to the 'golden goal' rule there was no opportunity for Alaves to reply. The cup was coming back to Anfield.

This is how David Lacey of the *Guardian* saw the game, 'So Liverpool have now created English football history by winning three cups in a season, and last night's triumph was achieved by a more adventurous approach than they had shown either in the Worthington Cup at the end of

February, when Birmingham City were beaten on penalties, or Saturday's FA Cup Final, when Michael Owen's two late goals scuppered Arsenal.'

It's true this was far from a typical Houllier performance. The Frenchman was famed for his team's defensive solidity. It was, though, the crowning moment of an incredible season and the red men would party all night long in Dortmund and back on Merseyside.

Gerard Houllier's treble heroes welcomed home: Liverpool's 2001 victory parade

Trophies are like buses: wait nearly ten years for one and three come at once. In 2001, Gerard Houllier led Liverpool to another treble-winning season. It was a truly remarkable year that added another League Cup, FA Cup and UEFA Cup to the club's trophy cabinet.

This was Houllier's second season in sole charge and his rebuilding job had delivered in spades. His team had defied expectations and gone on an incredible run in the cup competitions, but they had also secured third place in the Premier League, which meant a place in the Champions League awaited them the following season.

The supporters were jubilant and hopes that we were entering a glorious new period in our history began to rise.

Houllier had spent money in the transfer market, and the players he had brought in so far had gelled. Sami Hyypia and Stephane Henchoz gave the defence a solidity it had lacked previously and the likes of Markus Babbel and Christian Ziege brought class.

In midfield, the manager added Gary McAllister and Nick Barmby to Dietmar Hamann and Vladimir Smicer. Up front the experienced Jari Litmanen was added to the youth of Emile Heskey. All of this meant that Steven Gerrard,

Michael Owen and Danny Murphy were surrounded with quality and experience.

The *Liverpool Echo* declared 'Hip, Hip, Houllier' on its front page as it described the multitudes who turned out to welcome his all-conquering heroes home. Not since 1978, when Paisley's Reds had returned their second European Cup in as many years, had the city seen anything like this.

Official estimates put the numbers of those who turned out at nearly 500,000. The reality was that it may have been many more than that. Certainly, as the bus eased its way along the 17-mile route, huge crowds of cheering supporters, decked in red, clung to lampposts, hung out of windows and claimed whatever vantage point they could, just to catch a glimpse of the players and the cups. Young children – some on bikes, others on foot – gave the team an escort as they went.

There were also key points on the parade that saw huge crowds bring the bus to a standstill, with supporters desperate to see the players lift the trophies above their heads once more.

It was estimated that up to 100,000 gathered at the Jolly Miller and Pier Head alone. Local and national media covered the entire route and broadcast interviews with players and club officials on top of the bus.

McAllister in particular was simply blown away by the scale of the celebration. He spoke of the unprecedented nature of his team-mates' achievement and doubted whether it could ever be replicated again.

Club chairman David Moores talked about his love of the supporters and how the scenes made him want to do everything 'within his power to win things for them on a regular basis'. There was a carnival atmosphere to the whole event, evidenced by the fact that there was not a single arrest among half a million people.

This was what Reds supporters live for. It's what we dream of, a team that plays the Liverpool Way and brings championships home in May. No wonder the signage on the bus declared 'tell yer Ma we did it!' They certainly did.

Roma conquered as Gerard Houllier's triumphant return inspires Anfield to victory in 2002

On a night that Liverpool's assistant manager Phil Thompson would describe as 'one of the greatest in the football club's history', a frail-looking Houllier made his way to the Anfield dugout for the first time in five months.

The reaction of the crowd was thunderous and Liverpool's official TV station reported, 'The flags are out in force prior to kick-off and an impressive mosaic on the Kop heightens the sense of occasion. An electric atmosphere greets the players as they emerge on to the field and the noise inside Anfield reaches a crescendo with the first appearance of Gerard Houllier on the Liverpool bench since his heart operation.'

As the manager walked along the touchline he was embraced by his opposite number, Fabio Capello. All around there was a sense of history and portent and that simple walk from the dressing room to the dugout felt for all the world like a tactical masterstroke.

If Anfield was in need of inspiration, if the players needed a reason to fight, then Houllier had just delivered on both counts. Roma and their supporters wouldn't know what hit them.

It was all a far cry from the events of just five months earlier when the boss was rushed by ambulance to the nearby Royal Liverpool Hospital with a dissecting aortic aneurysm.

Liverpool were halfway through a game against Leeds United at the time and were a goal down. It was reported that before Gerard went under the anaesthetic, he had asked how the Reds got on.

He would have been relieved to hear that Danny Murphy had grabbed an equaliser in the second half but it would be months before the boss would be back in the hot seat. Thompson took the reins in Houllier's absence and did a great job, helping them to the second phase of the Champions League and keeping them in contention for the title.

Then, on 19 March 2002, the boss made the heroic decision to return. Thompson explained to the *Guardian* how it all happened, 'It was decided earlier in the afternoon and was special. He gave the players a pep talk at the hotel and we talked about it. Gerard said, "I fancy this!" It gave everyone a lift because Gerard inspires the players and the fans.'

He certainly did, with the atmosphere inside Anfield as good as anything that had gone before and the team sweating blood to get the win. It took just seven minutes for the Reds to break down Roma's defences.

Murphy was felled while attempting a shot from a John Arne Riise corner and the referee pointed to the spot. Up stepped Jari Litmanen to put Liverpool a goal up at the Anfield Road end.

An almighty roar shook the stadium, fists punched the air and supporters hugged and danced in the stands. The Italians were rocking, but somehow, they hung on until half-time and created a few chances. However, with Liverpool running into a Kop that was baying for blood, it would only be a matter of time before Roma would capitulate again.

The second goal came in the 63rd minute. Damiano Tommasi had brought down Litmanen, picking up a second yellow and receiving his marching orders. Murphy delivered a perfect cross from the free kick and Emile Heskey headed it home.

The roar that accompanied the ball hitting the net could be heard in the streets way beyond the stadium.

There was no way back for Capello's men and the Reds calmly saw out the remainder of the game. At full time the mood was jubilant with Liverpool through to the quarter-finals of the Champions League.

Thompson told LFCTV, 'This was a special atmosphere only Anfield can produce. This was Saint-Etienne part two and the fans cheered every tackle and it's one of the greatest nights in this football club's history.'

Capello admitted he had been outfoxed by Houllier's approach to the game, saying, 'I've never seen Liverpool play like this.' There was a real sense that the Reds could actually win the European Cup and the buzz around the ground as supporters poured out of Anfield and into the night, singing as they went, was intoxicating.

Alas, it wasn't to be, and this would prove to be one of the few remaining highlights of Houllier's reign.

Nevertheless, the night the Frenchman returned from his own personal battle to drive the Reds to victory will live long in the memory. Allez Les Rouges.

Neil Mellor in the realms of fantasy as Reds stun Arsenal with last kick of the game in 2004

Some moments in Liverpool's history are truly enormous. Often, they shape and define the club. Some concern trophies, heroic defeats, struggle and pain. Others are just joyous instances in time. They tell of unlikely heroes and unexpected victories. These singular gems are every bit as significant as all the rest.

This is the story of one such moment.

The 2004/05 season marked yet another changing of the guard at Anfield. The summer had seen the departure of

Michael Owen, who took up a new role on foreign shores as a bench-warmer at the Santiago Bernabeu in Madrid. In return Liverpool received a bag of magic beans and Antonio Nunez.

They would use those beans to slay the giants of Germany, Greece and Italy and they would use Nunez hardly ever. Still, he'll be able to tell his grandchildren he witnessed a miracle in Turkey.

In addition to Owen, Danny Murphy, Stephane Henchoz and Markus Babbel, who had all helped Liverpool secure a historic treble in 2001, departed along with their manager, Gerard Houllier.

The Reds replaced the Frenchman with a Spaniard, Rafa Benitez, and the Kop instantly warmed to the man whose unfashionable Valencia side had usurped both Barcelona and Madrid, winning two La Liga titles.

They would sing his name non-stop for about 20 minutes during one game in 2005. Of course, this season is best remembered for a certain game in Turkey, but long before that miraculous sunset Anfield would witness a fairytale worthy of any Boys' Own story.

On 28 November 2004, the 'Invincibles' of Arsenal visited Anfield. They boasted the likes of Sol Campbell, Robert Pires, Cesc Fabregas, Freddie Ljungberg, Patrick Vieira and Thierry Henry. Liverpool had Neil Mellor – he would be enough.

The Reds' league form hadn't been great up to this point. They were 13 games in and in fourth spot, 13 points off the top. Arsenal were second.

Liverpool had a decent spine, with Sami Hyypia, Jamie Carragher, Steven Gerrard and Xabi Alonso, but around the edges they oozed inexperience. In goal was Chris Kirkland and up front were two youngsters, who for all their promise were as green as the Anfield turf.

Florent Sinama-Pongolle and Neil Mellor certainly lacked experience and it felt like the Reds were hopelessly outgunned. As the game got under way the air of anxiety was palpable.

However, the Reds defied expectation and immediately took the game to the Gunners. For 40 minutes they attacked and late in the half they got their break.

Steve Finnan hit a long pass to Gerrard, who showed sublime vision by feeding Alonso, who drove a stunning shot beyond a despairing Jens Lehmann from the edge of the box.

The ground seemed to explode, then suddenly the half was over and the players left the field to rapturous applause. The joy was to be short-lived, though. Just 12 minutes after the Liverpool opener, a series of neat passes found Vieira in the box and he calmly slotted the ball past Kirkland.

It was like a gut punch and, in that moment, many inside Anfield would have gleefully taken the point. As the clock ran down, it seemed like that's exactly what they would get.

Cue Neil Mellor.

As the game moved into added time, the ball was down in the Reds' corner, between the Main Stand and the Anfield Road end. The referee had awarded Liverpool a free kick and Kirkland stood over the ball.

He probably should have hit it long to one of the Kop corner flags, allowing a forward to eat up the remaining time. Instead he launched it down the middle.

The ball seemed to hang in the air for an age. Harry Kewell and Sol Campbell both jumped for it and somehow it fell to Mellor. He looked out on his feet and roughly 30 yards from goal.

Ahead of him was a sea of players and the goal must have shrunk before his eyes. Time was up and somewhere in his tired mind a voice screamed shoot. He swung his leg at the ball and incredibly it flew into the net.

The roar that followed was ear-splitting. People would leap in the air and some would fall over their seats still hugging the person next to them. There was dancing in the stands and on the pitch the players piled on top of the unlikely hero.

Mellor had scored a winner in front of the Kop with literally the last kick of the game – it simply does not get better than that. The look on Sol Campbell's face spoke volumes. In such moments legends are created.

The night the famous Rafa Benitez went the pub to see the lads

Stories of Liverpool players and managers mingling freely with the supporters, drinking beer and swapping stories normally belong in a bygone age. However, in 2005 with Liverpool en route to a remarkable fifth European Cup, the famous Rafa Benitez went the pub to see the lads and the girls too.

This is what happened.

On Tuesday, 9 March 2005 the team were staying in the Hyatt Hotel in Cologne ahead of the Champions League last-16 second leg against Bayer Leverkusen on the Wednesday. They had arrived early in the day and stories suggest that a small group of fans spotted the boss outside the hotel.

'See yer in the pub later Rafa,' they shouted.

To their amazement, he replied, 'Yes.' Maybe he was being polite, but later on that night something amazing happened.

The management team wanted to watch the second half of Chelsea against Barcelona. The hotel had Manchester United versus AC Milan on. So, at half-time, Rafa, Pako

Ayestaran and Alex Miller decided to walk down the road to Jameson's Irish bar.

It turned out that the pub was also showing the United game, but that wasn't the only surprise awaiting the coaching team. The number of supporters estimated to be inside the bar that night varies, depending on who you speak to. Some say 200. However, judging by the number of fans who claim to have been there, it may be closer to 2,000.

Rumours had been circulating around the place for a while that Rafa was outside. You can imagine some supporters laughing it off as a wind-up, but then the door opened and in he walked.

At that moment Hernan Crespo scored against United and the bar erupted. The noise must have been deafening. Rafa had expected there to be a few people inside, but was completely blown away by the sight that greeted him.

He gave an interview to the club's website a few days later. This is how he described the incident, 'The atmosphere was amazing, and we could really feel it. Normally we only see or hear them in the stands, so it was fantastic to meet them close up.

'I was not expecting there to be so many Liverpool fans in Germany. Just before going into the Irish bar we thought there might be some fans in there but not that many!

'We tried to sneak in without anyone noticing and I said to the first fan, "Ssshhhhh, be quiet," but next thing the whole place erupted and everyone was singing "Rafa-Rafa-Benitez".'

The boss stayed for almost an hour, posing for photos, shaking hands and chatting to supporters. It's doubtful he got a round in, but then this was a man who, after 25 May 2005, would never have to buy a drink in Liverpool again. The night also gave birth to a new Kop chant. There's a couple of versions out there, but this one sounds about right:

> The famous Rafa Benitez went the pub to see the lads ...
> The famous Rafa Benitez went the pub to see the lads ...
> The famous Rafa Benitez went the pub to see the lads ...
> And this is what he said 'FUCK OFF'
> Who's that team they call United?

Liverpool avoid a Greek tragedy as Steven Gerrard leaves Olympiakos in ruins

Liverpool's run to the Champions League Final in Istanbul in 2005 is the stuff of legend, but they would not have made it were it not for Steven Gerrard.

'I don't want to be waking up tomorrow morning in the UEFA Cup.'

That was the message from Gerrard to his team-mates on the eve of their final Champions League group game against Olympiakos, in 2004. The Reds had struggled in the competition thus far, losing two of their five matches. The defeats came against Monaco and the Greek champions.

The mathematics meant that to ensure their captain got his wish, they would have to win by two clear goals. The atmosphere going into the game was one of cautious expectation. There was a rebuilding job taking place and this was Rafa Benitez's honeymoon.

Still, with the Reds' stuttering league form, an injection of hope was badly needed. The Greek fans were in buoyant mood, perhaps sensing a historic victory at one of the great cathedrals of European football.

Liverpool, with Chris Kirkland in goal, Djimi Traore and Antonio Nunez outfield and the likes of Josemi and Salif Diao on the bench, probably didn't have them trembling.

The Greeks had overlooked Florent Sinama-Pongolle, Neil Mellor, Steven Gerrard and an ear-splitting performance from the Anfield crowd.

The names Sinama-Pongolle and Mellor will probably fade in the memories of Liverpool supporters as time passes. They shouldn't though. Their contribution to this game and the whole run to Istanbul is immeasurable.

In the opening exchanges the atmosphere was pulsating, and the team responded in energetic style.

Liverpool flew at the Greeks and a succession of corners led to a disallowed goal from Milan Baros and a header wide from Sami Hyypia.

Liverpool soon faded though and Olympiakos got hold of the game thanks to their superstar player, Rivaldo. The Brazilian went close with one effort that sailed over the bar, taking a deflection off the top of Gerrard's head on the way. It would prove to be an early sighter.

On 26 minutes the Greeks won a free kick after the Brazilian was brought down by Hyypia about 20 yards from goal. The Finn had no choice as Rivaldo had already glided past four Liverpool players unopposed.

The resultant strike was a thing of beauty but Liverpool's wall had simply wilted in the face of it. Kirkland had no chance whatsoever. It was a huge body blow and it left the Reds needing three to qualify for the knockout round.

It was stick-or-twist time for Benitez at half-time. He opted for the latter, bringing on Sinama-Pongolle for Traore. Within two minutes the young Frenchman had dragged the Reds back into the game, converting Harry Kewell's cross at the near post. It was game on.

The crowd, who had been subdued by Rivaldo's earlier strike, burst into life. However, the Greeks wouldn't lie down and the game got physical with some hefty challenges going in, along with several off-the-ball incidents. This only served to crank up the noise levels in the stands.

Gerrard responded in typical style. He was all over the pitch, winning tackles and driving the team forward.

In the stands time seemed to have no meaning, as the growing sense that something magical was about to happen took hold. The skipper had a goal ruled out and the crowd's fury reached fever pitch.

This was turning into a classic that had the potential to rewrite history books, if only Liverpool could grab another. They did with just ten minutes left.

With the game eating up the clock, Benitez decided to roll the dice once more. He took Baros off, sending on another youngster in Mellor.

It took him two minutes to lash in Liverpool's second. Anfield exploded in colour and noise. The sound was incredible, and the Greeks in the Anfield Road end went quiet. Once again the Spaniard's substitution had paid instant dividends. The stage was now set for one of the most memorable moments in the club's history. Anyone who has watched the video will know these words by heart.

'Mellor, lovely cushioned header to Gerraaaaaaaaaard!' The camera is shaking, or is it the ground? 'Oooooooh you beauty! What a hit son, what a hit!'

They may have been the greatest words Andy Gray ever uttered. They describe perfectly the sumptuous quality of a captain's goal.

The Reds were through and the rest is wonderful, magical history. Gerrard would later describe it as the most important goal of his Liverpool career. But that night was about more than that, it was about the waking of a slumbering giant.

I'll leave the last words to stadium announcer George Sephton, who spoke to the departing Liverpool supporters,

'Thank you for the greatest night in more than 40 years of working for this club.'

Against all odds Liverpool, the players, manager and supporters, had delivered. Together that trinity would prove an unstoppable force in Europe that season.

Liverpool and Juventus; an encounter in memory and friendship

Twenty years on from the horror and devastation of Heysel, Liverpool and Juventus went head-to-head once more in European competition. The scene this time was Anfield and the occasion a Champions League quarter-final first leg.

Much had changed in football since that fateful day in 1985. However, for some among the visiting contingent the wounds still run deep.

The two clubs had made plans to publicly acknowledge the historic nature of the occasion. The *Liverpool Echo* ran a front-page apology, which was widely praised by the Italian media. And during a minute's silence to honour the 39 who died at Heysel, as well as Pope John Paul II, the Kop held aloft a mosaic that spelled out Amicizia (Friendship).

It was warmly welcomed by most Italian supporters but some chose to turn their backs. Their continued anger was understandable but Liverpool's fans hoped they had conveyed their sorrow and respect for those who had simply gone to a football match and not returned home.

The game itself got off to a frantic start. Future England manager Fabio Capello's men seemed ill-prepared to deal with a highly charged Anfield.

Gazetta dello Sport had this to say about the Reds' blistering opening, 'The fantastic atmosphere of Anfield was like an electric shock for the Liverpool players, who started the match at an astonishing tempo. They seemed unstoppable, while the Juventus players used neither their brains nor their legs.'

Juventus were in trouble almost from the kick-off. Brazilian midfielder Emerson slipped and gifted possession to Milan Baros, who charged at goal, winning the Reds a corner. Wave after wave of Liverpool attacks crashed on to the visitors' goal as the Italians struggled to deal with the pressure.

Their resolve lasted just nine minutes. Baros won another corner and from the resulting in-swinger, Sami Hyypia drove home with his left foot. Gianluigi Buffon could do nothing to stop it.

Inside the Kop, it had felt like being in a pressure cooker. As the ball hit the net it was as if the lid had come off. Sheer pandemonium broke out – none of us could believe what we were witnessing.

Barry Glendenning, updating in the *Guardian*'s live blog, wrote this, 'Liverpool's supporters are ecstatic, bellowing out a rousing rendition of "The Fields of Athenry", before singing manager Rafa Benitez's name to the tune of "La Bamba". Juventus, meanwhile, are totally rattled. They've failed to settle, and their defence is looking very shaky indeed.'

If we were ecstatic at going a goal in front, we entered dreamland in the 24th minute. Anthony Le Tallec, one of Gerard Houllier's 'gems', crossed the ball in from the right. It seemed to take a deflection and was met by Luis Garcia about 20 yards from goal.

The Spaniard unleashed a peach of a volley which looped over Buffon and nestled in the back of the net. Cue more unadulterated joy. The calmest man in the stadium was Rafa Benitez, his face an intense picture of concentration.

The Reds would make it to half-time two goals to the good. Nobody had given them a chance when the draw was made. Juventus were one of the strongest teams in Europe, had won their domestic league and, in Capello, had a tactical genius in the dugout. Liverpool had Rafa, though, and the Kop. That would prove decisive.

But Liverpool never do things the easy way and, true to form, they gifted Juve an away goal just after the hour mark. A tame Fabio Cannavaro header should have been easy to deal with but Scott Carson fumbled the ball into his own goal.

It set up a tense finale but the Reds hung on for a deserved home win. The second leg in Italy was a defensive masterclass by Benitez. Liverpool secured a goalless draw, booking a semi-final encounter with Jose Mourinho's Chelsea.

Luis Garcia's 'ghost goal' haunts Mourinho as Liverpool ascend to heaven

On the road to Istanbul, Liverpool had dispensed with the champions of Greece, Germany and Italy. Now it was the turn of the English champions. The first leg, at Stamford Bridge, had been a tense goalless draw and Liverpool relished the return at Anfield, where the fans could create some magic.

Anyone lucky enough to be there will remember this night forever. Anfield has witnessed some famous European nights down the years, but the semi-final against Chelsea in May 2005 is arguably the greatest of them all.

The call had gone out, urging supporters to get into the ground early to generate a special atmosphere. With a full 40 minutes to go until kick-off the noise inside the famous old stadium was deafening.

I remember walking through the turnstiles and feeling the atmosphere. It crackled and fizzed and, as I climbed the steps to my seat, the entire concourse under the Kop were singing.

This is how Jamie Carragher saw it, 'Even when we were warming up 40 minutes before the game, the crowd was as noisy as it's been for a long time. Normally you can hear DJ George playing his records, but even he was drowned out by the singing.'

By the time the game got under way, most of us were hoarse, others were exhausted, such was the raw energy expended. In all my years of watching Liverpool, I had never experienced such a sense of anticipation and nervous energy.

Rumours had swirled around Liverpool that Chelsea were so confident of progress they had booked the Blue Bar, on the Albert Dock, for their celebration. Everyone in the ground was determined to do their bit to wreck the party.

Chelsea won the toss and arrogantly decided to turn the Reds around. This meant Liverpool would be attacking the Kop end in the first half.

The opening minutes were a blur, with most supporters trying to catch their breath after almost an hour of constant singing. They would get no respite though, as in the third minute pandemonium broke out.

Milan Baros raced into the box, chasing a through ball from Steven Gerrard. He attempted to lob the advancing Petr Cech but was clearly brought down by the goalkeeper. A huge roar went up as Kopites screamed for a penalty.

Then suddenly Luis Garcia emerged and poked the ball towards the goal. William Gallas lunged at it, desperately trying to hook it clear, but Garcia wheeled away in celebration. Had the ball crossed the line?

Confusion reigned for a couple of seconds as nobody could work out if it was a goal or not. Then came an avalanche of noise as the referee indicated it was. Chelsea protested but Lubos Michel, the Slovakian official, was adamant – as he later recalled, 'I believe Chelsea would have preferred the goal to count rather than face a penalty with just ten men for the rest of the game. If my assistant referee had not signalled a goal, I would have given a penalty and sent off goalkeeper Petr Cech.'

Michel also commented on how the noise levels interfered with his ability to communicate with his linesman, 'I have refereed at places like Barcelona, Ibrox, Manchester United and Arsenal. But I've never in my life been involved in such an atmosphere. It was incredible.'

Liverpool had scored very early, though, and I would eat through my fingernails as the two teams sparred for another 93 minutes. When the fourth official indicated six minutes of added time it almost finished half the Kop off. Where did they get six minutes from?

Then there was a moment of sheer panic. The game was end-to-end and Djibril Cisse missed a chance to kill it off. Then Chelsea advanced and suddenly the ball fell to Eidur Gudjohnsen in the Reds' penalty area.

With the goal at his mercy, the Kop held its breath. Had he scored it would have been Chelsea in the final and I may have collapsed. Somehow, though, he missed, and the ball skidded past Jerzy Dudek's far post. The slightest deflection would have diverted it into the net but miraculously it went out for a goal kick.

John Arne Riise summed up how every Red was feeling in that moment, 'When Gudjohnsen had that chance at the end I was shitting myself. If he had scored I would have started crying. I would have retired on the spot or maybe even shot myself.'

Fortunately that wasn't necessary. The danger had passed and Liverpool were seconds from victory.

Dudek launched the ball upfield. Nobody could hear the final whistle but the sight of the Liverpool players throwing their arms in the air caused an explosion of noise the likes of which Anfield had never heard before.

All around me was an ecstasy of stumbling and falling as we hugged and danced. I remember tumbling backwards, my back crashing against my seat. I felt nothing until the following day, not that I cared. Liverpool were going to Istanbul and Chelsea would have to cancel their party.

Mourinho would complain about Garcia's 'ghost goal' for years to come, but even he had to admit that he had 'felt the power of Anfield and it was magnificent'.

Twenty-two days later, in Istanbul, Liverpool would ascend the steps of heaven.

Six minutes that shook football: Liverpool's magical night on the Bosphorus in 2005

On 25 May 2005, Rafa Benitez steered Liverpool to the biggest game in world club football, at the Ataturk Stadium in Istanbul. It was his first season in charge and standing in his way was arguably the best team in Europe, AC Milan. The game would become a seismic moment in the history of Liverpool Football Club.

Thousands of Reds supporters descended on the Turkish capital. Just as generations before them had done, they came from all corners of the world, by plane, train and automobile.

They outnumbered the Italians three to one. Back home, Liverpool was a city enthralled. Reds spent anxious hours in the build-up praying and running through pre-match rituals. Some anaesthetised themselves with alcohol. Meanwhile, Evertonians hoped for a Milan win.

Defeat in Turkey would have turned a season of promise into one of ultimate failure. Victory would restore the club to its European throne. The players and the manager would become immortals.

Steven Gerrard spoke of his desperation to lift 'Old Big Ears' as club captain. To do so, as a Scouser, would mirror a feat last achieved by Phil Thompson in 1981.

Jamie Carragher joked of going on an almighty bender if Liverpool won. Reds everywhere stood ready to join him. However, the first half of the game would leave many in Turkey wishing they followed a different sport.

At home, Reds watched that first 45 minutes in horror, through trembling fingers. AC Milan were simply majestic. It was a masterclass of the beautiful game and Liverpool were mere understudies. Within a minute Paolo Maldini put his team a goal up after Djimi Traore had conceded an early free kick.

Rafa's men held on for 38 minutes but then the floodgates opened. A one-goal deficit would have felt like a victory given the Italians' dominance but Liverpool gave themselves an Everest to climb in that second period.

Hernan Crespo was the destroyer, grabbing a further two goals in the last six minutes of the half. Andy Gray, commentating, declared, 'Game well and truly over!' He added, 'I hate saying that.' Yeah, right.

Back home, Everton supporters reached for their phones and filled their Red counterparts' inboxes with cruel text messages. Liverpool fans agonised over watching what might become a historic scoreline or turning the telly over.

In Turkey, a few Reds left the ground in tears. In the Italian end the Milan fans were jubilant and Carlo Ancelotti struggled to quell his team's sense of triumphalism.

Meanwhile, in the remaining two-thirds of the stadium someone started singing 'You'll Never Walk Alone'. At first it was a whisper, but it soon grew into a deafening chorus. Legend says that the players heard it and it lifted them to greatness.

What followed was six minutes that shook the world of football. This time though, it was the Reds dishing out the lessons. Ancelotti chewing furiously in front of a backdrop of Liverpool supporters in full fury is an enduring image. His look of disbelief told of a fightback so unexpected, so miraculous that songs will be sung about it for as long as football is played.

Gerrard's thumping header smashed the first hole in Milan's defences. Who can forget the commentator's words, 'Hello, hello,' as the Reds' skipper waved his arms at the Liverpool supporters, urging them to raise their game to new levels.

Then came Vladimir Smicer's strike. He picked the ball up 25 yards from goal and supporters yelled, 'Don't shoot!' He ignored them all and brought the tie to 3-2.

With 34 minutes remaining it was game well and truly back on, eh Andy? Fingernails were chewed, and foreheads rubbed in disbelief, while in the stands Liverpool supporters began to dream. Then, in the 59th minute, Liverpool won a penalty.

Back home, family members who had retired to their gardens at half-time were banished from returning in case they jinxed the comeback. Xabi Alonso first missed, and then hammered in the rebound. Across the world pandemonium ensued. The impossible had been achieved and AC Milan were rocking.

Everything else that followed pales by comparison with those glorious six minutes in the Ataturk. Dudek's miracle save, Carragher's heroics and Shevchenko's inexplicable penalty miss all play second fiddle to that astonishing fightback.

Within 360 seconds, Liverpool Football Club and its supporters had dragged themselves from the abyss. They would emerge with their hero holding aloft the greatest prize of all.

Milan's Kaka later summed up this miracle perfectly, telling Radio Cope in 2016, 'I still can't understand how we managed to lose that game. We had the best defenders in the world in that team.

'Our back four was Cafu, Jaap Stam, Alessandro Nesta and Paolo Maldini but we still let in three goals in six minutes. Something amazing happened that can't be explained.'

Oh yes, it can. It happened because we are Liverpool.

The mother of all homecomings in a season of miracles – Liverpool's 2005 Champions League parade

In the history of Liverpool Football Club, the year 2005 is a story of miraculous feats of sporting prowess, unshakeable belief, unbelievable support and more than a few miracles. This is a story that owes so much more to the journey than it does to the destination.

However, we'll cover that elsewhere. For this moment in the club's 125-year history we'll jump to the last page and pay homage to one of the greatest celebrations the city of Liverpool has ever seen.

It was a night when the pubs were drunk dry, and eateries ran out of food. More than a million people packed out the city centre on Thursday, 26 May 2005. When you consider that many Reds fans were still in Turkey and others had lined the route throughout the city, then you get an idea of the scale of this event.

I was among thousands of fans at the Jolly Miller on Queens Drive as the team bus went by. The look of disbelief on the faces of the likes of Xabi Alonso was a sight to behold. He had clearly never witnessed such adulation.

TV crews were everywhere, and radio journalists were wandering among the throng, attempting to grab snippets of excited fans waiting to see their heroes. The sense of history was palpable and the sheer joy in the crowd filled your heart to bursting.

Fathers and mothers had brought children, too young to remember the glory days, to witness scenes they had once taken for granted. Their children would now have their own stories to tell.

I was one of them and I'd been at many homecomings, especially in 1977, '78, '81 and '84. They were all amazing experiences, but they paled in comparison to the one in 2005. I was desperate to give my kids a taste of the joy I had known.

The difference between this and all the others though was the sheer unexpectedness of it, not to mention the monumental scale of the achievement. Maybe it felt like that in 1977, when Liverpool won their first European Cup, but even then, the city had grown accustomed to glory.

In 2005 Merseyside came out to welcome back players who had defied all the odds, not just in a final, but all the way through the competition. They had no right to be bringing that cup home, but they had earned it in fine style. The whole fan base wanted to thank them for it.

Few will forget the team bus edging its way slowly through the city streets, as hordes of jubilant supporters ran alongside it. Fans were perching on lampposts, hanging out of windows, leaning over bridges and risking life and limb in all manner of vantage points, just to get a glimpse of the heroes of Istanbul.

Then there's the sound of hundreds of thousands of supporters at St George's Hall, greeting the news that the team would be two hours late, with chants of '20 years, so

241

we'll wait two hours', a reference to their two-decades' long wait for a European Cup.

For me though, the abiding and most pleasurable memory of that night was standing outside the Jolly Miller on Queens Drive, with my daughters and son, welcoming that team home. My kids had been too young to fully appreciate Gerard Houllier's treble-winning season in 2001 and they had certainly never witnessed anything like the success I had down the years.

Seeing their excitement as the bus went by and hearing them shout and cheer brought tears to my eyes. They were a new generation baptised in glory. That might have been the greatest and most lasting of all the miracles of Istanbul.

Jamie Carragher almost loses his cornflakes as Steven Gerrard rejects Chelsea gold

It's July 2005, and just two months earlier a Steven Gerrard-inspired Liverpool had rescued victory from the jaws of defeat in Istanbul. Now, the club were on the brink of doing the exact opposite in terms of tying their heroic captain down to a new contract.

It was all a far cry from the interview Stevie had given in the immediate aftermath of Liverpool's European triumph over AC Milan. 'How could I leave after a night like this?' asked a joyous Gerrard. It was the equivalent of an open goal for the Reds' chief executive, Rick Parry.

Gerrard had been constantly linked with a move to Chelsea all season. In truth, he would have graced any team in world football.

We now know that the likes of Frank Lampard and John Terry had been bending the Reds' number eight's ear while on international duty, and Jose Mourinho clearly coveted the player. Now all that seemed behind us.

All Parry had to do was place that contract in front of his captain the moment that the plane touched down at Liverpool John Lennon Airport. Instead, he dithered. Maybe he was overly confident; perhaps he was reassured by Gerrard's positive comments.

Whatever the reason, Parry's prevarication unsettled the player.

The longer the saga went on, the more the speculation about Stevie's future increased. The famous 'sources close to the player' began briefing that he was unhappy, convinced the club wanted to sell him to raise cash for purchases.

Supporters went into meltdown with stories flying around that he was about to hand in a transfer request.

Rafa Benitez had always maintained an arm's length relationship with his captain. This was simply Rafa's way and it was a far cry from the arm-around-the-shoulder approach of his predecessor, Gerard Houllier.

Nevertheless, the Spaniard made a very public appeal to Gerrard to stay, stating he could have any role at the club he desired, including chief scout if he wanted it. The latter was an apparent reference to the player's expressed concern about the calibre of players the club was pursuing.

The whole sorry saga reached its nadir with Gerrard handing in a transfer request, immediately followed by a £32m bid from Chelsea. There was an air of choreography to events and it all left a bad taste in the mouth.

Sky Sports News immediately set up camp outside Anfield and even goaded some foolish kids into burning a replica of Gerrard's shirt. How embarrassing.

How had it come to this and how distant did those memories of the Ataturk seem? Parry was stung into a response, saying, 'I can confirm we have had a bid from Chelsea and that it will be rejected by us.'

Rafa echoed this saying, 'We don't need more money – we don't need to sell Stevie. My idea is that we want him to stay – that is what the chief executive and the board all want. We will talk with the player and the agent and we will try to find a solution. We will try right until the end.'

Unfortunately Gerrard's agents were having none of it and said that any offer by Liverpool would be 'too little too late and will be rejected'. A parting seemed inevitable and as Reds settled down for bed on 5 July the whole episode was a complete nightmare.

However, just as the second half in Turkey had produced a miraculous comeback, so did the morning of 6 July. And as Jamie Carragher sat watching Sky Sports News while tucking into his cornflakes, he watched as a smiling Rick Parry walked through the car park at the back of the Main Stand.

A gleeful journalist approached him and asked for an update. Parry simply replied calmly, 'Steven's decided to stay.' Apparently, his team-mate almost spat his breakfast at the TV screen. There are many rumours, mostly started by Evertonians, as to what prompted this last-minute U-turn. I prefer the explanation given by Stevie himself, 'No amount of honours won with any other club could ever mean as much as one won with Liverpool.'

That'll do for us, Stevie.

The Second Coming: Robbie Fowler's Anfield return in 2006

It is often said that you should never go back, but Robbie Fowler's return to Liverpool in 2006 provided the striker a heart-warming second coming.

Fowler burst on to the scene at Anfield as an 18-year-old prodigy in 1993. In just eight years he had replaced Ian Rush and amassed 236 Premier League appearances, scoring 120 times and winning five major honours. He was, at his peak, regarded as the most natural finisher in the game.

Fowler, or God as the fans called him, held the record for the fastest hat-trick in Premier League history, after a five-minute demolition of Arsenal in 1994. He was also a prolific marksman, becoming the only player to notch over 30 goals in his first three full seasons in English football.

Robbie was also a one-off in more than a footballing sense. In another game against the Gunners, he was awarded a dubious penalty after David Seaman was adjudged to have fouled him in the penalty area.

Instead of keeping quiet and burying the opportunity, he protested the goalkeeper's innocence and deliberately missed his spot-kick. Fortunately, Jason McAteer tapped in the rebound.

On another occasion, he courted controversy with football officials with his blatant support for striking dock workers in Liverpool. Then there was his now-legendary goading of Everton supporters after scoring in a Merseyside derby at Anfield.

Blues supporters had spread rumours that Fowler was addicted to cocaine; it was, of course, nonsense. Hilariously, the striker would shove their spite right back down their throats in glorious fashion.

As soon as the ball hit the back of the net, Robbie ran along the touchline at the Anfield Road end, falling to his knees and pretending to snort the white chalk line.

Everton fans were apoplectic. Gerard Houllier's attempted explanation, claiming Fowler was imitating Rigobert Song eating the grass, was even funnier.

The whole episode summed Fowler up perfectly: little more than a supremely talented supporter on the pitch.

Therefore, it was inconceivable that Fowler and Liverpool could ever part. The idea that the club would ever countenance selling him was ridiculous, but they did.

Things began to sour at the start of the 2001/02 season, although there were rumours that all wasn't well before that with Robbie frequently playing second fiddle to Michael Owen.

Stories of a training-ground spat between Fowler and Phil Thompson were rife and a tense standoff emerged, as it was reported the player had refused to apologise.

Suddenly the likes of Lazio, Arsenal and Leeds were circling, with Arsenal players reportedly briefing that Fowler was nailed on to sign for them. In the end, he signed for David O'Leary's Leeds for a bargain £12m. His last game for Liverpool came against Sunderland, in which he was taken off at half-time, meaning he never got to say goodbye properly to the supporters.

Fowler managed just 30 appearances in two seasons at Leeds but still scored 14 times before moving to Manchester City. At Maine Road he played 80 times and averaged a goal every four games.

Fowler never lost his love for Liverpool, though. He was actually in the Ataturk Stadium, as a fan, on that incredible night in 2005. Then rumours began to emerge the following season that Rafa Benitez could be interested in bringing Fowler back.

It seemed almost too good to be true, until some respected journalists suggested that the story might have legs. Then, on 27 January 2006, it happened. God returned home for one last hurrah and a chance to say a proper farewell to the club he loved.

He signed his short-term contract without even looking at it, so eager was he to grasp this chance.

His first game back came at Anfield, against Birmingham City. He came on as a substitute for Peter Crouch. The roar inside the ground as he ran on the pitch had to be heard to be believed.

A huge banner read 'GOD NUMBER ELEVEN WELCOME BACK TO HEAVEN'.

His return almost had a fairytale ending, too. Late on he scored a spectacular overhead kick at the Kop end only to have it mysteriously ruled out.

His final game would also end in frustration. Rafa had promised to take Fowler off with just a few minutes left, affording the legend an ovation he richly deserved. He hadn't scored but the emotional outpouring from the crowd must have been incredible.

However, as soon as the player sat down, Liverpool won a penalty. Harry Kewell scored it but a sense of what might have been hung in the air.

At least Robbie and his family would get to say a proper goodbye to the people who idolised him with an end-of-season lap of honour.

The records will forever show that Fowler, the self-styled 'cheeky kid from Toxteth' who went on to become a god, scored a total of 183 goals in 369 games for Liverpool. Not bad Robbie, not bad at all.

The Gerrard Final

On 13 May 2006, just shy of the first anniversary of Liverpool's heroic comeback in Istanbul, Steven Gerrard once again inspired an incredible fightback in a cup final. This was a performance so immense that they named the game after him.

The Gerrard Final, as it is now known, ended with Rafa Benitez securing honours for the Reds for a second successive season. However, it will be the contribution of his captain that echoes down the years.

Liverpool had overcome Chelsea at Old Trafford in the semi-final. With West Ham the opponents in the final at Cardiff, many Reds felt the cup was in the bag. Rafa's team had conquered all of Europe, they never knew when they were beaten, and few really believed that the Londoners would be much of a match for the likes of Reina, Hyypia, Carragher, Alonso and of course Gerrard. They were.

Up front for Liverpool that day were Djibril Cisse and Peter Crouch. West Ham had Dean Ashton and Marlon Harewood. In the dugout for the Reds was a European Cup and La Liga winning manager; for West Ham there was Alan Pardew. It should have been a cakewalk. It wasn't.

The game got off to a terrible start in the 21st minute thanks to an own goal by Jamie Carragher. Alonso gave away possession in midfield and Dean Ashton delivered an unbelievable pass to Lionel Scaloni on the wing. The Argentine's pass was diverted past the despairing Pepe Reina by Carragher for the Hammers' opener.

Soon afterwards, Reina fumbled a Matthew Etherington shot, allowing Dean Ashton to put the ball in the net for 2-0. What should have been a parade was turning into a disaster and the West Ham fans were filling their end of the stadium with bubbles.

'Why do we always do this to ourselves?' was the prevailing mood among Liverpool fans, but few will have panicked. This was the same Liverpool who had laughed at requiring three goals in 45 minutes to get past Olympiakos and who had won the biggest prize in football after being three down at half-time.

In both of those games they had relied on their inspirational captain to pull them back from the brink. And in this one he came up trumps once again to drag his side back into the game, making a mug of Scaloni and setting up Cisse to smash the ball home. Just over half an hour had elapsed and three goals had been scored in what was an incredible opening to a cup final.

This was a barnstorming game and for the neutrals it must have been a delight to watch. For Liverpool fans, it was another cardio workout.

Crouch was next to put the ball in the net, only to see his 'equaliser' ruled out for offside. Hammers supporters celebrated like it was full time. Then Ashton almost restored West Ham's two-goal advantage but his shot went wide.

By half-time the players looked like they had run a marathon. It didn't seem possible that they could replicate their efforts in the second half. They did.

Just nine minutes after the restart Liverpool were level. The BBC described Liverpool's captain as 'unstoppable' and the West Ham defence must have agreed as he smashed home a Crouch knock-down to make it 2-2.

Yet again Liverpool had overcome seemingly insurmountable odds and once more, Steven Gerrard had ridden to the rescue. There seemed to be only one outcome and most believed that the Reds would go on to destroy their opponents. They didn't.

Barely ten minutes later West Ham were in front again through Paul Konchesky. The defender attempted a cross from the wing. It flew towards Reina's goal and with the Spanish goalkeeper back-pedalling furiously the ball dropped over him and ended up in the back of the net. It was a hammer blow.

West Ham held out and with the game heading into injury time, a famous victory for the Londoners seemed on the cards. However, against Liverpool, until that final whistle blew no team could rest on their laurels, especially with Gerrard in the team.

The captain was out on his feet when the ball came to him, fully 30 yards out. He didn't have the energy to surge forward into the box as he would normally do. Instead, he just unleashed a ferocious shot which sailed into the bottom corner; 3-3 and the travelling Reds went crazy.

'Is this the best FA Cup Final in history?' asked legendary BBC commentator John Motson. It was.

The Reds survived a couple of scares in extra time and penalties beckoned. There wasn't a Liverpool supporter anywhere in the world who would have doubted for a second that the cup was coming home to Anfield. West Ham probably believed it too.

Liverpool won the shootout 3-1 and of course, Gerrard scored one of them. This had been an incredible game watched all around the world. The *Liverpool Echo* reported how even West Ham supporters were seen applauding their Liverpool rivals outside the ground.

What a remarkable game and what an incredible team captained by an all-time great, in Stevie G. It's little wonder the encounter will always be referred to as the Gerrard Final.

Little Boy Blue and Z Cars at Anfield

Rhys Jones was a passionate Everton supporter and, like all of us, lived for his team. He had hopes and dreams, but they were ended in a senseless act of violence.

On 22 August 2007, Rhys, aged just 11 years old, was walking home from football practice in the Croxteth area of Liverpool when a youth on a mountain bike fired three shots with a handgun, murdering the young Evertonian.

It broke his family's hearts and the whole of Liverpool, red and blue, felt their pain. In times of tragedy, the people of this city gather at places of worship, the two great cathedrals, Anfield and Goodison.

Everton had already paid an emotional tribute to the young fan in a league game against Blackburn Rovers. His idols had laid flowers at the scene of his murder.

The murder of a young child transcends footballing rivalry and Liverpool supporters had also been deeply moved by the tragedy. All of us knew what it was like to follow your team. We all felt that common bond and of course, as human beings, we could all walk in his parents' shoes.

Liverpool were due to play a Champions League game against Toulouse at Anfield in midweek. It was the perfect opportunity for the club to offer its solidarity.

Tony Barrett, a lifelong Red and then a reporter for the *Liverpool Echo*, lobbied the club to pay its own tribute to the youngster and his family. His suggestion was that 'Z Cars', the tune that ushers the Blues on to the Goodison turf every home game, should be played at Anfield before kick-off.

The *Echo* reported that the club was also inundated by requests from Reds fans asking them to play the song. Rhys's uncle, Neil Jones, broke the news of the planned tribute to Rhys's parents. He spoke to the *Echo*, 'When I told them about the proposed tribute at Anfield, Melanie [Rhys's mother] said playing "Johnny Todd" at Anfield would be a unique event, a complete one-off, just like Rhys, and a fitting tribute to him as it was his favourite tune.

'She's also pretty sure he'll have a little mischievous grin on his face at the thought of being the cause of it.'

For that reason, if for no other, it was worth doing.

I was at that game. I stood in Block 109 of the Kop, facing the Main Stand. I saw Rhys's parents and brother brought on to the pitch. Rafa Benitez walked towards them and they embraced.

Then they stood on the touchline, holding hands, heads bowed. A garbled announcement explained what was about to happen, but there was no need. We all knew.

As the teams came out the tones of 'Johnny Todd', the theme to the TV show *Z Cars* thumped out at Anfield for the first time ever. The whole ground stood and applauded.

As the song finished, 'You'll Never Walk Alone' began and it seemed as if the Kop were singing it directly at the family. As it finished there was hardly a dry eye in the ground. I looked at my phone. It was full of text messages from Reds and Blues overwhelmed by the gesture.

Rhys's mum Melanie took great comfort from it and speaking to the *Echo*, she said, 'Liverpool were really amazing with us. They were fantastic from start to finish ... When we got out of the car, we were given a massive round of applause by everyone. It knocked us back. It was just the most amazing thing.

'When we got to pitchside, the noise was deafening. We couldn't even hear "Z Cars" being played but my brother assured me it was.'

Rest in peace, Little Boy Blue.

The birth of 'Spirit of Shankly', the first Liverpool Supporters' Union, in 2008

This moment in Liverpool's history is a story of resistance and protest, and of distant owners with scant regard for the concerns of supporters. It also marks a historic schism between the club and its supporters. It would end with one set of American owners replaced by another, after a tumultuous day in the High Court.

In 2007, Liverpool had been taken over by American investors who had 'come to win' and who spoke of how they understood the dreams and aspirations of its devoted followers. In truth they had purchased the club via a leveraged buyout.

Their intention was to use the profits of the club to pay off the loan they had taken out in order to buy it. What could possibly go wrong?

At first George Gillett and Tom Hicks were given a cautious welcome. However, the lessons of history had taught supporters to judge others by their actions, not their words.

Initial attempts at engagement were positive, but things soon went awry. It would eventually become clear that money and profit were the overriding concern for Hicks and Gillett.

There were promises of a new stadium, and spades in the ground within 60 days. What they delivered was the most expensive set of drawings ever made. Supporters soon realised that the club's manager, Rafa Benitez, was also unhappy and the Kop began chanting 'Liverpool Football Club, is in the wrong hands'.

With news of mounting debt and a lack of financial support for the manager, supporters' patience reached breaking point. In 2008, they convened a meeting in the Sandon pub, the historic birthplace of Liverpool Football Club. The players would change there before games in the late 19th century.

The room was a mixture of anger and despair, with fans venting their rage at the direction the club was taking. Calls for protests were met with mixed responses, with some opposed to protests at matches.

Initial chanting at the games, in opposition to the new owners, had been met with boos and jeers. However, the meeting still voted in favour of forming a Liverpool Supporters' Union.

Initially it was named 'Sons of Shankly', but soon 'Sons' was changed to 'Spirit'. A movement was born: Spirit of

Shankly (SOS). The organisation enjoyed great support locally and internationally, but some supporters criticised their approach.

The club's rivals in Manchester were having similar difficulties. Their supporters had rallied against the Glazer family and their campaign appeared slick and the organisation allegedly even had a CEO.

As Reds fans organised protests, boycotts and marches while wearing jeans and trainers, United's wore green-and-gold scarves as a mark of defiance. Some took to internet forums to criticise SOS.

A barrage of ridicule came their way on some forums and via social media. They were accused of not doing enough, then of going too far. They were called fools for thinking they could take on such a powerful foe, or condemned by some for damaging the very thing they were fighting to protect.

Eventually Hicks and Gillett were driven from the club, cursing the band of 'internet terrorists' who defeated them as they left. They were referring to SOS.

Their campaign, which involved bombarding e-mail servers of major banks, had even persuaded financial institutions not to lend the Americans money.

So, it was with great pleasure that SOS organised a busload of supporters who travelled to London to wave the Americans goodbye at the High Court.

In the early days of the FSG ownership, John W. Henry reportedly told representatives of the union that he would not be there if it wasn't for their actions.

Meanwhile, there are some United fans still wearing green-and-gold scarves, while the Glazers remain deeply ensconced.

What a story this is, a modern-day David and Goliath tale. It is a victory for the common supporter over big business. Not only did they fight off the club's owners – who were armed with expensive lawyers and deeper pockets – they ultimately proved their doubters wrong.

SOS set a benchmark for future supporter campaigns. They created a model for all fans looking to have a say in the clubs they love. They have scored victories on ticket pricing, organising a walk-out during games and are now recognised and engaged with by the club.

They may be a long way from achieving their ultimate aim of 'supporter ownership of Liverpool Football Club', but no one can doubt that supporter representation has never been higher on the political agenda.

We owe that to campaigning groups like Spirit of Shankly.

When Rafa's Reds crushed Real Madrid in a 2009 Anfield classic

Its 2009, the scene is a floodlit night at Anfield, the opponents are European royalty and Rafa Benitez's Liverpool are about to serve up a footballing lesson.

This was a time when the Reds were regulars in the knockout phase of the Champions League and were feared throughout Europe.

Anfield had a fearsome reputation that was well-earned. Chelsea could testify to that, succumbing to the cauldron of noise and passion in two semi-final encounters. Stories of teams falling apart under an intense barrage from the Kop are of course legendary.

However, none of that seemed to bother Real Madrid or the Spanish press.

Despite their team being a goal down from the first leg at the Santiago Bernabeu – thanks to a late Yossi Benayoun goal – and facing an intimidating away tie on Merseyside, Madrid newspaper *Marca* ran with a headline, 'This is Anfield, So What'.

It was like a red rag to a bull and with the Kop baying for blood and an energised Fernando Torres – a former hero of Real's rivals Atletico Madrid – only too eager to satiate their desire, Liverpool served up a footballing masterclass. Madrid simply wilted.

English newspaper the *Guardian* described the Reds' captain Steven Gerrard as a 'wrecking ball' who had turned Madrid to rubble. Liverpool, it said, were 'walking on air'.

It was the perfect description of the game with our inspirational number eight pulling the strings and orchestrating Torres's demolition of the enemy. This was a Madrid side filled with stars, such as Iker Casillas, Sergio Ramos, Wesley Sneijder, Raul, Arjen Robben and Gonzalo Higuaín. However, Rafa had constructed a formidable side himself. It included the likes of Pepe Reina, Alvaro Arbeloa, Xabi Alonso, Javier Mascherano and Fernando Torres, allied with Reds heroes Jamie Carragher and, of course, Steven Gerrard.

This was a real 'clash of the titans'.

From the kick-off Torres tormented his foe, scoring the first after just 16 minutes. The stadium practically lifted out of the earth, such was the explosion of joy as the ball hit the net. The Spaniard raced along the touchline, in front of the Madrid fans, tormenting them by gesturing to the name on his shirt.

Torres continued to ruffle feathers in the Madrid defence and in the 28th minute they gave away a soft penalty. Alonso sent a pass into the box which ricocheted off the chest of Arbeloa and it was adjudged to have struck the arm of Gabriel Heinze. It looked harsh, with the ball appearing to hit his shoulder instead. Nevertheless, the referee pointed to the spot. Up stepped Gerrard who slotted the ball home with aplomb.

Despite this apparent injustice, Liverpool were fully deserving of their half-time lead. Anfield simply popped and crackled with anticipation for the second half.

As the game resumed, it was clear Madrid were incapable of containing the Reds. Within just two minutes the home side were three up. Ryan Babel had the Spanish defence tied in knots on the left-hand side and his pass to Gerrard was volleyed into the back of the net.

This was effectively game over and Benitez would rub salt in his former club's wounds by taking his captain off and replacing him with rookie Jay Spearing in the 73rd minute. To heap misery on humiliation the game was wrapped up in the 89th minute with an Andrea Dossena goal sealing an emphatic 4-0 rout.

The victory started a sequence of results that would see Liverpool score 13 goals in three games. They followed this up with a 4-1 win at Old Trafford and a 5-0 demolition of Aston Villa at Anfield. They went close in the Premier League that season and ultimately bowed out in Europe at the hands of Chelsea after a thrilling 7-5 aggregate defeat in the quarter-final.

Regardless, this was undoubtedly a glorious period for Liverpool.

Old Trafford empties as Reds humiliate Manchester United

It's March 2009. Liverpool, under Rafa Benitez, are in imperious form and are about to face their arch-rivals, Manchester United, in a crucial game in the title race.

Just a few days earlier they had dispensed with the might of Real Madrid, winning 4-0 at Anfield. Fernando Torres, playing like a man possessed, had destroyed the Spanish giants. He would prove equally important in the encounter at Old Trafford.

This was a lunchtime kick-off and featured live on TV. Liverpool's XI featured Sami Hyypia, Jamie Carragher and Steven Gerrard, who were all veterans of that historic night in Istanbul. Since then Rafa had added Pepe Reina, Javier Mascherano and Torres, along with the relentless Dirk Kuyt.

United boasted a team of seasoned internationals and champions, with Edwin van der Sar, Rio Ferdinand, Wayne Rooney, Carlos Tevez and Cristiano Ronaldo lining up against the Reds.

This was a real clash of the titans, with little love lost on the pitch, in the stands or in the dugout.

For United fans, who had consoled themselves before the game by saying Madrid must have been rubbish because they had conceded a fourth to Italian defender Andrea Dossena, there was a special gift in the 90th minute.

This was truly poetic. Mind you, by then the Theatre of Screams was already half-empty. Liverpool suffered an early setback after 23 minutes though, going behind to a penalty, which Ronaldo dispatched. In typical fashion United sought to press for a second and Martin Skrtel broke up one attack by lumping a clearance upfield.

Nemanja Vidic looked favourite to get to it, but he inexplicably allowed the ball to bounce. Torres was on it like lightning, robbing the defender, before bearing down on goal.

He had a lot to do, but van der Sar had no chance as Fernando put the ball in the far corner; 1-1 and it was game on. In the away end, Liverpool were bouncing.

Things were about to get a whole lot better as the Spanish scorer turned provider.

With the clock ticking down towards half-time, Torres clipped a delightful through ball for Gerrard to chase and the Scouser got to the ball ahead of Patrice Evra.

Gerrard felt contact and went down in the box. The referee pointed immediately to the spot. The sight of Gerrard doing a starfish in the penalty area at Old Trafford was sublime; magical stuff.

Without an ounce of nerves, the captain stepped up and put Liverpool in front. It was perfect timing and probably swung the game decisively in favour of the visitors. Then came the sight of Stevie kissing the badge, and then the camera, gleefully mocking the Stretford End, all of which just added to the moment.

As the second half got under way, United rallied. Rooney found himself on the end of a Ronaldo cross at the far post but failed to profit. The Reds were holding firm through a mixture of fortune and hard work and soon United's fightback fizzled out.

Vidic was having a horrendous game already but it was about to get a whole lot worse. Outwitted by Gerrard, he allowed the number eight to race clear. Knowing he was beaten and certain Gerrard would fashion another goal, the defender dragged him back.

Gerrard went to ground, hands in the air, and the referee obliged with a red card. United were down to ten men and Liverpool had a free kick about 25 yards out.

Up stepped Fabio Aurelio. The Brazilian was quality but he was dogged by injuries. He put all of that aside though as he swept the ball into the net, to the astonishment of everyone watching.

Sir Alex Ferguson was stood on the touchline, his face turning a crimson shade of purple. The players danced on the pitch and in the away end it was pandemonium.

With just under a quarter of an hour to go, Old Trafford emptied.

And Liverpool were far from finished. As the game moved into the 90th minute, Reina punted the ball forward. Dossena, only on the pitch as a 68th-minute substitute for compatriot Albert Riera, somehow found the legs to chase it. The ball looped over his shoulder and he met it delightfully on the half-volley. It flew over the despairing van der Sar and into the net.

What was left of the Mancunian army held their heads in their hands, while Liverpool players danced on the pitch and the travelling Mersey hordes went crazy.

Mind you, United must have been pretty rubbish if Dossena could score past them, right?

Titanic struggle at Stamford Bridge sees Rafa Benitez's Liverpool bow out with honour

Between 2005 and 2010, Liverpool and Chelsea played out a fierce rivalry that would see them face each other in one cup final and three semi-finals. Amazingly, during this spell, Rafa Benitez's side had defeated Mourinho's Blues on their way to two Champions League finals, in Istanbul and Athens, and an FA Cup Final at Wembley.

However, in 2009, Liverpool bowed out of the Champions League at the quarter-final stage after a titanic and emotionally charged struggle at Stamford Bridge.

The game took place on 14 April 2009, the eve of the 20th anniversary of the Hillsborough disaster.

The Reds had lost the first leg 3-1 at Anfield. They would need a miracle if they were to progress, and they were at a ground where they had tasted so little recent success.

Still, such was the European pedigree of Rafa's Reds that many supporters felt they could pull it off. History will show that Chelsea ultimately prevailed but Liverpool would leave the tournament with their heads held high.

Without their inspirational captain, Steven Gerrard, Liverpool were led by Jamie Carragher. In goal was Pepe Reina, Xabi Alonso and Javier Mascherano patrolled the midfield, and up front were Fernando Torres and Dirk Kuyt.

However, it was a piece of Brazilian magic that set Liverpool on their way and left many Reds feeling that the impossible could once again be achieved.

In the 19th minute, Liverpool won a free kick about 20 yards out. Fabio Aurelio stood over it and the Chelsea defence jostled for position with the Liverpool attack. Everyone expected the Brazilian to whip in a cross.

However, the angle was so inviting and goalkeeper Petr Cech had left his near post unguarded. Fabio opted to shoot and the ball went straight in. The Liverpool end went crazy and on the pitch the players danced with joy.

Just nine minutes later the fans' hopes soared even higher as the team won a penalty. Alonso put it away to level the tie numerically, but Chelsea had three away goals so Liverpool needed one more to avoid an exit.

As the whistle sounded for half-time it seemed destiny was once more on the side of the Reds. However, three second-half goals from Drogba, Alex and Lampard had Chelsea firmly back in control by the 76th minute.

The score was 3-2 on the night and 6-3 on aggregate. It was a hammer blow and nobody would have blamed the players, who were out on their feet at this point, if they had just seen the game out without conceding again.

Instead they found it within themselves to mount yet another fightback. In the 81st minute Lucas levelled on the night and just two minutes later Kuyt put Liverpool 4-3 up.

One more goal would level the tie overall, with the Reds progressing thanks to their five away goals. The sense of anticipation in the away end was palpable. The panic in the Chelsea ranks would reach epidemic proportions. After all, Liverpool had form: they were Europe's comeback kings.

In the Champions League at least, they were also Mourinho's nemeses. They fought heroically until the last, but an 89th-minute Frank Lampard goal secured a 4-4 draw and the tie for Chelsea. The Reds were out but nobody was down.

If you're going to lose a game, at least leave the opponent knowing they've been in a fight. Liverpool had done just that.

The following day, on the 20th anniversary of the Hillsborough disaster, the *Liverpool Echo* declared, 'On a day when the Liverpool anthem "You'll Never Walk Alone" takes on even greater emotional significance, it is particularly apt that the club's players and supporters can hold their heads up high today.

'Last night, pride came after Liverpool's fall.

'Rafa Benitez's team produced one of the most heroic performances in the Reds' illustrious history as they came agonisingly close to conjuring up the kind of sensational result which would have stunned football.

'It is Chelsea who take their place in the last four of this season's Champions League, but it is Liverpool who again defied logic and who almost created a tale of the unexpected to rival even that which was written in Istanbul.'

Speaking for the Hillsborough families from the front of the Kop, at the 20th memorial service at Anfield, Trevor Hicks and Margaret Aspinall thanked Benitez and his players for their fighting spirit. 'You did us proud,' they said.

Now that is high praise indeed.

From Dubai to Texas and the sublime to the ridiculous: Liverpool's tortuous ownership saga

In January 2007, Liverpool Football Club seemed on the brink of a takeover by Dubai International Capital. The company claimed vast assets and held out the prospect of multi-million-pound investment in the playing squad.

Chairman David Moores had recognised that he was no longer able to compete with the new breed of billionaire football owners. Roman Abramovich's takeover at Chelsea had set a new benchmark in spending and the days of the wealthy local fan owning their club were over.

Moores, as majority shareholder, would grant DIC exclusivity, allowing them to carry out due diligence. However, he would become uneasy about the length of time it took and also cited difficulties in communicating with them. Then there was the alleged discovery of a document outlining the company's exit strategy from Liverpool.

DIC eventually made an offer to the club and Moores prevaricated, asking for more time to consider it.

He was also keen to explore a rival offer from American George Gillett. His request was not well received and on 31 January the proposed deal collapsed. DIC's statement read:

'Dubai International Capital LLC today announces that it has decided to end negotiations with Liverpool FC and Athletic Grounds plc about a possible investment in the club.'

A spokesman for the Dubai investors would later accuse Moores of suffering a 'mental aberration'. Moores said he was acting in the best interests of the club. Whatever his reasons, Reds supporters were furious and internet forums went into meltdown.

Soon news of Gillett's bid emerged, along with the fact that this rival offer would net Moores £8m more than the Dubai bid. To add salt to already painful wounds the

DIC chief executive was a reputed Liverpool supporter and issued this statement, 'Liverpool ... exists to win things for its supporters. It deserves to be in the hands of people who support it, who understand its history and legend and who share the enthusiasm and passion of its fans ... As fans, we hope that the new owners would share the same vision as we had for LFC.'

The overwhelming feeling that the club had somehow snatched defeat from the jaws of victory took hold. There was a real sense of chaos and genuine fear for the future. In that context, the arrival of Gillett and Tom Hicks was greeted with a measure of relief by some.

The two American owners' offer of £174.1m was formally accepted on 6 February 2007. In truth, they hadn't used a penny of their own cash.

Instead they borrowed the money, which they would later load on to the club's debt. The overall loan covered the purchase price for the club, £11m for legal fees, £44.8m to take over the club's debt and £70m for a stadium they would never build. In all the club owed almost £300m to the banks.

This was nothing more than a confidence trick. Supporters were justifiably angry with Moores, who they felt had at best been duped. At worst, many suspected he had chosen the two hucksters for personal gain.

The Americans came armed with grandiose plans and huge promises, including this one from Tom Hicks, 'We are going to build the finest team for the finest stadium in the Premier League and that is Liverpool.'

It was no more than hot air. However, the quote that would come to define their era would be this one, uttered by Gillett, 'The shovel needs to be in the ground in the next 60 days.'

Such a self-imposed benchmark was foolhardy, particularly because neither he nor Hicks possessed the wherewithal to deliver on it. Gillett was also responsible for the immortal line, which promised that 'if Rafa wanted to buy Snoogy Doogy we would back him'.

Unfortunately, in no time Hicks was telling the boss to quit asking for more players and concentrate on coaching the team. That prompted one of the most bizarre press conferences Benitez ever gave.

Angered by the rebuke, the Spaniard would answer every question with this phrase, 'I am concentrating on managing and coaching my players.'

Supporters knew exactly what the boss was getting at and, fearful they may lose him, threw their support behind the Spaniard.

In terms of the Americans, the mask had truly slipped. Liverpool supporters' groups, headed by Spirit of Shankly, campaigned strenuously to rid the club of the two Americans.

Liverpool hadn't won a single trophy under their 'custodianship' and the much-vaunted new stadium, on Stanley Park, would prove no more than an expensive set of drawings. Their lasting legacy is the atmosphere of mistrust and cynicism that dogs the club's current ownership.

Hicks and Gillett's reign would end in infamy and humiliation, at the High Court in London. Reds supporters will never again be taken in or taken for granted. Sadly, today's Kopites will always have one eye on the pitch and the other off it.

Rise of the 'Rafatollah' – how Benitez won the hearts and minds of Liverpool supporters

Following the departure of Gerard Houllier in 2004, Liverpool appointed a manager who would lead them back to the pinnacle of Europe: Rafa Benitez. Liverpool supporters have always had a special bond with their managers. Ever since the days of Shankly, there has existed a 'holy trinity' at Anfield: the players, the supporters and the manager.

Sometimes this borders on genuine devotion, but occasionally the supporters take the adulation to truly comical levels. When it comes to football, Liverpool supporters don't do things by halves.

A great example of this came in 2005 when a group of Liverpool fans took a picture of Rafa Benitez to the League Cup Final against Chelsea, at Cardiff.

This wasn't any old photo or banner though. It was a classic portrait, set in a heavy golden frame, the sort of picture you see carried by Middle Eastern crowds celebrating a religious leader.

It was nicknamed the 'Rafatollah', a play on the word Ayatollah, which describes a high-ranking Muslim cleric. Soon it was seen at stadiums all over Europe and began to take on a legend of its own.

It would reach its zenith in 2007. Liverpool were facing Barcelona in a Champions League tie at Anfield and would progress to the next round on the away goals rule despite a 1-0 defeat.

However, the most memorable moment took place before the kick-off. With the big game approaching a group of Liverpool supporters, dressed as 'Red Cardinals', led the portrait through the streets of Liverpool, from Williamson Square in the city centre all the way to Anfield.

Crowds laughed and snapped pictures on their phones, as Rafa's image was paraded around Anfield.

It all added to the allure of big European nights and the genuine carnival atmosphere that sprung up around these games. Liverpool fans loved Benitez back then, but this wasn't really fanaticism. It was a truly Scouse tribute, that managed to both pay homage and take the mickey at the same time.

The events unfolding outside the ground caught the attention of the media and Rafa was asked about it in a press conference. His grin was as wide as the Mersey. He got it and joked that he had never seen anything like it before, except maybe in Iran.

Later that year the picture was seen again, only this time the fun was over. Stories were rife that the club was considering parting company with its Champions League-winning manager, and were even considering Jurgen Klinsmann as a potential replacement.

Supporters were carrying the picture alongside other banners declaring their support for the boss and warning the club's American owners not to sack their hero.

Chants of 'they don't care about Rafa, they don't care about fans, Liverpool Football Club is in the wrong hands' filled the air.

One of the supporters who organised the protest, John Mackin, told the *Liverpool Echo*, 'We did this to display to Rafa, and to anyone else, that getting rid of him would be disastrous. The man is held in such high esteem by supporters.'

Sadly the owners would simply bide their time and Benitez eventually left in 2010. He continues to hold Liverpool Football Club and its supporters in the highest regard. For the overwhelming majority of us, that feeling is mutual.

How a lone cry for justice started a chorus that convinced a minister to act

On 15 April 2009 the people of Liverpool, along with friends and supporters from all over the country, gathered at Anfield in solidarity with the families of the 96 who perished and the survivors of the Hillsborough stadium disaster.

Just as they had done every year since 1989, they came together in love and remembrance, but this time the seething anger, that had lurked beneath the surface for 20 years, burned brighter than ever before.

For two decades they had seen doors slammed in their faces, heard platitudes and been told to move on. Enough was enough.

Around 30,000 people poured into Anfield. Among them were two men whose actions would prove crucial in breaking the political inertia that had stood in the way of justice for so long.

Both were born in Liverpool. One was Reds supporter Roy Dixon, the other was an Evertonian and Secretary of State for Culture, Media and Sport, Andy Burnham MP.

Countless others had spent years piling pressure on authorities, fighting tirelessly for the truth and to clear the names of their loved ones. Every one one of them should be immensely proud.

Sometimes though, when the tide has been so strong for so long, it takes just one final blow to break the dam and, once it goes, the resultant wave becomes irresistible. And so it would prove to be on that day.

Burnham had been invited to attend by Liverpool MP Steve Rotheram and the Mayor of Liverpool, Joe Anderson. He hadn't fancied it. He was worried about breaking down as he delivered his address, but he knew the people would want more than words.

This is what he told the *Liverpool Echo*, 'I could never have lived with myself if I'd not been there. I'd been thinking in the run-up that, in some way, this could be fate – that I was being put there for that moment in time.

I was thinking, "Is there some way I can now open up Hillsborough again?"

'I felt more nervous than I had ever felt before in my life. But, knowing the city as I do, I thought I will take what comes – I'll deal with it as best I can. I sensed, "This has to happen – this feeling people have of a huge sense of injustice and a lack of a resolution has to have its voice."'

As he gave his speech, the crowd sat patiently at first, but their tolerance was wearing thin. Then, as Burnham relayed a message from Prime Minister Gordon Brown, something snapped inside someone in the crowd.

That man was Roy Dixon. He had escaped Hillsborough because he was working that day. However, his nephew had been injured and, like so many others, had struggled to come to terms with it ever since.

So Roy had sat there listening to another politician seemingly going through the motions, words he had heard before. We had all heard them before and in a spontaneous act of defiance, this man spoke for all of us. His words would force a government to think again.

He shouted, 'Justice!'

Immediately, others joined in and soon it was an almighty chorus, speaking truth to power and forcing power to yield. Burnham stopped his speech and bowed his head, listening, his face etched in sorrow and humility.

Then, as the cries subsided he nodded and acknowledged the moment. He had heard their cries and he would act upon them.

This is what he said later, 'I was there as his minister, but I've always said, if I wasn't the minister, I'd have been one of those shouting at the minister.'

Little did anyone know that Mr Brown had been watching on TV. Minutes later, as Burnham entered the Main Stand, his phone rang. It was Brown, calling to thank him for doing the right thing and attending the service.

The next day the Cabinet met. Hillsborough was on the agenda. That lone cry for justice had set in motion a chain of events that would ultimately lead to the publication of the Hillsborough Independent Panel report and the inquest that eventually quashed the original verdicts and cleared the fans of any blame for the disaster.

Five years later, at the 25th-anniversary gathering, Burnham would again address the assembled crowd. 'Wherever you are out there Roy Dixon, take a bow,' he said.

Roy today is full of praise for the former minister, telling the *Echo*, 'I will give Andy Burnham his due because he said he would find out what went on and he did. He was a man of his word. And I have got the greatest respect for him now. It just shows you that one voice in the crowd can make all the difference.'

Take a bow Roy, one more voice that refused to be silenced.

Reds in turmoil as Rafa Benitez is sacked – Liverpool FC in summer 2010

The dismissal of Rafael Benitez took some time to get over, both for a section of fans and for the club itself.

Benitez replaced Gerard Houllier as manager of Liverpool in 2004.

The Frenchman had endeared himself to Reds supporters by solving the club's defensive woes and ending their wait for silverware, but things would eventually sour as he failed to live up to his own dazzling standards; a parting of the ways became inevitable and Liverpool turned to Benitez to rebuild the team and to ensure regular Champions League football at Anfield.

Rafa arrived with an incredible pedigree. He had transformed an underachieving Valencia side into title winners. This was an achievement made all the more remarkable by the calibre of his rivals in La Liga – Benitez had eclipsed Real Madrid and Barcelona, winning Valencia's first title in three decades.

He came with a reputation though. The Spaniard was a political animal and not above a public spat with his club, if it got him what he wanted. For a long time, it worked, and the man delivered in spades.

Rafa embraced Liverpool from the moment he walked through the door and the Kop loved him. They sang his name relentlessly to the tune of 'La Bamba'.

In 2004 you could taste the optimism surrounding the club. The arrivals of Xabi Alonso and Luis Garcia added to this and, although it took time for the Reds' league form to improve, in Europe they were a revelation.

Benitez gave an early indication of his intent by taking Liverpool to the League Cup Final with only half a season under his belt. That game would end in heartbreak but there was more, so much more to come.

Under Rafa, Liverpool climbed to the summit of European football – and it happened in breathtaking style with that monumental comeback against AC Milan in Istanbul.

The Reds had waited 20 years to taste such sweet glory and their fifth European Cup. For this alone he should forever be regarded as a legend.

The club remained at the top of European football throughout his reign, regularly reaching the latter stages of the Champions League. He reached another final in Athens, won an FA Cup and came agonisingly close to winning the Premier League.

These achievements are all the more spellbinding given the chaos the club was in throughout his stint as manager.

Some may say he contributed to that, regularly falling out with the owners and publicly criticising them. However, in doing so he was perfectly in tune with Reds fans and many felt he was their representative within the club.

Sadly, in his ongoing conflict with the club's hierarchy, there was only ever going to be one winner. A combination of mismanagement by absent owners off the field, and poor results on it, meant Rafa would be forced out in 2010. His parting gift was a £96,000 donation to the Hillsborough families and the survivors of the tragedy.

He has gone on to win trophies at home and abroad and retains the respect and admiration of most Reds supporters. Despite the rancour that surrounded his departure, Benitez's reign can be regarded as a glorious period in the club's history. His sacking is all the more senseless given the man Liverpool chose to replace him with.

That's a whole other story, though.

El Pistolero shoots down Stoke City in dream debut

It's 2 February 2011 and Anfield is about to witness the emergence of one of the most talented and turbulent stars ever to wear the red shirt, Luis Suarez.

Unbeknown to the 40,254 supporters who turned up to see Suarez's debut appearance, against Stoke City, the self-styled 'El Pistolero' was about to unleash his scintillating genius and tempestuous temperament on the Premier League.

It was barely a month since Kenny Dalglish had taken over from the banality of Roy Hodgson in the dugout and two since Fenway Sports Group – or New England Sports

Network as they were known then – had replaced Hicks and Gillett in the boardroom.

It was a period of upheaval that ultimately led to the loss of Fernando Torres to Chelsea, in a deal worth £50m, during the same window that ushered in Suarez.

Liverpool supporters, who may have become used to maddening chaos off the pitch, would soon be seeing it on the field of play.

Suarez could evoke both delight and despair, but his wonderful skill and ability would instantly endear him to the Kop, who for two-and-a-half years simply could not get enough.

During that spell he scored an amazing 82 goals in 133 appearances. Arsene Wenger, who later tried to sign Suarez for Arsenal for the embarrassing sum of £40m plus one pound, once said of him, 'I think that every defender in England hates playing against him. He has a strong, provocative personality. From the information I gathered on him it appears that on a day-to-day level he is really easy to work with.

'Also, that he's respectful, he loves training, he's an angel. He turns into a demon when he's on the pitch. We all dream about having players like that.'

Liverpool saw his demonic side several times before he left for Barcelona in 2014 but against Stoke he was an angel in disguise. As the game got under way, with Liverpool languishing in seventh place and Dalglish trying to restore some pride to a club that had been through the mill, there was at last a sense of genuine excitement among the fans. Suarez started on the bench after his £22.8m signing from Ajax.

The first half of the match was nothing to write home about, but within two minutes of the second, Raul Meireles put the Reds 1-0 in front. Luis entered the fray to huge cheers just over 15 minutes later.

Sixteen minutes after that, he put his new team 2-0 up, replicating the achievements of the man he had replaced. Fernando Torres had scored exactly 16 minutes into his debut also. The *Guardian* remarked, 'Liverpool mourned when Kevin Keegan left and replaced him with the finest player in their history. Liverpool despaired when Ian Rush joined Juventus and replaced him with arguably the most attractive team in their history. Last night, thanks to Luis Suarez's fairy tale introduction to the Premier League, Liverpool hardly gave Fernando Torres second thought.'

In truth, the Uruguayan would score far better goals in his Liverpool career. *The Times* commented on the somewhat unspectacular nature of the strike, 'Suarez came off the bench and, after under-hitting his shot, was grateful for a botched clearance by Andy Wilkinson, but do not expect anyone – not even the Premier League "dubious goals panel" – to try to deprive the man of his moment.'

Luis was delighted to be off the mark for his new club, saying: 'I think it is a dream debut, anyone would say it is a dream debut. Just to be on the field for a few minutes and to manage to score in front of the Kop, it's what dreams are made of.'

Suarez was a rare talent, the likes of which we won't see at Anfield too often. However, to paraphrase Steven Gerrard, we can consider ourselves lucky that our lives coincided with the emergence of his genius at Anfield.

The Kop sings Happy Birthday to Kenny Dalglish

In the history of Liverpool Football Club, there are many men who have not only embodied the ethos of Anfield but redefined it. Bill Shankly is an obvious example. However, older supporters will point to Billy Liddell, who for a period simply was Liverpool; or, in the words of the Kop, Liddellpool.

For those who grew up watching the Reds conquer all before them in the 1970s and 80s, that man would be Kenny Dalglish, a player and a manager who was even cooler than 'The Fonz'. The relationship between Kenny and the Kop transcends football.

When he left the club in 1990, carrying the scars of two of football's biggest tragedies and clearly in need of a break, many of us felt like a piece of the club had been ripped from us. Football and Liverpool would never be the same again. For a long time, we were right. When he returned, he lifted Anfield from a self-inflicted malaise and gave new hope to a fanbase on the brink of revolt.

Many of us could see that Kenny had unfinished business but this was a move that carried its own risks. Some felt his return was doomed to failure and his bond with the supporters could be tarnished as a result.

'Do you worry that your reputation may be damaged, in the eyes of the fans, if this doesn't work out?' asked one journalist.

'I worry more about what they would think of me if I didn't come back and help when I am needed,' was his reply.

This summed up the man's selflessness and dedication to Liverpool, the club and its people; a fact not lost on the fans. His glowing reputation has never and will never be dimmed.

If anyone ever requires evidence of this basic fact, simply point them to a moment in time, in which the personal bond between supporter and manager has never been more evident. The moment the Spion Kop sang 'Happy Birthday' to Kenny Dalglish.

Sure, Liverpool's supporters have a reputation for deifying the man in the dugout. They have invented whole stanzas for the likes of Shanks, Paisley, Houllier and Benitez. But many of those songs were about footballing achievements. This was something affectionate and playful, something you do for a loved one.

The date was 7 March 2011. The game was against Manchester United and Liverpool were destroying the enemy. Dirk Kuyt fired the easiest hat-trick of his career and Luis Suarez had provided all the ammunition.

Anfield was in a jubilant mood and King Kenny had turned 60 a week earlier. The manager was patrolling the technical area and the supporters, who had not yet had the chance to acknowledge this milestone, took their chance to serenade their idol.

It started low and slow at the back of the famous old stand and built into a crescendo. 'Happy birthday to you, happy birthday to you, happy birthday King Kenny, happy birthday to you.'

The boss later admitted to feeling 'a bit emotional' at the tribute and joked that they might not have done it if the Reds had been losing. Don't bet on that, Kenny.

The madness and genius of King Luis

With 82 goals in 133 appearances for Liverpool, including a season where he managed an astonishing 31 goals in 33 games, there is no doubting that Luis Suarez is a genius. However, as a great banner on the Kop once declared, 'No great genius has ever existed, without a hint of madness'. During a turbulent three years on Merseyside, King Luis provided more than a hint of both.

Liverpool knew exactly what they were getting when they paid the bargain price of £22.8m for him in January of 2011. Suarez was known as a fierce competitor, both in training and competitive outings. He would do absolutely anything to win. This hunger came at a price though. In Holland he had been branded the 'Cannibal of Ajax' by Dutch newspaper *De Telegraaf*, after biting PSV's Otman Bakkal on the shoulder. He ended up banned for seven games and fined by his club.

However, the Reds were convinced they could polish this rough diamond and he would become a key figure under both Kenny Dalglish and later Brendan Rodgers.

Liverpool supporters simply adored the Uruguayan and adapted an old Depeche Mode song, 'I Just Can't Get Enough', in his honour.

> 'When he scores a volley
> or when it's with his head
> I just can't get enough, I just can't get enough
> He scores a goal and the Kop go wild
> and I just can't seem to get enough of
> Suarez, do, do, do, do, do, do, Luis Suarez'

It wasn't long, though, before the player found himself mired in controversy once more. After a 1-1 draw with Manchester United at Anfield on 15 October 2011, Suarez was accused of racially abusing Patrice Evra.

He vehemently protested his innocence and the club and supporters threw their weight behind him.

Nevertheless, a three-man FA panel found him guilty, banned him for eight games and fined him £40,000. Many Liverpool fans felt he had been unjustly treated and continued to support the player, while vocally opposing racism, singing 'we're not racists, we only hate Mancs'.

For many, this was a typically Scouse attempt at irreverence that masked embarrassment at being associated with bigotry. It should be said, though, that both players have maintained their respective positions on this, with Suarez continuing to maintain his innocence.

They are perhaps the only two people who know what was said that day.

Unfortunately the pair would spark further media fury the next time they met, with Luis appearing to avoid shaking the Frenchman's hand during the modern pre-match ritual for the cameras.

For many this was a storm in a teacup, but Suarez and his manager Kenny Dalglish were forced to apologise later. Interestingly, in 2016, Suarez won the Golden Shoe for his exploits with Barcelona. Patrice Evra posted this comment on his Instagram page, 'In my Instagram there is only love and never hate!!! Luis, you're a great player and the best No 9. Congratulations Luis @luissuarez9. I love this game !!! hahahaah.'

Whatever happened on the pitch at Anfield in 2011, Evra has been able to get past it and recognise Suarez's brilliance as a player.

Suarez won his only trophy for Liverpool in the spring of 2012 when he lifted the League Cup. He would also score an equaliser against Everton in the semi-final of the FA Cup in the same year. The Reds went on to the final, but lost to Chelsea.

A second bite incident occurred against Chelsea in April 2013 during a 2-2 draw at Anfield. Video evidence showed Suarez biting Branislav Ivanovic.

Even the then-Prime Minister, David Cameron, jumped on the bandwagon at this point, urging the FA to act. They obliged and banned Suarez for ten games. The player decided enough was enough and openly declared his desire to leave, prompting a farcical approach from Arsenal.

This was rebuffed by Liverpool, whose principal owner suggested that the board at the Emirates might have been intoxicated. In the end Luis accepted he was going nowhere, at least for a while. That was the thing with Suarez, no matter what was going on off the pitch or in his head, the player never gave anything less than 100 per cent, either during training or in a game. That's partly why Liverpool supporters love him.

Suarez went on to play a pivotal role in the 2013/14 near miss when the Reds fell at the final hurdle and narrowly missed out on the Premier League title.

Luis finished as top scorer and Player of the Season having struck 31 times. New boss Brendan Rodgers acknowledged his contribution, saying, 'He has shown in his time at Liverpool in the last year or so that he is near unplayable. He on his own can occupy a back four with his movement and his cleverness.'

In the end Liverpool couldn't hang on to their troublesome star. A further biting incident during the 2014 FIFA World Cup saw him banned from all football activities for four months.

Such was his stock as a player though, Barcelona were still prepared to pay £75m for his services.

He remains one of the top three strikers in world football today, and is still adored by Liverpool fans across the globe.

King Kenny's tears of joy as Liverpool secure Wembley berth for first time in 16 years

After the debacle of the Roy Hodgson months, a Liverpool legend arrived to steady the ship: Kenny Dalglish once more came to the Reds' aid. He did more than that, of course, and led the club to two cup finals at Wembley in the same season.

Liverpool lost the 2012 FA Cup Final against Chelsea in May but had won the League Cup earlier in the season after a penalty shootout. On their way to their first cup final in the capital for 16 years they faced a resurgent Manchester City in a two-legged semi-final.

The first leg finished 1-0 to the Reds thanks to a Steven Gerrard penalty. With a return leg under the Anfield floodlights beckoning, Kopites could almost taste the Wembley air.

As is often the case, the game didn't quite pan out as we all expected.

With the atmosphere inside the ground typically raucous, the Reds flew at City. However, it was the side from Manchester who took the lead through Nigel de Jong with a 25-yard shot on the half-hour mark.

It was a hammer blow and could easily have deflated the Kop. It didn't though, and within ten minutes Liverpool were ahead in the tie once more.

Micah Richards handled a Daniel Agger shot and the referee pointed straight at the spot. Nobody else was required other than club captain Steven Gerrard, who stepped up to fire the Reds back in front.

The two teams would finish the half with a goal each on the night so it was a case of back to the drawing board for City manager Roberto Mancini, who changed tactics in the second period.

His tinkering would pay off, too, and City went back in front through Edin Dzeko in the 67th minute. This was a disaster as Mancini's two away goals threatened to put City in the final.

However, Liverpool were not finished. All they needed was a single goal and the glory would be theirs.

So they just kept going, egged on by a vociferous Kop. And it took only seven minutes for them to race back into the lead. This time it was former City player Craig Bellamy who did the damage. Here's how the *Liverpool Echo* described his finish, 'It was a well-worked goal, too. Fed by Kuyt inside the area, Bellamy exchanged passes with Johnson to lose his marker and fire beyond Hart.'

The celebrations that greeted the goal were only dwarfed by those at the final whistle. It was a momentous occasion, with the Reds back in a cup final for the first time in six years and back at Wembley for their first visit since 1996.

The twin towers were gone but the national stadium had lost none of its allure to supporters, who once routinely referred to the old ground as 'Anfield South'.

Lost in the melee of those frenetic final moments was the image of Kenny Dalglish in contemplative mood on the touchline. As the minutes ticked down, the enormity of his achievement began to sink in.

It may have only been the League Cup but the Reds had been through the mill in the years that preceded the King's return.

He knew the supporters had placed a lot of faith in him and, though he wouldn't complain, the pressure must have been immense. All that was gone now though, and he had fulfilled his sacred mission, the one laid down by Shankly all those years ago, to make the people happy.

Liverpool and their supporters were back at Wembley thanks to his leadership, and they were delirious. As all of that began to register his eyes welled with tears of joy. His emotion betrayed his deep connection with the club and the city.

He would later compose himself and tell the waiting media, 'It's great for the people who have stood by us because it has not been too easy a time for Liverpool Football Club over the last few years. I don't know the last time we went [to Wembley] but we know where we are going. Maybe we've forgotten the route but I'm sure the driver will remember!'

Mission accomplished, Kenny.

The 2012 League Cup Final – Dalglish returns silverware to Anfield trophy cabinet

Liverpool hadn't tasted trophy success for six years by the time 2012 arrived. Despite the recruitment of Luis Suarez, along with then record signing Andy Carroll, the Reds' league form had been patchy at best. So it was on the cup competitions that Liverpool supporters pinned their hopes.

The Reds were seven times winners of the League Cup and were desperate to add a record eighth. It was also their first final at the new Wembley. As my son and I got off the coach for his first cup final, we noticed a great banner hanging from the concourse declaring, 'We're back, love what you've done with the place.'

There was a nice symmetry to the fixture given that our recent domestic cup successes had all come at Cardiff's Millennium Stadium. The Welsh capital's side were basking in their underdog status and were clearly the nation's favourites for the cup. This point wasn't lost on our players. At full time, an emotional Jamie Carragher reflected on how defeat would have been unthinkable given how everybody was rooting for Cardiff.

The game looked like it might be easier than it turned out to be when Glen Johnson hit the woodwork early on, but within 20 minutes Liverpool were behind after a mix-up in defence. It seemed to spark the Reds into life but they couldn't find the breakthrough and as they came out in the second half you just couldn't see them finding the equaliser.

However, this is Liverpool and it was inevitable we would see more drama before the curtain finally fell. On the hour mark, Martin Skrtel levelled. Carroll had headed on a whipped corner from Charlie Adam and Suarez clipped the post. The ball rebounded to the Slovakian who hammered it home.

Our end of the ground was an explosion of relief and joy; probably more relief if truth be told. However, the remaining half-hour was a lesson in frustration and after we had survived a late effort from Kenny Miller, extra time beckoned.

Liverpool were clearly the more experienced and fitter of the two sides. Despite not being able to see off their opponents in normal time, I was fairly confident we would have too much for their tired legs. I was wrong; Cardiff never gave up.

Suarez had one cleared off the line and Liverpool's momentum was building. Then, three minutes into the second period of added time, it looked like Kuyt had won the cup. His weak shot came back to him and, despite stumbling, he managed to summon the strength to beat the keeper from 18 yards.

With the game ebbing away we were starting to believe the silverware was heading back to Anfield. Was this the start of another glorious era under the King, Kenny Dalglish?

Yes, but not before more drama. This is Liverpool after all.

With two minutes to go a goal-line scramble saw Kuyt clear the ball for a corner. Surely that was it. Just defend the set piece and the cup is ours. In swung the ball and Aron Gunnarsson headed on target, only for Kuyt again to clear. His heroics were in vain though as Ben Turner poked the rebound home.

Cardiff were jubilant; 2-2 and penalties beckoned.

Strangely I was supremely confident. Liverpool were masters of the shootout and had won many finals via this cruel 'lottery'.

This is Liverpool though and it's never easy.

What followed was agony. First Steven Gerrard missed, and red heads went into hands. Then Cardiff missed, and hope was restored, before Adam dashed it in spectacular fashion. His spot-kick is still rising and probably passing Pluto by now. Then Don Cowie put Cardiff ahead.

What we needed was a hero with ice in his veins. Up stepped Kuyt for 1-1. The Bluebirds missed their next and the balance once more shifted in Liverpool's favour. The next three were scored and with the shootout at 3-2 to Liverpool, it was left to Anthony Gerrard, cousin of Steven, to take the next for Cardiff. If he missed it was all over.

Few of us had any sympathy for him as the ball skidded wide of Pepe Reina's upright. Football is a ruthless game and the youngster sunk to his knees as Reds player piled on top of their keeper. After all the pain and turmoil of the previous six years, the silverware was back, and it felt good.

How Jamie Carragher hung up his boots after a trophy-laden Liverpool career

On 7 February 2013, Jamie Carragher announced that he would retire from football at the end of Liverpool's 2012/13 campaign. His decision brought the curtain down on a career that spanned 25 years.

As a youngster he had won the FA Youth Cup in 1996, before going on to collect 11 major honours for Liverpool. His crowning glory was a seminal performance in Istanbul in 2005 during which he fought through muscle cramps to repeatedly deny AC Milan in the closing stages of the Champions League Final.

His exertions in the Ataturk Stadium that night had taken such a heavy toll on his body that he was barely able to stand for the trophy presentation.

After that game, Carra declared that he would never leave Liverpool for another club, saying, 'When I say life, I mean it. I want to stay here. When I say that, it's not talk, I really mean it. I mean I'm not kidding myself, I don't think I'm going to go any higher than Liverpool. If your club's in the Champions League that's the ultimate and obviously you want to win trophies.'

Carragher was an honest player and once said of his career, 'There may be more skilful players in the squad, but no one can ever say I don't give 100 per cent.' The supporters recognised that and regularly sang that they dreamt of a team of Carraghers.

He may have started out as a Blue but he grew into one of the most loyal and passionate Reds on the face of the earth. In a statement announcing the decision to retire, he said, 'It has been a privilege and an honour to represent this great club for as long as I have.'

In all the lad from Bootle played 737 times for the club, a feat achieved through sheer hard work and determination. The total was only topped by Ian Callaghan's incredible 857 appearances, and Kenny Dalglish marked Carragher's revelation with a tweet, 'Sad day for Carra announcing his retirement. He'll be missed but he can be very proud of everything he's done for Liverpool.'

Many, including Michael Owen and Rio Ferdinand, speculated that Carragher would go straight into management at the end of the season. Ian Ayre, Liverpool's managing director, hinted that the club would offer him some sort of role after he ended his playing days.

Who knows if that ever happened, but if it did Jamie opted for a career in the media instead.

Carragher's final game came on 19 May 2013, against Queens Park Rangers at Anfield. Before kick-off, the Kop held up a mosaic spelling out 'JC 23' and both sets of players formed a guard of honour. It was an emotional occasion but the tough-tackling Scouser had refused to entertain talk of tears.

Gerrard and Callaghan presented Carragher with a special award on the pitch before the game got under way. Liverpool won 1-0 and while nobody expected Carragher to score, he came agonisingly close by striking the post from 30 yards out.

Had it gone in, the roof would probably have come off the Kop. It wasn't to be though and in the 87th minute, Brendan Rodgers took the player off for an emotionally charged ovation from all four sides of the ground and the other 21 players on the pitch.

An era was over and one of the most respected players in the game was off to pastures new. Carragher's contribution to Liverpool is immeasurable and difficult to capture in a short piece like this. Perhaps it's best, then, to leave it to Alan Hansen, arguably the greatest centre-half ever to wear the red shirt, to sum up Jamie's qualities and standing in the game.

After witnessing the defender's heroics against Chelsea in the semi-final of the European Cup at Anfield, the legend said these words, 'Carragher is ten times a better defender than I could ever be. He is a completely different player. He is a great defender whereas I was not. My strengths were on the ball, positional sense and recovery pace.

'The way he held Chelsea at bay was unbelievable. I'm sitting there in awe of how many times he intercepted, blocked and covered.

'I think if we look at Liverpool greats over the years – and there have been a lot of them – Carragher is up there with the best of them.'

FSG's bold move appointing Brendan Rodgers as Liverpool manager in 2012

It's 1 June 2012 and Liverpool are emerging from another tumultuous period in their history. It's been a disastrous spell. The club's ownership has changed hands twice in just over three years. It has flirted with administration and lost key playing talent. In the dugout, the situation has been far from stable. The Reds have sacked a Champions League-winning manager, Rafa Benitez, and replaced him with Fleet Street favourite Roy Hodgson.

When that didn't end well, the new owners turned to Liverpool legend Kenny Dalglish, only to sack him a year-and-a-half later. This ushered in Brendan Rodgers, the Reds' 23rd manager in 120 years and their first from Northern Ireland.

His interviewers were apparently impressed with his dossier on the club. In it he had detailed a plan to take the Reds from eighth place to Champions League contenders once more. He almost went a step further, narrowly missing out on the Premier League at his second attempt.

Brendan was welcomed with open arms by Liverpool fans and his ability to embrace and understand the club's psyche won him many admirers early on. One song created by the Kop went like this, 'Brendan Rodgers' Liverpool are on their way to glory, built a team like Shankly did, so the kids would have a story.'

Supporters, though, often have revisionist tendencies. Some will claim today that they never liked Rodgers. However, in that second season, you would have been hard pressed to find any of them. Banners celebrating the Irishman adorned the Kop and the Anfield Road end, as his all-action team destroyed sides at will.

Brendan's stated aim was to make games at Anfield the longest 90 minutes of an opponent's life. For one glorious and ultimately agonising season he delivered. Many will say it was all down to the genius of the mercurial Luis Suarez, but that seems unfair.

Suarez was indeed a game-changer for Liverpool but he had to be managed and coached. He was far from happy at times and had even asked to leave. Rodgers dealt with that situation and ultimately the Uruguayan knuckled down and delivered.

In the end Brendan would have to find his level in another league. However, for all the disappointment associated with that failed title tilt in 2013/14, few of us can deny that he delivered one of our most exciting teams in recent history.

His Liverpool may have fallen catastrophically short but perhaps, after the turmoil that preceded him, we were expecting a little too much. Or, maybe we owe him a little for lifting us from the gloom and making us dream again. In the end, it's the hope that kills you, but you can't deny that Brendan Rodgers, albeit briefly, reminded Liverpool supporters of what they had been missing for such a long time.

Anne Williams, the real Iron Lady

Anne Williams passed away on 18 April 2013 after a battle with cancer. She had devoted a quarter of a century of her life to the fight for justice for her son.

Kevin Williams died at Hillsborough. He was just 15 at the time of the 1989 disaster. The official record stated that he was dead or beyond saving by 3.15pm on the day, but his mother believed he was alive beyond this point and could have been saved.

Police officers were put under enormous pressure to alter statements and were discouraged from giving evidence that might incriminate the police and emergency services. However, despite this, one female officer would later corroborate Anne's version of events. Kevin had called out 'Mum' long after the arbitrary 3.15pm cut-off point, imposed at the inquest.

This was crucial to Anne's quest to have the verdict of accidental death, that sat like a stain on her son's death certificate, changed. If Kevin was dead by 3.15pm there was nothing anyone could have done to save him, but if he was alive that changed everything.

Anne, an ordinary mother, had been forced to turn detective and lawyer in the 24 years that followed the loss of her precious son. She fought a heroic campaign along with the Hillsborough Justice Campaign (which she chaired initially) and later Hope for Hillsborough.

Time and time again she had judicial doors slammed in her face. She simply went home to gather more evidence, before returning to bang at those doors once more.

She took her case to the European Court of Human Rights, only to be told she was 'out of time'. If she had thrown in the towel at this point, nobody could have blamed her. Instead Anne fought on.

'I knew what they were doing,' she said. 'They were trying to wear me down. But I just thought I'll wear you down before you get to me. I was never going to give in.'

Nelson Mandela once said, 'Judge me not by how many times I am knocked down, but by how many times I get back up again.'

Anne Williams can be compared favourably to any of history's great champions of justice. Her life's achievements still echo through time. She is a model for any parent fighting for a child who has been wronged.

Inevitably her death, coming just a day after the funeral of Margaret Thatcher, the self-styled 'Iron Lady', led many on Merseyside to draw comparisons. Ironically speaking on the steps of St George's Hall after the release of the Hillsborough Independent Panel report, Anne railed against the idea of a state funeral for the former Prime Minister.

A petition to honour Thatcher had inspired her to start her own petition, calling for the Attorney General to reopen Kevin's case. It attracted more than 100,000 signatures.

After her death, many claimed that Anne was the real 'Iron Lady' and she is now immortalised as such on a banner displayed proudly on the Kop. There, she sits proudly alongside the greats in Liverpool's illustrious history.

It's easy to be strong when you have the full weight of the state, the police and the media on your side. Try doing it when you're a mother fighting a lone battle to win justice for your son.

They probably thought they could break her, but they picked on the wrong mum. Anne was not for turning and she would eventually see her son's verdict of accidental death overturned. Hers was a truly inspiring victory.

After the death of Thatcher, Liverpool City Council declined to fly its flag at half-mast. The reason? 'This is an honour reserved only for the death of royalty.'

The following day it was lowered in honour of Anne Williams. Enough said.

How Brendan Rodgers's explosive Reds destroyed the Gunners in 2014

'I'm trying to think of a performance I can remember in the last 15 years. Maybe one or two in the Champions League got close but that was as explosive as it gets.'

That's how Steven Gerrard described Liverpool's 5-1 demolition of a full-strength Arsenal side at Anfield in February 2014.

The Reds had given a hint of their attacking prowess against Everton 11 days previously. The Blues had been utterly blown away, conceding four without reply. However, the next game, against West Brom, had ended in a disappointing draw.

The Gunners, sitting at the top of the table, were a different proposition. Everyone expected a close, tricky encounter. What they got was a masterclass in attacking football, full of pace, power and devastating finishing.

Liverpool flew straight out of the traps and in the first minute were a goal up through Martin Skrtel, who then doubled the lead nine minutes later. Within 20 minutes Liverpool were 4-0 up thanks to further goals by Raheem Sterling and Daniel Sturridge.

This was unreal. The Liverpool supporters couldn't believe what they were seeing as they sang 'poetry in motion tra la la la', and danced joyously in the stands. The Gunners were shell-shocked and the game looked well and truly over.

Mikel Arteta summed up their feelings in a painful post-match interview, 'After 19 minutes, we were 4-0 down and it was like a car crash. The manager was really upset at half-time, that's normal because it wasn't good enough for this football club. It was the angriest I have seen him.'

No doubt the sight of the entire stadium, Arsenal fans aside, rising as one, with a minute of the half remaining, to give the Reds a standing ovation must have infuriated Arsene Wenger. It was a complete humiliation and there was still a full 45 minutes to go.

Within seven minutes of the restart, Liverpool were 5-0 up through Sterling, and it was starting to look like Wenger's worst fears were about to be realised. Liverpool's jubilant supporters were beginning to dream of a cricket score.

Arsenal clearly decided on damage limitation at this point and concentrated on restricting Liverpool's chances. In truth, the Reds eased off themselves.

In the 69th minute the Gunners won a penalty from seemingly nothing. Alex Oxlade-Chamberlain looked to be going nowhere inside the box when Gerrard was adjudged to have brought him down. Arteta scored with ease from the resulting spot-kick.

It was frustrating but, despite the fans from north London singing – with a heavy dose of irony – 'we're going to win 4-3', it would prove only a consolation. Wenger's post-match analysis was damning.

'We were feeble,' he moaned. 'Feeble in every important domain of playing at the highest level: concentration, strength in the challenge and naivety. So, from that moment on it's impossible to win a game when you're playing at that level.'

Understandably, Brendan Rodgers preferred to talk about his own side's performance than focus on the ineptitude of their opponents, 'We were brilliant. The performance level was absolutely out of this world.'

It was Brendan, it certainly was.

The end of an era: Steven Gerrard calls time on his Anfield playing days

Steven Gerrard played his last game for Liverpool on 16 May 2015, signalling the end of an era for one of the club's bona fide legends. It was an ignominious end for a player who had lit up Anfield from the moment he joined the club as an eight-year-old – as Liverpool were crushed 6-1 by Stoke City and in a team of hopeless underachievers – but it was Stevie who got the Reds' only goal.

Gerrard grew up in the Huyton area of Liverpool and would go on to conquer Europe in a red shirt, with a Liver Bird on his chest. In a career that spanned 17 years he played 710 games and scored 186 goals. For Reds supporters everywhere, his leaving Liverpool was a bitter blow.

It may all have been different, of course, had the club offered him a contract the previous summer, but for whatever reason they dallied too long, and a club icon decided it was time to move on. He would leave temporarily for the United States and LA Galaxy, but the call of Anfield would eventually prove too loud to ignore and he returned in 2017 to manage Liverpool's under-18s.

Many of us will view it as an utter privilege that our lives coincided with the emergence of Gerrard's legend at Anfield. Clearly he is a player who will be spoken of with reverence for as long as Liverpool Football Club exists. Such an honour far exceeds any trophy or title.

As such, the Anfield Road end at Anfield has a lot in common with the Wirral peninsula on Merseyside. Both gaze upon the greatest sights anywhere in the world. Of course, one of them looks out over the mighty River Mersey, at the finest waterfront in the world. The other gazes upon the greatest football terrace in all of football.

It was from a seat in the Anfield Road end that I was privileged to witness the goal Steven Gerrard regards as his best. *What a hit, son!* Of course, I'm talking about the 84th-minute strike against Olympiakos that set us on our way to Istanbul.

In years to come it will be a source of disappointment to Gerrard that he never won the Premier League title. However, he is regarded as a living legend irrespective of that gap in his medal collection. Gerrard is simply the greatest player to have not won that medal. For a spell of five years he would have walked into any team in world football.

Steven Gerrard was Liverpool Football Club. He was a Liddell or a Dalglish, because he embodied the spirit and ethos of the institution. They named the team Liddellpool after Billy Liddell, and for Steven Gerrard they renamed an FA Cup Final.

Kenny Dalglish might have been cooler than 'The Fonz' but there are few childhood Dalglish disciples who'd have any qualms in declaring Stevie as the greatest player to pull on the red shirt. After all, our legendary number seven was always surrounded with greatness. Gerrard would often have to elevate the club beyond its station.

He won every cup it was possible to win and scored in the final of every competition. In all he amassed nine major honours, including two FA Cups, three League Cups, the Champions League and the UEFA Cup. He was also a three-time runner-up in the Premier League.

To Liverpool supporters, Gerrard is a captain, a Red and a Scouser born and bred. He has achieved what every kid growing up in the red half of the city dreams of. It is no surprise to see him return to the club in a coaching capacity and nobody would bet against him one day managing Liverpool in the future, and lifting the Premier League championship that evaded him during his playing days.

From doubt to belief: a new era begins, with the arrival of the 'normal one'

On 8 October 2015, Liverpool appointed Jurgen Klopp as the 24th manager in the club's history. The Brendan Rodgers era had burned brightly for one glorious season but it had come to an end.

Rodgers had followed up his scintillating 2013/14 title tilt with a hugely disappointing sixth-place finish in 2014/15, which had ended with an ignominious 6-1 thrashing at Stoke City.

In addition, Liverpool had crashed out of the League Cup and FA Cup in the semi-finals. In the Champions League they had failed to get out of the group stage, finishing third in a group that featured Ludogorets and Basel. They were then dumped out of the Europa League by Besiktas in the round of 32.

It was all a far cry from the heady days of the previous season. Liverpool had lost Luis Suarez and, in many people's eyes, failed to spend the cash wisely. Therefore, it was a surprise to most Reds that the club didn't part company with Rodgers in the summer of 2015.

Jamie Carragher summed up Liverpool's malaise. 'We think we're a big club, but we're not,' he said. Being a Liverpool supporter had started to feel like a chore to many.

Rodgers would limp on until October 2015. It would take an awful draw with Everton to force the owners' hand. They had been long-term admirers of Klopp but he had been taking a break from football after he had left Borussia Dortmund.

It seemed, however, that he was getting bored and had indicated that he may be ready to return to management. With many other clubs potentially in the market for a new manager, the owners decided to make their move.

Rumours suggested that Rodgers had been sacked over the phone with Ian Ayre left to negotiate his severance package. Newspapers reported that captain Jordan Henderson broke the news to the squad.

Liverpool appeared to be floundering and directionless. This was Fenway Sports Group's third managerial sacking since they took over in 2010.

They simply had to get the next appointment right. Klopp was the supporters' preferred choice and any club with ambition would have had the German on their shortlist.

Somehow, to the surprise of many supporters, the owners managed to persuade him to join the Reds. His eventual unveiling was like a shot of adrenaline to a fading heart. It was absolutely clear that this man completely understood the club, but more than that he knew what was ailing it.

Ex-players like Mark Lawrenson were gushing in their praise. Roy Evans, a man who had worked with greats such as Shanks and Paisley, claimed to have a lump in his throat after hearing Klopp being interviewed in the media. David Fairclough and Gary Gillespie were 'inspired' and all struggled, and ultimately failed, to avoid drawing comparisons with a certain great Scotsman from Glenbuck.

The German had only been at the club a matter of days and he had already proved a headline writer's dream, producing enough soundbites to last a lifetime. Every one of them was sincere and brilliant. There was not a cliché in sight.

For many, though, it was one message, delivered with a twinkle and a smile, that resonated most. At the end of Klopp's first interview for LFCTV, Clare Rourke asked the now standard question, 'So what message do you have for those Liverpool supporters?'

Klopp thought for a moment. This was his opportunity to speak directly to the fan base. He could have trotted out the same old guff about what an honour it was for him blah blah.

Instead he looked directly at the camera and cut directly to the problem facing the entire club in that moment. 'You must change from doubter to believer – now!'

It had been 25 years since the Reds had won the title. It was a millstone that has dragged every manager before him down and weighed heavy on too many of the players also. The supporters had turned too many corners, only to find themselves in another blind alley. Belief was in short supply.

He continued, 'If someone thinks we have waited long enough for the title – then restart and then everything can happen.'

So began a new era at Liverpool Football Club. The past might be glorious, but it was only to enjoy. Liverpool were now in the future business. Supporters had been transformed, at least for a while, from doubters to believers. Each of us strapped in for what promised to be a wild ride.

Liverpool supporters tell owners that 'enough is enough' on ticket prices

The bond between the club and its supporters has propelled Liverpool on to the world stage. It has sustained players, managers and the boardroom through good times and bad. However, it has never been as severely tested as in the opening decades of the 21st century.

The roots of this disconnect can be traced back to the growing wealth inequality between Liverpool and their rivals. The club, owned for decades by the Moores family, was slipping behind and in 2007 chairman David Moores began looking for a buyer who could take things forward.

It led to a failed takeover by Dubai International Capital that effectively left Liverpool at the mercy of George Gillett and Tom Hicks. They did untold damage to the club, and the net effect was to undermine the trust supporters had placed in the club for more than a century.

When new owners eventually emerged from the ashes of the debacle, there was a mountain to climb in regaining that trust. However, in 2016 they miscalculated spectacularly when announcing a new ticket pricing structure.

Supporters revolted and for the first time in the club's history there was talk of boycotting games. This culminated in a planned walkout against Sunderland at Anfield on Saturday, 6 February 2016.

The protest was timed for 77 minutes, a reference to the cost of a new premium ticket, priced at £77. The whole city knew about the planned walkout. Support was overwhelming.

The call to arms had been issued by two independent supporters' groups, Spirit of Shankly and Spion Kop 1906. At the turnstiles, before the game, supporters talked openly about the walkout.

One overheard conversation went along the lines of, 'I'm walking out like. But if you'd come all the way from Australia or something and you had a young kid with you, would you walk out?'

The reply was emphatic, 'Too right I would. I'd tell the kid I'm doing it for him. So he can go to games in the future.'

For many the game felt like an afterthought, a sideshow to a drama being played out in the stands. The Kop was devoid of the usual colourful banners. Instead black flags were being unfurled.

One banner bore an image of a Liver Bird holding a Kopite upside down; money tumbling from his pockets. The relationship between supporter and club artistically summed up.

In the Main Stand, to the right of the directors' box, a group of fans had rolled out another message for chief executive Ian Ayre. 'Football without supporters is nothing.' There were also other smaller banners around the ground.

As the game was about to start the Liver Bird banner was carried to the back of the Kop, a black flag in pursuit. Those carrying them were applauded as they went.

There was some unease at the idea of a protest though. Another conversation between friends broke out about the value of the walk out.

One supporter was clearly torn, 'I've been thinking about this all day. Even now I'm not sure what I'm going to do. It's not like me to walk out of a game and it kills me to even think about it.'

Another spoke up, 'Look mate, I understand why people are doing it, but I'm not walking out. I don't agree with it.' There was sadness in his voice and he was almost apologetic.

His friend replied, 'I know what you mean, but we've got to do something. Don't get me wrong it's not about us, it's about the poor supporters who'll be charged £77.'

The debate went back and forth and although it was friendly, it was plain it was causing anguish for some. The game was a mere sideshow.

As the 77th minute approached, the tension started to build. First just a few people got up and started making their way for the exits. There were chants of 'Liverpool' before an early rendition of 'You'll Never Walk Alone' as fans sought to affirm this was not a protest against the players.

Then another song started at the back of the Kop. It grew until it was booming. People stood up and began moving as one. 'You greedy bastards, enough is enough!'

A similar exodus was taking place in the Main Stand. Under the Kop, the concourse was filled with supporters leaving the ground. They began chanting and the sound in that confined space was thunderous. It continued outside in the streets.

Supporters had sent a clear message. Enough was enough. To their credit the owners listened and while many still doubt their commitment to the club, there's no doubt they now understand how committed the supporters are.

Truth and justice: the people of Liverpool pull off the greatest sporting victory ever

The events of 15 April 1989 led to 96 innocent football supporters being unlawfully killed as a result of the

Hillsborough disaster – but it would take 27 years until the truth was finally heard in court.

Men, women and children – the youngest just ten years old, Jon Paul Gilhooley, the cousin of Steven Gerrard – were cruelly taken away from their loved ones.

The tragedy cast a shadow of lies and smears across an entire city. In the immediate moments after the disaster struck, the establishment set about encasing the truth of the catastrophe in a shell of lies, distortions and cruel slander.

The toll of the tragedy goes way beyond the 96 who perished. Countless survivors have had lives blighted. Many were unable to live with the lies, told by the guilty, that made them feel responsible for the deaths of their fellow supporters. Some resorted to suicide.

Whole families were robbed of the potential of loved ones. Future graduations, weddings and the birth of grandchildren were stolen from them and they were left to grieve in smouldering anger. Such a loss would be intolerable in any circumstances, but to suffer the double injustice of having the deaths of those you mourn described as an 'accident' was a great insult that couldn't be allowed to stand.

What followed was a 27-year campaign that simply refused to go away. The first cracks in that establishment shell appeared in 2012 with the publication of the Hillsborough Independent Panel report, which led to a public apology by the Prime Minister David Cameron. They had picked on the wrong city, for sure.

At a new inquest into the tragedy in 2016, doubt and worry about whether another 'accidental death' verdict could be handed down set in. What if they somehow managed to still blame supporters again? It was unbearable.

Instead, on Monday, 26 April 2016, in a courtroom in Warrington, the jury passed what amounted to complete and utter vindication of those who died; the survivors, the families and all those who had fought so hard for truth and justice over more than a quarter of a century.

The 96 had been unlawfully killed and the supporters had played no part in the disaster, they declared. The verdict confirmed what Liverpool supporters had been saying for decades. The truth was out and surely justice must follow.

That evening the city of Liverpool held a vigil in the shadow of St George's Hall, often a symbol of protest, heroic homecomings and historic victories. That night it celebrated the greatest sporting triumph of all time, truth and justice for the 96 and justice for all.

Speech after speech told of a city's pride and damned those in the media, the establishment and the South Yorkshire Police. They had held their tongues for too long – now with the gag removed, they let rip and there was no hiding place for those responsible.

The final word on a momentous moment in the history of Liverpool Football Club goes to Sheila Coleman, of the Hillsborough Justice Campaign, as she reflected on an old saying that talked of the ability of evil to prosper when good men do nothing.

'Well, we are good men and good women,' she said, 'and we did something.'

We certainly did, for the 96, the families and the survivors.

Total Eclipse of *The S*n*

In the aftermath of Hillsborough, the people of Liverpool were reeling. With a population at the time somewhere in the region of 300,000, almost everybody would have been touched by a disaster that ultimately cost the lives of 96 people and injured 766.

Liverpool is a proud city and its people are passionate and strong. Like other great working-class regions, they place great value in the principles of fairness and solidarity. So, when disaster strikes or when people find themselves in hardship it's natural for them to come together and support one another.

This was evidenced by the mass outpouring of grief that turned Anfield into a shrine. The barriers on the Kop were decked in scarves and poems. People etched the names of the victims into the paintwork, in the places where they normally stood on matchdays. The pitch was covered in floral tributes, all the way to the halfway line.

This was normal to the people of Liverpool. It's what you do for people when they are struggling or in pain. However, it seemed utterly alien to the establishment and to a newspaper editor who had ice running through his veins and a swinging brick in place of a heart.

With the city of Liverpool on its knees, desperately trying to make sense of the senseless, Rupert Murdoch's media chose to put the boot in. Many newspapers let themselves down at the time, some more so than others. However, for sheer brutality and dishonesty, none could hold a candle to Kelvin Mackenzie's S*n.

Under a banner headline 'The Truth', itself an affront to journalism, the paper claimed that supporters had urinated on lifeless bodies, had beaten up police officers attempting to help victims and stolen from the dead or the dying. These were vicious lies, now exposed as a cynical attempt to divert blame for the disaster on to the supporters.

This was a shameless act, cruel and calculated. It shocked everyone in Liverpool regardless of footballing allegiance. Reds and Blues could see this for what it was and those feelings of solidarity and grief soon turned to anger. Everton supporters immediately understood that the paper was attacking them too.

The Blues had played in the other semi-final and only a toss of the coin had prevented them from being at Hillsborough. Many also had family members and mates in Yorkshire for the game. The rag was accusing people they cared about of barbarity.

If the headline was intended to divide and demoralise, it had the opposite effect. Within hours a boycott of the tabloid was organised, that is as strong today as it ever was.

Posters began to appear in newsagent windows, asking people not to buy the rag, 'in solidarity with our brothers and sisters who died at Hillsborough'. The campaign bit hard and *The S*n*'s sales plummeted on Merseyside.

Numerous attempts to revive it, with mealy mouthed non-apologies and even an appeal to club manager Kenny Dalglish, failed. The paper contacted Kenny in the early days of the boycott and asked if there was any way it could repair the damage. It was rebuffed after it refused to run a similar headline, admitting it lied.

Rather than wane with the passing of time, the campaign has gathered momentum. Merseyside postal workers threatened to strike rather than deliver free copies in Liverpool. *The S*n* was forced to withdraw its mail drop as a result.

Small shops and even large chains in the city no longer stock it, thanks to the 'Total Eclipse of the S*n' campaign, organised by locals. Taxi drivers carry 'Don't Buy the S*n' signs on their cabs and Liverpool, Everton and Tranmere Rovers refuse to allow reporters from the paper on their premises.

This is possibly one of the greatest boycotts ever organised. Many people on Merseyside believe the paper will never recover there. Children and grandchildren who weren't even born at the time of the disaster can tell you exactly why their parents won't buy it.

Now it seems the rest of the football world is beginning to realise what Scousers have known for almost 30 years, that the paper is no friend of ordinary people. Seventy football supporters' groups, including Manchester United and Chelsea, recently took the decision to boycott the rag too.

Mackenzie and Murdoch picked on the wrong city.

Philippe Coutinho's Brazilian magic stuns Old Trafford as rivals meet in Europe for the first time

There have been many titanic struggles between Liverpool and their arch-enemies Manchester United down the years – but only twice in Europe.

Ever since the clubs first met at Anfield, in the Second Division in 1895, the two have been fierce rivals. That game ended 7-1 to Liverpool, by the way.

However, for all their domestic battles, they had never met in European competition. That is until they were drawn against each other in the last 16 of the Europa League on 10 March 2016.

Jurgen Klopp immediately saw the importance of the tie and, sensing the opportunity to whip the Kop into a frenzy, described it as the 'mother of all games'.

He didn't need to, they could do that themselves, but this was vintage Klopp.

Jurgen is never a cliché and, where other managers might seek to downplay the importance of such a game in an attempt to ease the pressure, he sought to turn it to his advantage. It worked a treat.

The first leg took place at Anfield and Liverpool ran out comfortable 2-0 winners thanks to goals from Daniel

Sturridge and Roberto Firmino. The game lived up to Klopp's description with United unable to settle thanks to a tremendous performance from all four corners of the ground.

'That's the worst Man Utd performance I've ever seen,' said Paul Scholes, who was working as a pundit for BT Sport. 'They're destroying the Man United legacy now ... I don't think the manager knows how big this game is.'

In truth, Liverpool made United look poor. The press had Klopp's men in the driving seat and most Liverpool fans could sense a memorable night at Old Trafford beckoning. They were right but there would be a scare on the way too.

United had left Anfield without a precious away goal. Still, as Liverpool supporters knew only too well, all they needed was an early goal and the game could easily be turned on its head.

The United fans attempted to replicate the majesty of the Kop in an effort to intimidate their rivals. However, the paltry sprinkling of banners was more than a little embarrassing. It invoked more hilarity than horror among the Red hordes.

Nevertheless, United would strike fear into Liverpool hearts just after the half-hour mark. Anthony Martial's trickery on the wing goaded Nathaniel Clyne into a lunge that upended the Frenchman. The referee signalled a penalty and the travelling Kop held their breath.

He scored, and suddenly it was game on. Liverpool's defence had been a problem for some time and there was real fear that United, with their tails up, would launch a panic-inducing barrage. Could the Reds really hang on for an hour?

They would do more than that and, on the stroke of half-time, Philippe Coutinho scored a goal he had absolutely no right to finish. The *Telegraph* headline said it all, 'THEY DINK IT'S ALL OVER; Coutinho touch of genius is too much for United'.

Klopp described it as the 'perfect goal', saying, 'What he did was brilliant. Phil had a genius moment. It was the most unexpected thing he could do in that situation.'

It certainly was. With seconds remaining before the break, Coutinho ran at the United defence and left Guillermo Varela embarrassed as he homed in on David de Gea's goal.

The Spaniard had been in inspirational form thus far, he had the near post covered and the angle was extremely tight.

Somehow, miraculously, stupendously, the Brazilian did what no other player would have done and the absolute last thing de Gea thought he could do; he chipped him at the near post.

As the ball hit the net, joyous scenes broke out in the away end. Liverpool had that all-important away goal and United needed to score three more to progress. All they had to do was sit back and hit their opponents on the break.

In truth Louis van Gaal's men threatened little and with 15 minutes left on the clock the United fans headed for the exits. This passage from the *Guardian* described the scenes and is particularly pleasing, 'As a measure of how Liverpool saw off their old enemy, nothing summed it up more than the break of play, with a quarter of an hour still remaining, when the first Manchester United supporters decided they had seen enough and the queues started forming at the exits.

'This was the club that once prided themselves on late feats of escapology – Barcelona in 1999, "Fergie Time" and all the rest – but those days have gone and Liverpool's supporters certainly enjoyed waving them goodbye before the burst of jubilation at the final whistle.'

So sweet!

Dejan Lovren breaks Dortmund hearts as Jurgen Klopp's Reds mount heroic fightback

Time and again Liverpool are driven to the brink of defeat, only to refuse to accept their fate. Countless encounters, from Auxerre to Milan, demonstrate their never-say-die attitude.

On Thursday, 14 April 2016, Borussia Dortmund came to Anfield for a Europa League quarter-final that gave a new generation of Kopites stories to tell.

With 45 minutes to go before kick-off, the pavements outside the ground were crammed. Supporters were animated in conversation and, delirious with anticipation, revelled in the occasion.

Anfield Road was jammed as Reds and Yellows alike posed for selfies and laughter filled the air. I moved through the 'tunnel' under the new Main Stand, still under construction, weaving my way through the throng, before emerging near The Albert.

A sign was hanging in front of a shop, next to the Hillsborough Justice Campaign store. It read 'Willkommen In Liverpool'.

The sound of singing from inside pubs drifted into the street and joined the smell of beer and chips. A cacophony of accents surrounded me: English, Scouse, German and Irish.

It really was all nations, all cultures, in one place and dreaming of glory. This was European football. This was Anfield.

I walked on past The Park pub. The door was open but the place was rammed and it looked raucous inside. Songs were being sung and a crowd was bouncing in front of the bar, beers and phones in the air.

Across the road was the Kop, with the usual build-up inside and outside the gates. Shankly was mobbed, as he always was, arms outstretched glorying in eternal adulation.

Far above him were the metal panels that helped to lock in the atmosphere. By 7.30pm I could hear fists and boots banging against the steel; a chant of 'Liiiiiverpool!' audible in the street.

Inside I was greeted with Dortmund's 'Yellow Wall' at the opposite end of the pitch, a magnificent sight. I turned my head left and gazed down on our own 'Red Wall'.

Reggae tones wafted lazily from the loudspeaker system and spread throughout the ground. Kopites inhaled them deeply, swaying and singing 'Don't worry about a thing, 'cause every little thing is going to be all right.'

It was a carnival of football.

None of the bitterness and intense rivalry of a Chelsea or United encounter could be found. It was like footage of 1960s Scousers, in love with life, music and football and singing Beatles and Cilla Black tunes.

The first half was a European masterclass. Dortmund were immense and fully deserving of their 2-0 lead. They simply blew Liverpool away and half-time was a blessed relief.

Just as in 2005, the Reds faced a second half in need of three goals. At Anfield against the Greek champions and in the Ataturk against Italian giants they found a way back; could they do it again?

Divock Origi pulled one back early in the second half. Hope sprung eternal. However, it's just not in Liverpool's DNA to coast. A victory without struggle is easier on the heart but it doesn't taste anywhere near as sweet.

So there was an air of inevitability about Marco Reus's heartbreaker and Dortmund's third. It failed to dampen spirits, though. Instead the Kop roared back and Jurgen

Klopp was going crazy on the touchline, gesturing and orchestrating both the crowd and his team.

Liverpool responded and suddenly Philippe Coutinho was free with the ball at his feet. He had a lot to do but he somehow slotted the ball past the goalkeeper for 3-2; was the impossible really happening again?

There was an ecstasy of stumbling and falling, of hugging each other, fist-pumping and screaming 'yiiiiiiiiiiiiiirrrrrs!' at the top of our lungs. Then scarves were spinning and 'Ring of Fire' erupted around the stadium.

The Germans stood in stunned silence. Perhaps they knew. Perhaps their team did, too. Liverpool won a corner. Coutinho chipped it in to the near post and Daniel Sturridge glanced it back into the six-yard box.

There followed a scramble of legs and Mamadou Sakho's long limb prodded the ball into the net. Liverpool had drawn level. The roar that ensued was incredibly loud and suddenly, belief soared.

However, with the game almost done, Liverpool needed another goal to progress. Up stepped Dejan Lovren, who rose from within a clamour of players to smash home a James Milner cross and drive Anfield crazy with joy. Only Liverpool, only Anfield, can produce nights like this.

Jubilation greeted the final whistle. 'You'll Never Walk Alone' rang out once more and all around me were stunned and ecstatic faces. One guy just looked at me, speechless, his fist pounding against his chest.

He didn't need to speak. I knew what he meant.

Jurgen Klopp's inspirational speech to broken players after Europa League heartache in Basel

The Jurgen Klopp era exploded into life in the 2015/16 season with the charismatic German leading Liverpool to two cup finals in his first full term. Both ended in bitter disappointment. However, the second of those defeats would end with the manager delivering a blood-curdling speech to his players that would lift them from their anguish and prepare them for the many battles that lay ahead.

The game in question was the 2016 Europa League Final in Basel, against Sevilla. Liverpool had marched triumphantly to the final, disposing of Manchester United, Borussia Dortmund and Villarreal on the way.

So momentous was their push to Switzerland that many Reds sensed victory was written in the stars. However, Liverpool's preparations had hardly been helped by UEFA incompetence in the handling of an alleged failed drug test by Mamadou Sakho. The authorities had incorrectly sanctioned the defender for testing positive for a substance that, it later turned out, wasn't even on the banned list.

Liverpool responded by removing him from the squad until the matter was settled. It meant he would miss the final. This was a blow as the defender had played a crucial role in the progress to the showpiece occasion.

Still Liverpool supporters were in a confident mood. They had, after all, witnessed their team's storybook dismantling of much tougher opposition than Sevilla along the way.

As the first half got under way, it seemed their confidence had been well placed. Liverpool dominated the first half and were duly rewarded with a goal of sublime quality from Daniel Sturridge.

Here's how *The Times* described the goal, 'The goal was designed by Brazilians and finished by an Englishman. The ball was moved slickly from right to left, from Roberto Firmino to Philippe Coutinho, who controlled it with his left and then very deliberately side-footed it on right-footed to Sturridge.

'The ball suddenly appeared at pace, carving its passage through the air, beating the outstretched left hand of the diving Soria and flying in.'

The sense that Klopp's first full season was about to end in glory was palpable. Text messages flew around the globe, as Reds supporters sensed another chapter in the club's history was being written.

Inside the stadium there were scenes of joyous delirium. The choice of venue for the game had raised more than a few eyebrows, with a capacity of just 35,000. More than three-quarters of those were Liverpool fans and it must have felt a very lonely place for the Spaniards in the stands.

As Sturridge peeled away in celebration, the Liverpool bench spilled on to the pitch with Klopp turning to the crowd to punch his fists in the air. This was a manager in communion with his supporters.

The script was written. Liverpool were on their way to victory, or so it seemed.

However, from that point the story was one of squandered opportunities and a tale of what could have been. In truth, the Reds should have been two or three up by half-time, such was their dominance. They had two clear penalties waved away and a second Sturridge strike ruled out for offside.

As they went in at half-time with only a single goal to their name, an ominous sensation descended.

The premonitions of Liverpool fans watching in the stadium and on television sets around the world were justified. The second half was a nightmare. Within a minute Sevilla were level through Kevin Gameiro. Liverpool's defence had capitulated far too easily, and Alberto Moreno had been culpable. His errors would see him replaced at left-back the following season by James Milner, a natural midfielder.

Still, there was a whole half remaining and there should have been no excuse for the collapse that followed. Yet the men in red seemed equally beset with the same dark forebodings as their supporters.

During a six-minute spell that resembled an evil mirror image of the Reds' own comeback in Istanbul 11 years previously, Sevilla raced into a 3-1 lead through Coke. His goals in the 64th and 70th minutes would clinch the cup for the Spaniards and break Liverpool hearts.

The *Guardian* captured the mood in the Liverpool camp perfectly. This was a golden opportunity missed, 'They stood in the rain with runners-up medals around their necks, watched Sevilla hoist the Europa League trophy for the third year running, and promptly disappeared down the tunnel.

'Jurgen Klopp and his Liverpool players had no appetite for standing on ceremony after their European dreams were shattered by Sevilla's second-half transformation and their own inability to withstand it.'

Liverpool supporters traipsed out of the ground. Some would make their way home, others would return to hotels and bars to drown their sorrows. They would be unaware that in the team hotel, the Liverpool manager was preparing to give a stirring speech that would lift his players and turn a bitter defeat into a footnote in a much bigger story, yet to be told.

Within days of the final, stories began to emerge on social media and in pubs and internet forums, of Klopp's heroic oratory. Of course, like the fabled tale of Rafa Benitez's half-time team talk in the depths of the Ataturk, only those present know if the stories match reality. For supporters like me though, that's irrelevant. What matters are the folklore and the legends they create.

The tales that emerged in Liverpool in the aftermath of that game go like this:

The players were sat around, their heads down, faces a portrait of misery. Some were drinking, and others were arguing. Klopp and his team were sat in a corner, deep in contemplation.

Then the boss got up and spoke. Everybody else stopped and listened. He said, 'Three hours ago, I was a broken man, two hours ago I felt a little better, but still heartbroken, one hour ago I lifted my head and thought of the future. Now I am ready to fight again for you, to fight for Liverpool. We are going to fight for everything next season.'

It is said that the place erupted in song and cheers and that the players started singing Liverpool songs. The defeat was far from forgotten, but crucially attention had already turned to the season ahead and future battles to be fought.

Did it happen? Maybe it did, maybe it didn't. But, in the telling of the story, many supporters were able to lift their heads and think of the future once more. What will it bring? Well if it is half as glorious as the past, then that will do me.

The new Main Stand, a new era and an emphatic win over the champions

Anfield's Main Stand was constructed in 1894, at a total cost of £1,000. Its modern-day expansion would cost £100m. The original stand was largely made of timber and remained unmodified until the 1970s. In the middle of the stand roof was a semi-circular gable, which later included a crest, containing the words Liverpool Football Club.

In 1973 it was expanded to include more seats, better facilities for players and a TV gantry. And so, it remained that way until 2016, when new owners Fenway Sports Group made good on their promise to stay and expand Anfield.

The additional seats created raised the capacity to 54,000 and, with the possible expansion of the Anfield Road end, the stadium could eventually seat upwards of 60,000 supporters.

The work was completed in a year, with the new stand constructed from behind the old during the 2015/16 season. Liverpool started their 2016/17 season with three away games, to allow the finishing touches to be completed.

Their first home game in the shadow of the new three-tier stand was against champions Leicester City. It was a remarkable occasion and the Reds made sure they weren't upstaged by the bricks and mortar.

At midday Anfield was resplendent, bathed in sunshine, with barely a breeze in the air. Supporters gathered, posing for pictures in all the familiar places, then they stood staring and snapping images of the new construction.

It was monumental, magnificent and imposing, yet still incomplete in areas; words that could easily be applied to the squad that would blow the champions of England apart that day. With Dejan Lovren sporting a black eye, Ragnar Klavan still struggling with injury and James Milner's continued reinvention as a left-back, Liverpool's back four remained a work in progress.

Lucas Leiva, absent for so long and narrowly avoiding a transfer to Turkey in the summer, was pressed into centre-back as Jurgen Klopp attempted his own reconstruction job on the Reds' defensive line.

In the run-up to the game such matters seemed secondary to the occasion. This felt like a cup final or even a festival. Liverpool Football Club had taken a giant leap into the modern era.

Liverpool's season hadn't been disastrous to that point. They had secured four points out of a possible nine and a victory in this game would make it a very respectable start.

Leicester managed to live with them for the first ten minutes or so, but they couldn't cope at all after that. But for an inexplicable gift from Lucas, they'd have barely made an impression on the game.

The demolition job started on 13 minutes. Milner broke on the left and delivered a delightful diagonal to Roberto Firmino. The Brazilian's deft touch took him past Robert Huth and gave him the time and space to slide the ball past Kasper Schmeichel.

The ground exploded and the sound felt genuinely enormous. The away end had been indulging in clichés about atmospheres only seconds earlier, words that were now being rammed right back down their throats.

Liverpool's second arrived thanks to an assist from Jordan Henderson, who sent Sadio Mane and Daniel Sturridge racing towards goal. It looked like Daniel would score but he unselfishly clipped the ball with his heel to Sadio, who lifted the ball over the hapless goalkeeper.

The Reds were comfortable but a defensive lapse let the visitors back in. Liverpool were attempting to play the ball out from the back when Lucas found himself in two minds. He hesitated and instead of listening to Joel Matip, who was imploring him to put it out, he decided to play the ball across his own six-yard box. Jamie Vardy probably couldn't believe his luck as he stroked the ball home.

Football has no rhyme or reason sometimes and Leicester, having barely threatened, were right back in it.

Lucas looked disconsolate, devastated. Then something truly magical happened. While some supporters were losing their heads, the Kop began singing his name. It was a gesture as heart-warming as it was generous.

In the second half Liverpool extended their lead through Adam Lallana in the 56th minute. His blistering diagonal shot from the edge of the box was a real settler and the Reds grew in stature after that.

Leicester looked like they could concede any time yet they held out until the dying moments of the game. Henderson launched a pass to Mane, who showed great pace and strength to outdo the Leicester goalkeeper, who had rushed out of the 18-yard box.

Supporters rose from their seats in anticipation, but instead of shooting, he unselfishly squared the ball to Firmino. The Brazilian outsmarted his marker and planted the ball into an empty net.

At 4-1 it was game over and a new era at Anfield was off to a flying start.

Afterword

SO, we have reached the 2017/18 season, the club's 125th year in existence. For now our journey must end. However, Liverpool Football Club will go on. New stars will rise, classic games await us, and before long new pieces of silver will surely adorn the trophy room.

As I write, Liverpool continues to be blessed with players of phenomenal talent. Mohamed Salah, Sadio Mane, Philippe Coutinho and Roberto Firmino routinely have the Kop on the edge of their seats. Allied with burgeoning local talent such as Trent Alexander-Arnold and Ben Woodburn, they ensure that the club has a bright future.

Liverpool Football Club has returned to elite European competition. The travelling Kop will continue to journey to distant lands and at home we can dream of spectacular nights under Anfield floodlights. The Saint-Etiennes, Chelseas and Dortmunds of the future are lying in wait.

Just as they have throughout its history, the Reds' fortunes continue to ebb and flow. There will always be dark times followed by periods of recovery, defeats and victories. The capitulations to Manchester City and Spurs, and the destruction of Arsenal and Brighton are all evidence of this. But through all of that, Anfield and the supporters will endure.

In writing this, I have rediscovered exactly what it is I support, why I follow this great club and why after almost three decades without a league title, I still begin every season believing that drought will end.

In recent years, I came close to falling out with the club. Owned by distant businessmen, bought and sold like any other commodity and fought over in the High Court, Liverpool FC, in so many ways, couldn't have seemed more removed from the object of my childhood obsession, than it does today. Even the very Liver Bird upon my chest has become a trademark, a brand.

In truth, it has always been this way. The club, after all, was born out of a boardroom battle. Just as Hicks and Gillett fought with John Henry on matters of finance and football in this new century, so too did John Houlding and George Mahon at the end of an old one. It is not these men though who define our club; significant though their contributions may have been, theirs are just stories like all the rest. And it is all of these stories, woven together, that have seared this club into my heart.

No doubt I've missed countless tales that give our club its sense of otherness. There will have been players who inspired wonder and supporters whose life stories are every bit as epic as the heroes they followed; alas it would take several volumes to do them all justice.

So, I offer this as my contribution to a great odyssey that is already 125 years in the making. I hope that, as we celebrate this milestone, the tales unearthed and remembered here will remind you all who we are. We are Liverpool and we have dreams and songs to sing.

You'll Never Walk Alone.